Large-Scale Assessment and Accommodations:

What Works?

Edited by

Cara Cahalan Laitusis
Linda L. Cook

Council for
Exceptional
Children
The voice and vision of special education

ETS

CollegeBoard
connect to college success

NATIONAL INSTITUTE FOR
URBAN SCHOOL
IMPROVEMENT

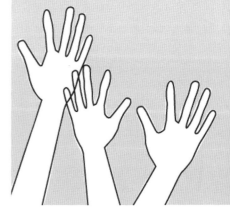

College Board, AP, PSAT/NMSQT, and SAT are registered trademarks of the College Entrance Examination Board.

ISBN 0-86586-430-6

Copyright 2007 by Council for Exceptional Children, 1110 North Glebe Road, Suite 300, Arlington, Virginia 22201-5704

Stock No. P5834

All rights reserved.

No part of this publication may be reproduced, stored in a retrieval system, or transmitted, in any form or by any means, electronic, mechanical, photocopying, recording, or otherwise, without prior written permission of the copyright owner.

Printed in the United States of America

10 9 8 7 6 5 4 3 2 1

To our husbands
Vytas Laitusis and Daniel Eignor
for their support, both personal and professional

Cara Cahalan Laitusis is a research scientist in the Research and Development Division at Educational Testing Service in Princeton, NJ. She received a Ph.D. in school psychology from Fordham University in 2003 and her B.S. in psychology from Trinity College (Hartford, CT) in 1993. Her research interests include investigating validity and fairness issues in large-scale assessments, with a primary focus on students with disabilities. She is currently a project director and principal investigator on the Designing Accessible Reading Assessments and the Technology Assisted Reading Assessment (TARA) projects, which are both funded by the U.S. Department of Education.

Linda L. Cook is a principal research scientist in the Research and Development Division at Educational Testing Service in Princeton, NJ. She received her Ed.D. in educational measurement and statistics from the University of Massachusetts in 1979; her M.E.D. in education of the deaf from Smith College in 1972; and her B.S. in chemistry from Ursinus College in 1960. Her primary research interests are the fairness, validity, and accessibility of tests for students with disabilities, test equating and scaling, and cross-cultural issues in testing including adapting and linking tests given to examinees of different languages and cultures. Cook is co-director of the Designing Accessible Reading Assessments Project.

Contents

Preface

KURT F. GEISINGER
The University Nebraska

Societal views, like everything else in the world, change over time. In the last third of the 20th century, members of society in the United States made their views known by urging that individuals with disabilities be assured the same opportunities to fulfill their potential as members of society as their nondisabled peers. In order to act upon this prevailing sentiment, the U.S. government passed legislation to provide rights and services to individuals with disabilities so that they could participate and compete, to the fullest extent possible, in American society. The Rehabilitation Act of 1973 (Section 504) and the Americans with Disabilities Act (ADA) of 1990 codified much of this change in societal orientation toward equity for individuals with disabilities. Both of these acts are far reaching and address many educational rights and services for people with disabilities, including assessment opportunities.

Pullin (this book) points out:

The ADA includes a specific provision governing examinations "Any person that offers examinations or courses related to applications, licensing, certification, or credentialing for secondary or post-secondary education, professional, or trade purposes shall offer such examinations or courses in a place and manner accessible to persons with disabilities or offer alternative accessible arrangements for such individuals." (42 U.S.C. 12189)

She also points out the importance of the Individuals With Disabilities Education Act (IDEA, 2004), which stipulates that states must include students with disabilities in state education reform initiatives, while ensuring compliance with requirements for individualized educational opportunities.

The provisions of the ADA, Section 504 of the Rehabilitation, and the IDEA legislation are very important for people with disabilities because educational assessments are used in part to determine who gains access to various educational programs, who completes various educational programs successfully, and who may have access to a broad range of employment opportunities.

The manner in which educational and psychological assessments are administered to individuals with disabilities changed after passage of the above-cited laws. People with disabilities now receive tests with changes to the standard test administration process that permit them to be tested in a manner that helps ensure that their disability does not interfere with the fair and valid measurement of their skills or abilities. Recently, the focus on changes to the standard testing procedures used for large-scale assessments administered to examinees with disabilities has been brought to the forefront because of the No Child Left Behind Act (2001). As a result of this legislation, state departments of education are held accountable for testing students with disabilities and must carry out such testing in compliance with the ADA. The need to test children covered by ADA and to provide them with assessments that are true measures of their skills and abilities, impacted as little as possible by their disabilities, has become an important challenge for both psychometricians and practitioners. (See Geisinger, 1994, 1998a, 1998b; and Tenopyr, Angoff, Butcher, Geisinger, & Reilly, 1993 for discussions of some of the challenges.)

The major challenge faced by psychometricians and practitioners is to find an answer to the question of how to provide accessible assessments to examinees with disabilities while maintaining the validity of the inferences based on the scores from these tests. Finding an answer to this question has led to the recent use of two descriptive terms related to changes to the test or test administration conditions: accommodations and modifications.

Accommodations are normally perceived as adaptations to the test or to the test administration process that do not or minimally change the construct measured by the test, and permit the individual with a disability to be tested validly. Accommodations may be given to test takers with perceptual, physical, cognitive, or emotional disabilities. For example, individuals who are blind or visually impaired may take the test in Braille, with a tape recorder, with a human test reader and recorder, or in large-print type. For other test takers who may be deaf or hard-of-hearing, a sign language interpreter could administer the test. The time of day when a test is administered could be changed for groups of test takers with certain other disabilities or they could receive additional rest pauses. Perhaps the most controversial alteration of test administrations involves providing additional time on timed or speeded tests to individuals with disabilities including those who are learning disabled; this change is the most frequent accommodation of standard testing procedures. These are but a few of the accommodations that are provided to examinees with disabilities who are taking academic assessments. (These accommodations and psychometric data supporting their use are discussed in Willingham et al., 1988, and updated in Pitoniak & Royer, 2001; Sireci, Scarpati, & Li, 2005; and by Sireci & Pitoniak, this book.)

Some individuals differentiate accommodations, as described previously, from modifications, where the construct being assessed may be changed in some way because of the change in the test or the testing procedure (see Sireci et al., 2005). It is necessary to obtain empirical evidence of the impact of the changes to the test or testing procedure on the scores of the assessment in order to determine if the change can be categorized as an accommodation or a modification and this distinction may not always hold.

Although it is very important to study the impact of these test administration changes on test scores, there are serious difficulties in obtaining empirical evidence that scores from accommodated tests are equivalent to scores from standard administrations and can thus be considered the result of an accommodation rather than a modification.

One reason it is difficult to study the impact of accommodations on test scores is that the numbers of individuals with specific disabilities are often small and such group sizes do not support the application of many statistical and psychometric procedures. Also, differences in degrees of severity of a particular disability make the formation of what is considered the accommodated group difficult. Difficulty in defining the study group complicates comparisons with the nondisabled group and also limits the generalizability of the results of any study based on groups that are formed and end up being heterogeneous in nature. In addition, there are issues involved in deciding whether to group together individuals with different disabilities who have received the same test accommodation. Finally, identifying criteria to use to validate accommodated assessments is difficult. For example, criteria, such as grade-point average, may not always have the same meaning for students with and without disabilities who take the assessment of interest. These are only a few of the problems related to providing evidence that assessments administered to individuals with disabilities provide fair and valid scores. Moreover, the nature of the tests themselves (e.g., speeded or not) may impact the generalizability of the findings.

The purpose of this book is to provide the educational practitioner with information about the nature and use of accommodations and modifications with large-scale assessments that will be of assistance when that practitioner has to make decisions about the administration of such assessments to students with disabilities.

The book is separated into three sections. The first section contains chapters that focus on state and federal *Policy*, and how these policies have evolved over time and what their impact has been on accommodating large-scale assessments. The second section of the book is devoted to *Research*, and how this research can inform

the practitioner who must make decisions about accommodations for large-scale assessments. Finally, the third section of this book is devoted to chapters that focus on *Practice*, and how both researchers and practitioners have addressed some issues associated with accommodating assessments that are administered to examinees with disabilities and English-language learners.

This author urges readers of this book to keep in mind a few primary points. First, the testing of individuals with disabilities has increased dramatically in the recent past in the United States, and most of the current thinking related to accommodations is still in the formative stage. The key issue that we need to continue to contemplate and study is whether the accommodation being considered is appropriate or whether it appears to change the construct to be tested. In considering this question, it would be prudent to consider use of principles such as universal design to make tests maximally accessible and appropriate for all test takers. We should also acknowledge that test changes that are appropriate for individuals with disabilities may also prove useful for English-language learners, a quickly growing component of our population.

Finally, this author hopes that both society and educational institutions will continue to stand for equity and fairness, and that educational institutions will prize excellence, help every student succeed to the best of his or her ability, and permit individuals to make the contributions to society that they wish. It is hoped that the information provided in this book will facilitate these important societal values.

REFERENCES

Americans With Disabilities Act of 1990, 42 U.S.C., 12101 *et seq.* (1990).

Geisinger, K. F. (1994). Psychometric issues in testing students with disabilities. *Applied Measurement in Education, 7,* 121–140.

Geisinger, K. F. (1998a). Psychometric issues in test interpretation. In Sandoval, J., Frisby, C. L., Geisinger, K. F., Scheuneman, J., & Grenier, J. R. (Eds.), *Interpretation and diversity: Achieving equity in assessment* (pp. 17–30). Washington, DC: American Psychological Association.

Geisinger, K. F. (1998b). Testing accommodations for the new millennium: Computer-administered testing in a changing society. In Niyogi, S. (Ed.), *New Directions in Assessment for Higher Education: Fairness, Access, Multiculturalism & Equity* (FAME). The Graduate Record Examination FAME Report Series, No. 2 (1998), 12–20.

Pitoniak, M., & Royer, J. (2001). Testing accommodations for examinees with disabilities: A review of the psychometric, legal, and social policy issues. *Review of Educational Research, 71*, 53–104.

Section 504 of Rehabilitation Act of 1973, 29656 U.S.C., 701 *et seq.* (1973).

Sireci, S. G., Scarpati, S. F., & Li, S. (2005). Test accommodations for students with disabilities: An analysis of the interaction hypothesis. *Review of Educational Research, 75*, 457–490.

Tenopyr, M. L., Angoff, W. H., Butcher, J. N., Geisinger, K. F., & Reilly, R. R. (1993). Psychometric and assessment issues raised by the Americans With Disabilities Act (ADA). *The Score, 15*(4), pp. 1–2, 7, 15.

Uniform guidelines on employee selection procedures (1978). *Federal Register, 43*, 38290–38315.

Willingham, W. W., Ragosta, M., Bennett, R., Braun, H., Rock, D. A., & Powers, D. E. (1988). *Testing handicapped people*. Needham Heights, MA: Allyn & Bacon.

Acknowledgments

The chapters in this book are based on invited presentations made by leaders in the fields of special education and educational research that were prepared for the "Accommodating Students With Disabilities on State Assessments: What Works?" conference held in Savannah, Georgia in March 2006. The conference was attended by nearly 300 teachers, administrators, university and college professors, researchers, test developers, measurement specialists, and others committed to learning about testing accommodations and large-scale assessments. The conference provided a unique opportunity for this diverse group of committed individuals to share their knowledge and to learn from each other.

We would like to thank the sponsors of the conference (Educational Testing Service, the Council for Exceptional Children, the College Board, and the National Institute for Urban School Improvement) for providing the support needed to move this conference from an idea to a reality. In particular we would like to thank the representatives of these organizations that we worked with, Ida Lawrence, Wayne Camara, Richard Mainzer, and Shelley Zion, for their contributions in conceptualizing and planning the conference. We would also like to thank Kitty Sheehan and Kathy Howell for their efforts in carrying out all the logistics that are such an important component of any successful conference.

The most important group that we would like to thank are the authors of the chapters in this book. As the editors of this book, we had the privilege of working with a small but committed group of individuals focused on improving educational assessments for all students. We would like to express our gratitude to these authors for their excellent and important contributions to this book. It has been our pleasure to work with every one of them.

It is our hope that this collection of chapters on policy, research, and practice will help both practitioners and researchers to advance assessment for learning, not only for students with disabilities but for all students.

Cara Cahalan Laitusis
Linda L. Cook

Selecting and Using Testing Accommodations to Facilitate Meaningful Participation of All Students in State and District Assessments

STEPHEN N. ELLIOTT
Vanderbilt University

Documenting the achievements and educational progress of students is a critical aspect of an appropriate education and is required by law for students with disabilities. Assessment practices, especially district- and statewide testing, is one of the primary methods educators use to collect evidence of students' learning. Typically, however, when educators think of testing students with disabilities, they think about individualized, norm-referenced tests of cognitive abilities, achievement, and social and adaptive behavior. Such tests are often helpful in identifying students with disabilities, but are of limited use as evidence concerning educational progress because they usually do not contain specific content that is aligned with what students are being taught on a daily basis. In addition, such tests do not easily allow for progress comparisons to other students in the same schools or to established achievement standards.

Today, all students in Grades 3 to 8 and 10 or 11 are expected to be included in large-scale assessments, but historically not all students have been included in many of the statewide or schoolwide assessment programs. Participation rates for students during the past several years in statewide assessments have ranged from a low of 40% to a high of 99% (Elliott, Braden, & White, 2001). Many of the students who did not participate were students with disabilities or with limited English proficiency. There are several reasons for these varying participation rates. The reasons typically given for excluding students like these from testing programs include:

- The concern that students with disabilities will lower a school's mean score.

- The desire to "protect" students with disabilities and English language deficiencies from another frustrating testing experience.

- The perception that the tests are not relevant, especially to students with disabilities.

- The fact that some parents do not want their child spending valuable class time

1

taking a test that doesn't count toward a grade.

- The belief that the guidelines for administering standardized tests prohibit, or at least greatly limit, what can be changed without jeopardizing the validity of the resulting test score.

The limited participation of students with disabilities and with limited English proficiency in state and district assessments results in (a) unrepresentative mean scores and distributions (norms), (b) beliefs that these students cannot do challenging work, and (c) undermining of inclusion efforts for many students. However, if educators and other educational stakeholders who aspire to high standards for all students are to have a meaningful picture of how well students are learning and applying valued content knowledge and skills, all students need to be assessed periodically.

Making decisions about including students with disabilities in assessment programs and implementing assessments validly can be challenging and requires teachers' active involvement on individualized education program (IEP) teams. One of the first challenges confronting educators is to determine the "right" assessment program for students with disabilities. Practically speaking, students with disabilities could participate in (a) the general education achievement test without accommodations, (b) the general education achievement test with testing accommodations, (c) an alternate assessment, or (d) part of the regular assessment with testing accommodations and the remainder in an alternate assessment. In making this participation decision, educators consider an array of factors including (a) the alignment between a student's IEP goals, classroom curriculum, and the content of the test; (b) a student's reading ability; and (c) the nature of instructional accommodations a student typically receives. The purpose of this book is to provide information that will

aid practitioners in making decisions regarding the appropriate assignment of accommodations. This chapter serves as an introduction to the other chapters in the book and focuses on the overall appropriateness of the selection of test accommodations in school districts.

TESTING ACCOMMODATIONS: INCREASING STUDENT PARTICIPATION AND TEST SCORE VALIDITY

As noted in IDEA '97 and in most state's testing guidelines since the law was enacted, testing accommodations and alternate assessment are two possible methods educators can use to facilitate the participation of all students with disabilities in assessments and accountability systems. Therefore, every teacher who works with one or more students with disabilities should know about testing accommodations and alternate assessment if they want to facilitate their students' meaningful involvement in assessment programs.

Definition of Testing Accommodations

One of the most frequent steps for increasing accessibility and the meaningful participation of students with disabilities in assessments is allowing some changes to testing procedures. Such changes are commonly referred to as *testing accommodations*. Testing accommodations *are changes in the way a test is administered or responded to by a student*. Testing accommodations are intended to offset distortions in test scores caused by a disability without *invalidating* or changing what the test measures (McDonnell, McLaughlin, & Morison, 1997). When appropriate testing accommodations are used, the resulting test scores are considered to be more valid indicators of a student's knowledge and skills.

Federal laws (i.e., IDEA and NCLB) require participation in statewide assessments, but do not define what constitutes an appropriate accommodation. To ameliorate this definitional dilemma, Hollenbeck and associates (Hollenbeck, Rozek-Tedesco, & Finzel, 2000) specified four test alteration attributes that help define appropriate accommodations:

1. *Unchanged Constructs:* The alterations must not alter the measured construct(s).

2. *Individual Need:* Test alterations must be based on individual need.

3. *Differential Effects:* Test alterations must produce differential effects by student or group.

4. *Sameness of Inference:* Test alterations must generate similar inferences based upon generated scores.

The degree that these four attributes are in consensus, the test alteration is more likely to qualify as an accommodation and less likely to be a modification. Modifications are not allowed because the nature of what is measured by the assessment is changed, thus undermining the comparability of the assessment results for those students who received the alteration and those students who did not receive it.

Accommodations are commonly grouped into four categories: (a) accommodations in timing, (b) accommodations to the assessment environment, (c) accommodations in the presentation format, and (d) accommodations in the recording or response format. Figure I-1 provides some specific examples of each of these categories of accommodations.

Purpose of Testing Accommodations

It is important to note that not all students with disabilities will need testing accommodations to participate and provide a valid or accurate account of their abilities. On the other hand, for a small number of students with more severe disabilities, testing accommodations will not be appropriate or reasonable. These students' educational goals and daily learning experiences concern content that may differ significantly from that contained in state or district content standards. Although many of the IEP goals of these students should be aligned with the state's academic content standards, a student's current performance may differ significantly from the performance standards expected for a given student's grade level. Consequently, students in this situation will need to participate in an alternate assessment to meaningfully measure their abilities and provide valid results.

Although accommodations should not change the construct being tested, they should provide differential effects for a student's or group's performance (Tindal, Heath, Hollenbeck, Almond, & Harniss, 1998). If the test alteration works for all or nearly all students or fails to work at all, then the alteration would not be considered an allowable accommodation. Agreeing with the differential performance perspective, Fuchs and associates (Fuchs, Fuchs, Eaton, Hamlett, & Karns, 2000) suggested that a student's accommodated performance on a test must exceed the increase attained by students without disabilities to be considered a legitimate accommodation.

Many different testing accommodations are allowable as long as they do not change the meaning of the content being assessed (i.e., reduce the validity of the test scores). IEP teams are entrusted to determine the appropriate testing accommodations for individual students with disabilities. Most state departments of education have extensive rules or guidance about testing accommodations that are highly consistent with recommendations made by test companies (e.g., see CTB/McGraw-Hill's *Guidelines for Inclusive Test Administration* at www.ctb.org) and the National Center on Education Outcomes (NCEO; see Thurlow, House, Boys, Scott, & Ysseldyke, 2000 at http://education.umn. edu/nceo/), a U.S. Department of

Time Accommodations

- Administer a test in shorter sessions with more breaks or rest periods.
- Space testing sessions over several days.
- Administer a test at a time most beneficial to a student.
- Allow a student more time to complete the test.

Setting Accommodations

- Administer the test in a small group or individual session.
- Allow a student to work in a study carrel.
- Place student in a room or part of a room where he or she is most comfortable.
- Allow a special education teacher or aide to administer the test.

Format Accommodations

- Use an enlarger to facilitate vision of material.
- Use a Braille translation of a test.
- Give practice tests or examples before actual test is administered.
- Assist a student to track test items by pointing or placing the student's finger on items.
- Allow use of equipment or technology that a student uses for other school work.

Recording Accommodations

- Use an adult to record a student's response.
- Use a computer board, communication board, or tape recorder to record responses.

FIGURE I-1

Examples of Accommodations Frequently Considered Appropriate for Students With Disabilities

Education-funded resource center at the University of Minnesota.

Tests and assessment programs can be altered in a variety of ways to facilitate the participation of students with disabilities and provide valid results. As increasing numbers of students with disabilities are included in assessment programs and take the same tests as their peers without disabilities, teachers and other members of IEP teams will need to consider the use of testing accommodations. It is important to understand that accommodations are intended to maintain and facilitate the measurement goals of an assessment, not to modify the actual questions or content

of the tests. Accommodations usually involve changes to the testing environment (e.g., Braille or large print materials, the amount of time a student has to respond, the quietness of the testing room, assistance in reading instructions) or the method by which a student responds to questions (e.g., orally with a scribe, pointing to correct answers). Testing accommodations should not involve changes in the content of test items. When this occurs, the test is very likely to be measuring different skills or different levels of the same skills, and consequently the conclusions made from the results are likely to be invalid.

Accommodations generally result in some minor changes in the procedures for administration or response upon which a test was standardized. Consequently, because many educators have been taught to follow standardization procedures exactly, there may be some reluctance to use accommodations. The keys to the selection and appropriate use of testing accommodations are fivefold. First, accommodations must be determined on a case-by-case basis for each student. Second, knowledge of the instructional accommodations a student currently receives should guide considerations of testing accommodations. Third, accommodations are intended to make the test a more accurate measure of what a student knows or can do. That is, IEP teams must select accommodations that are likely to facilitate a student's participation in a testing program, but not likely to change or invalidate the intended meaning of a test score. Fourth, the accommodations must be implemented as planned. This is not always easy given the testing demands on many educators to accommodate multiple students during the same test or because of a lack of receptivity on the part of some students, especially adolescents (Feldman, Elliott, & Kim, in press; Lang, Elliott, Bolt, & Kratochwill, in press). Fifth, and finally, it is critical that educators document the accommodations which seem to effectively facilitate access and responding for students. The use of an accommodation decision and documentation tool like the *Assessment Accommodation Guide* (Elliott, Kratochwill, & Schulte, 1999) provides a method for documenting effective accommodations and communicating with educators who support students in subsequent years.

MAKING DECISIONS ABOUT THE SELECTION AND IMPLEMENTATION OF TESTING ACCOMMODATIONS

Among measurement experts there is a consensus that the purpose of using testing accommodations is to increase the validity of the inferences one makes from the test scores of students with disabilities (Elliott, McKevitt, & Kettler, 2002; Linn & Gronlund, 2000). This relationship between testing accommodations and the validity of the resulting scores is theoretically sound and starting to be documented in data-based reports (e.g., Elliott, Kratochwill, & McKevitt, 2001; Elliott & Marquart, 2004; McKevitt & Elliott, 2003; Pitoniak & Royer, 2001; Schulte, Elliott, & Kratochwill, 2001; Tindal et al., 1998). Meanwhile, educators on the front lines who are administering tests to all students must make test participation decisions for students with disabilities and then select and implement testing accommodations that are judged a priori to be valid. Educators are very capable of making participation decisions and are knowledgeable about the instructional accommodation needs of their students, but are often challenged to make accommodation decisions that lead to "good" (i.e., valid) test scores.

In working with thousands of educators who are responsible for administering large-scale assessments to students with disabilities, this author has found that they needed a wide range of knowledge to successfully select and use testing accommodations reliably. In particular, educators collectively need to have the following:

- Knowledge of the student's abilities and disabilities.

- Knowledge about the student's instructional accommodations.

- Knowledge about the state's or district's testing guidelines.

- Familiarity with the test's item content and format.

- An understanding of the concept of validity and what it means to invalidate a test score.

- Knowledge of any previous accommodations successfully used with the student.

Understanding that decisions about testing accommodations and their effect on a student's test performance, however, are highly individualized events so research on testing accommodations is unlikely to be directly prescriptive. All is not lost, if you have a clear understanding of what a test or subtest measures, then many of the decisions about appropriate (i.e., accommodations that do not change the construct that the test is measuring) become rather straightforward. For example, reading questions and answers on a reading test designed to measure sight vocabulary and comprehension would certainly invalidate interpretations of the resulting score because these accommodations are changing the skills or competencies that the test is designed to be measuring. Conversely, reading a complex story problem on a test designed to measure mathematics reasoning and calculation could be appropriate for some students with disabilities. In this latter case, assistance with reading is designed to increase the likelihood that the test score is a better indicator of what the student has learned in mathematics. If the accommodation does this, then the test score is said to be valid.

Many educators find it difficult to make decisions concerning the selection and use of testing accommodations with students. They also find it difficult to explain the use of testing accommodations to other educational stakeholders. As a result of numerous discussions about testing accommodations with teachers, parents, and testing experts, two metaphors that are useful for thinking about the role and function of testing accommodations are suggested.

The first metaphor for testing accommodations concerns *eyeglasses*. Look around any room with other adults present and you will see at least one third and maybe one half of them wearing eyeglasses to correct for vision impairments. Eyeglasses are an accommodation for imperfect or poor vision. If you wanted to test the natural vision ability of a

person who wears glasses for driving and outdoor activities, then wearing glasses during a test of distant vision would invalidate the test score assuming your purpose is to make an inference about the person's natural or uncorrected vision. On the other hand, if your purpose was to determine the same person's driving ability, then wearing the glasses during the driving test that he or she wears daily would be an appropriate accommodation because it would facilitate a more accurate assessment of the person's driving skills by minimizing or eliminating problems due to vision impairments.

The second metaphor about testing accommodations is an *access ramp*. As a point of fact, an access ramp can be conceptualized as part of a package of testing accommodations for individuals with significant physical impairments. If individuals can't get to the testing room, then they certainly can't demonstrate what they know or can do! The conceptual value of an access ramp has additional meaning, however, when addressing issues of construct validity. Testing accommodations facilitate access to a test for students with a wide range of disabilities just like a ramp facilitates access to a building for individuals with physical disabilities. The tests that students are required to take are designed to measure some specific *target cognitive skills or abilities*, such as mathematical reasoning and computations, but almost always assume that students have the skills to access the test, such as attending to instructions, reading story problems, and writing responses. Thus, knowledge and concepts tests like those included in most large-scale achievement tests target broad constructs like mathematics, science, and reading and are used to determine how students are doing in these subjects. Some students, in particular many students with disabilities, have difficulty with the *access skills* needed to get "into" the test. Thus, appropriate testing accommodations, just like an access ramp, should be designed to reduce problems of access to a test and enable students to demonstrate what they know and can do with regard to the skills or abilities the test is targeting.

By now, you should have a good understanding of what testing accommodations are and how they should function to improve the validity of a student's test score. In addition, you should be aware that testing accommodations are sanctioned by federal and state policies, and that IEP team members are responsible for selecting and implementing them for qualified students. But you can legitimately ask, "How do you go about selecting specific testing accommodations for specific students with specific disabilities and well defined instructional plans?" The keys to selecting and implementing testing accommodations for an individual student lie in the classroom(s) where that student is taught each day and having a good understanding of what the test they will take actually measures. The instructional accommodations that teachers frequently use to facilitate the teaching-learning interactions for a student are prime candidates as accommodations when that same student is participating in a state- or districtwide test. This premise is reasonable, particularly when there is good alignment between what is taught in the classroom and what is on the test. This does not mean, however, that all accommodations used to support a student during instruction will result in appropriate accommodations for testing.

As a summary, think about the list of "Dos and Don'ts in Testing Accommodations" offered by Thurlow, Elliott, and Ysseldyke (1998, pp. 61–62):

- *Don't* introduce a new accommodation for the first time for an assessment.
- *Don't* base the decision about what accommodations a student will use on the student's disability category.
- *Don't* start from the district or state list of approved accommodations when con-

sidering what accommodations a student will use in an upcoming test.

- *Do* systematically use accommodations during instruction and carry these into the assessment process.
- *Do* base the decision about accommodations, both for instruction and for assessment, on the needs of the student.
- *Do* consult the district or state list of approved accommodations after determining what accommodations the student needs. Then, reevaluate the importance of the accommodations that are not allowed. If they are important for the student, request their approval from the district or state.

This guidance from Thurlow and colleagues is as good today as it was nearly a decade ago when it was first offered. Thus, as you work with students to provide testing accommodations, revisit this list and try to add to it.

PREPARING STUDENTS TO TAKE TESTS AND USE TESTING ACCOMMODATIONS

Test preparation is a frequent concern of many educators and parents and should be considered a reasonable step for both teachers and students when testing accommodations are going to be implemented. As Feldman et al. (in press) have documented, the self-efficacy of many students with disabilities is low when they consider their test-taking skills. Many adolescents actually reject IEP suggested testing accommodations during the testing event apparently because they don't need them or don't want to be seen by others as needing additional help. Therefore, I believe it is worthwhile for students to understand the role of testing accommodations and for this understanding to be part of test preparation. For many students, it is wise to do some practice testing with accommodations prior to the actual testing event.

Sound test preparation practices may appear to be common-sense activities, however, experience with many educators suggests otherwise. Ultimately, the issue of proper test preparation is to ensure the validity of the resulting interpretations of test scores. That is, the assessment of student achievement should provide a fair and representative indication of how well students have learned what they have been taught, and to do this, test questions must focus on knowledge and skills similar to those that were taught during instruction. Perhaps the most important word in the previous sentence is *similar*. There is an important ethical difference between teaching to the test (and content standards) and teaching the test itself! Teaching to the standards that a test measures is a desirable practice and involves teaching students the general knowledge and skills that they need to answer questions on the test and to succeed in future education and work settings. Teaching the test itself involves teaching students the answers to specific questions that will appear on the test. This is neither pedagogically appropriate nor ethical because it can result in a distorted or invalid picture of what students have achieved.

Good test preparation should enable students to show what they have learned in classes over the past year and to get comfortable with any testing accommodations that have been suggested by IEP teams. Therefore, it is helpful for all students to understand that when taking a test they should:

- Be well rested and comfortable at the time of testing.
- Attend carefully to test directions and follow directions exactly.
- Ask questions when they are unsure of what to do.
- Find out how questions will be scored.

- Pace themselves so they do not spend so much time on some questions that they cannot get to other questions.
- Plan and organize essay questions before responding.
- Act in their own interest by attempting to answer all questions.
- Check often to make certain they are marking their responses accurately and in the correct place
- Communicate with their teacher about accommodation strategies that are acceptable and likely to be effective.

Many good test-taking skills can be mastered by virtually all students, but students, especially many students with disabilities, need some practice to develop these skills and confidence in using them. Consider spending instructional time a couple weeks prior to an important test discussing and modeling good test-taking skills for students and talking directly with students who will be receiving accommodations. Test preparation and test-taking skills are designed to increase the validity of students' test scores, not necessarily to increase their scores. Thus, testing accommodation plans should be part of test preparation for both the students who receive them and the educators who implement them on behalf of their students.

A CONCLUDING THOUGHT

Educators are now empowered and entrusted to include all students in the various assessment systems that have been implemented in their districts and states. To achieve this expectation, new policies and practices have been advocated that involve testing accommodations and alternate assessments. In this introduction, the rationale for using testing accommodations has been explored as a primary tactic to facilitate the meaningful participation of students with special needs in assessments. Subsequent chapters in this book will examine what research tells us about testing accommodations, accommodation policies, and accommodation practices. Throughout the chapters of this book, it will become clear that wise use of assessment accommodations rests upon an understanding of the concept of test score validity and an appreciation that good assessment is part of good instruction.

REFERENCES

CTB/McGraw-Hill (2001). *Guidelines for inclusive test administration.* Monterey, CA: Author.

Elliott, S. N., Braden, J. P., & White, J. (2001). *Assessing one and all: Educational accountability and students with disabilities.* Alexandria, VA: Council for Exceptional Children.

Elliott, S. N., Kratochwill, T. R., & McKevitt, B. C. (2001). Experimental analysis of the effects of testing accommodations on the scores of students with and without disabilities. *Journal of School Psychology, 39*(1), 3–24.

Elliott, S. N., Kratochwill, T. K., & Schulte, A. G. (1999). *The Assessment Accommodations Guide.* Monterey, CA: CTB/McGraw-Hill.

Elliott, S. N., & Marquart, A. M. (2004). Extended time as a testing accommodation: Its effects and perceived consequences. *Exceptional Children, 70,* 349–367.

Elliott, S. N., McKevitt, B. C., & Kettler, R. (2002). Testing accommodations research and decision-making: The case of "good" scores being highly valued but difficult to achieve for all students. *Measurement and Evaluation in Counseling and Development, 35,* 153–166.

Feldman, E., Elliott, S. N., & Kim, J. S. (in press). *Attitudes and reactions to large-scale assessments: An experimental investigation of the effects of accommodations on adolescents' self-efficacy and test performance.* Unpublished manuscript.

Fuchs, L. S., Fuchs, D., Eaton, S. B., Hamlett, C., & Karns, K. (2000). Supplementing teacher judgments of test accommodations with objective data sources. *School Psychology Review, 29,* 65–85.

Hollenbeck, K., Rozek-Tedesco, M., & Finzel, A. (2000, April). *Defining valid accommodations as a function of setting, task, and response.* Presentation at the annual meeting of the Council for Exceptional Children, Vancouver, BC, Canada.

Lang, S., Elliott, S. N., Bolt, D. M., & Kratochwill, T. R. (in press). The effects of testing accommodations on students' performance and reactions to testing. *School Psychology Quarterly.*

Linn, R. L., & Gronlund, N. E. (2000). *Measurement and assessment in teaching* (8th ed.). Englewood Cliffs, NJ: Merrill.

McDonnell, L. M., McLaughlin, M. J., & Morison, P. (Eds.) (1997). *Educating one and all: Students with disabilities and standards-based reform.* Washington, DC: National Academy Press.

McKevitt, B. C., & Elliott, S. N. (2003). The use of testing accommodations on a standardized reading test: Effects on scores and attitudes about testing. *School Psychology Review, 32*(4), 583–600.

Pitoniak, M. J., & Royer, J. M. (2001). Testing accommodations for examinees with disabilities: A review of pyschometrics, legal, and social policy issues. *Review of Educational Research, 71*(1), 53–104.

Schulte, A. G., Elliott, S. N., & Kratochwill, T. R. (2001). Effects of testing accommodations on students' standardized mathematics test scores: An experimental analysis. *School Psychology Review, 30*(4), 527–547.

Thurlow, M. L., Elliott, J. L., & Ysseldyke, J. E. (1998). *Testing students with disabilities: Practical strategies for complying with district and state requirements.* Thousand Oaks, CA: Corwin Press.

Thurlow, M. L., House, A., Boys, C., Scott, D., & Ysseldyke, J. (2000). *State participation and Accommodation policies for students with disabilities: 1999 update* (Synthesis Report 33). Minneapolis: University of Minnesota, National Center on Educational Outcomes.

Tindal, G., Heath, B., Hollenbeck, K., Almond, P., & Harniss, M. (1998). Accommodating students with disabilities on large-scale tests: An experimental study. *Exceptional Children, 64,* 439–450.

Law, Policy, and Large-Scale Assessment

Section I of this book provides the reader with an overview of recent federal education reforms and legislation (ADA, IDEA, and NCLB) that have had a significant impact on the inclusion of students with disabilities and English language learners in large-scale assessments. The three chapters in this section contain discussions of the implications of these education reforms for educational practitioners, policy makers, and researchers.

In Chapter 1 of this section, Thurlow provides an overview of state policies for providing accommodations on assessments and focuses on three main topics. These topics include a review of the numbers of students who are using accommodations on state assessments, a summary of state policies and guidelines addressing which accommodations are permitted and which are not permitted on these assessments, and a discussion of some of the issues and implications surrounding the use of accommodations on assessments. Finally, Thurlow identifies areas that will need additional work in the years to come, including research on the impact of testing accommodations, professional development for the individualized education program (IEP) teams selecting accommodations, and finally improvements to documentation of which accommodations a student is approved for and which accommodations the student actually uses in practice. She makes the point that continued improvements in the accessibility of assessments for students with disabilities must be made.

In Chapter 2, Abedi provides a review of state identification and testing accommodation policies for English language learners (ELLs). Abedi's review provides a sobering summary of the current state of affairs as it pertains to the testing of students with disabilities who are also ELLs. In addition Abedi outlines three critical points of interaction (classification, accommodation, and assessment) that influence performance outcomes for ELLs with and without disabilities taking large-scale assessments. Abedi discusses the implications of these critical points of interaction for policy makers, researchers, and practitioners.

In the final chapter of this section (Chapter 3), Pullin provides a framework for taking into account legal, educational, and policy issues stemming from the provision of testing accommodations for students with disabilities. The chapter begins with an introduction to the current public education reforms (e.g., NCLB and IDEA) and their public policy goals. Pullin discusses the consequences of including students with disabilities in the general education reform initiatives. After the introduction to education reforms, she focuses on the legal and technical requirements of these education reform initiatives for students with disabilities. Finally, Pullin discusses the legal and technical implications of recent education reforms for policy makers, educational practitioners, and researchers.

CHAPTER 1

State Policies and Accommodations: Issues and Implications

MARTHA L. THURLOW
University of Minnesota

Providing accommodations to individuals while they are taking assessments is not something new, yet it is something that has become a hotbed of activity in the K–12 education world. This is particularly true within the context of the Individuals with Disabilities Education Act (IDEA), which requires that all students with disabilities who have individualized education programs (IEPs) participate in state- and districtwide assessments, and the No Child Left Behind Act (NCLB), which requires not only that students participate but also that schools, districts, and states be held accountable for their participation and their performance.

Accommodations are viewed in many different ways by schools, test developers, and those who use the accommodations. State policies about accommodations are a window into some of the views that exist. These policies reflect many of the issues that surround testing today. They also suggest some topics we, as educators and assessors, need to think about for students as they move beyond the K–12 educational system. There is no end to the interesting findings

and implications that are embedded in or suggested by accommodations policies. This chapter will examine some of these key issues and implications.

Accommodation policies have come a long way since 1992 when the National Center on Educational Outcomes (NCEO) first started studying the policies and guidelines that states developed to help districts and schools determine which accommodations were acceptable for students with disabilities to use during testing and which were not (Thurlow, Ysseldyke, & Silverstein, 1993, 1995). Even the way that the field views accommodations has changed. In the early 1990s, accommodations were considered almost solely as a way to gain access to the assessment, and of course to make instruction meaningful for students. For assessment this meant that accommodations gave the student a way to participate in the assessment. The primary thought was not about what the construct was. Rather, it was about what needed to be done so that the student could sit down to take the paper and pencil test. Did a reader have to be provided?

Did the special education teacher have to give the test? Did testing have to be provided over multiple days?

Today, most definitions of accommodations recognize the importance of the construct being assessed. Accommodations are defined in terms of avoiding the effects of *construct irrelevant variance*. Construct irrelevant variance is the increase or decrease of test scores due to factors other than the student's actual knowledge or skills (e.g., changes in the test administration). A definition used by Tindal and Fuchs (1999) recognized the importance of removing the construct irrelevant variance, but also suggested that an accommodation would be effective for the student with the disability and not effective for other students. This aspect of the definition is being revised as the notion of differential boost is introduced, where both youngsters with disabilities and those without show some effect of the accommodation, although the boost is larger for those with disabilities (Sireci, Scarpati, & Li, 2005).

Accommodations policies and practice in K–12 education are very different today than they were 15 years ago when NCEO searched test manuals and asked state personnel whether they had anything available on their testing accommodations policies. Today these policies are almost always available on state Web sites, and often in a variety of other formats designed for parents, teachers, and students.

This chapter provides an introduction to the topic of state policies and accommodations by touching on three main topics:

- How many students are using assessment accommodations?

- What do state policies/guidelines tell us about accommodations—which are allowed and not allowed by states?

- What are some of the issues and implications that surround the use of accommodations?

These topics provide the basis for a meaningful conversation about research on accommodations. For research to be meaningful, however, we need to know what is happening when tests are actually given to students.

USE OF ACCOMMODATIONS

In the past, there were no requirements to track the use of accommodations. Based on state policy, we knew that certain accommodations were most frequently allowed (e.g., Braille, large print). But this information had no relationship to which specific accommodations were used most often or how many students were using them.

In 1999, NCEO attempted to document the percentages of students using accommodations through a state survey (Thompson & Thurlow, 1999). At that time, only 12 states were able to provide information on either the numbers or percentages of students using accommodations during state testing. Rates varied from 8% to 84% of students in a state at a grade or school level. There are many confounds in these data; what actually counted as an accommodation varied from state to state. For example, in one state allowing students to take extra breaks was considered an accommodation and counted as such. In another it was considered good testing practice and not counted as an accommodation. These kinds of differences affect not only the numbers of accommodations that are received, but also the numbers of students who receive accommodations. Such confounds existed in 1999 and still exist today.

When IDEA was reauthorized in 2004, a requirement was added that states report on the number of students who use accommodations to participate in the regular assessment. NCEO's 2005 survey of state directors of special education (Thompson, Johnstone, Thurlow, & Altman, 2005) indicated that about half of the regular states (*n* = 26) and

TABLE 1-1

Percentage of Students With IEPs Using Accommodations During the Regular Assessment

		Elementary	Middle	High School
Reading				
	States Reporting	34	34	29
	Mean Percent	65.2	64.3	61.8
	Range	21.4–100.0	12.3–100.0	13.0–100.0
Math				
	States Reporting	35	35	29
	Mean Percent	65.8	64.2	61.1
	Range	25.9–100.0	17.9–100.0	5.8–100.0

Note. From Annual performance reports: 2003–2004 state assessment data (Table 3, p. 21) by M. L. Thurlow, R. Moen, & J. Altman, (2006) Minneapolis, MN: University of Minnesota, National Center on Educational Outcomes.

2 of the 10 unique states have the capability to report on specific accommodations. (Unique states are those entities that receive U.S. special education funding: American Samoa, Bureau of Indian Affairs, Commonwealth of the Northern Mariana Islands, District of Columbia, Federated States of Micronesia, Guam, Marshall Islands, Palau, Puerto Rico, and the Virgin Islands.) Another 12 regular states can report on nonspecific accommodations used (i.e., they can indicate the number of students using accommodations), and 8 regular states can report on the number using standard versus nonstandard accommodations. Those states that cannot report often have local summaries that are not yet reported back to the state.

Data on the percentages of students using accommodations for the testing year 2003 to 2004 (Thurlow, Moen, & Altman, 2006) indicate that the rates of use of accommodations across states are highly variable, regardless of the level of schooling (elementary, middle, high school). These data are shown in Table 1-1.

Approximately three fourths of the regular states are represented in these data. The average percentage of students using accom-modations is about 65% at the elementary school and 64% at the middle school, virtually the same. The 61% at the high school level is not that far below the elementary and middle school levels either, regardless of whether the content is reading or math. This latter finding is in contrast to previous findings that show quite a difference between the elementary and the high school level in terms of percentages of students using accommodations (Thurlow, 2001).

The range in accommodation rates is interesting and something of concern. The numbers in the range reflect the rate of use for a single state at a single grade level (e.g., in one state in Grade 4). Thus, for elementary reading, in one state 21.4% of students in the elementary grade tested used accom-modations and in another state 100% of students in the elementary grade tested used accommodations. In the analyses repre-sented in Table 1-1, Grade 4 was used as the common grade for the elementary level unless the state did not test in that grade, then Grade 3 was used. If neither Grade 3 nor Grade 4 was available, then Grade 5 was used. The important point to pull from these numbers is that the range in provision of accommodations across states is tremendous.

What do such wide differences in the provision of accommodations mean? Does it reflect huge differences in policy, which make it unlikely that students will use accommodations in some and very likely that almost all students will use accommodations in others? Is it an implementation issue having nothing to do with what the policies are? It is important to have a better understanding of the policies to understand these answers.

STATE POLICIES

State policies and guidelines on accommodations serve a number of purposes including determining who may receive accommodations during testing and outlining the parameters of the use of each accommodation. These policies and guidelines provide a basis for identifying issues and implications that surround accommodations today.

States vary in who they allow to use accommodations during testing. In several states, testing accommodations are not limited to those students who have IEPs or to those students who have 504 accommodation plans. Of course, many states also allow English language learners to use accommodations during testing (Rivera, Collum, Willner & Sia, 2006). The focus of this chapter is on accommodations for students with disabilities.

Two states allowed all students to use accommodations in 2005. Both Oregon and Wyoming did so without any restrictions on the accommodation, other than to indicate that the student must need the accommodation and it must have been a part of the student's regular instruction. Six states indicated that any student could use accommodations with qualifications on their use (Colorado, Kansas, Montana, New Hampshire, Rhode Island, and Vermont), with the qualifications generally limiting the students to standard accommodations, and also requiring that the accommodations must

have been used for regular classroom instruction. Several states' accommodation policies (n = 11) specifically recognized the need to provide accommodations under special circumstances, such as when the student breaks an arm, or is hospitalized for an extended amount of time.

Criteria that states indicated in their written policies that can be used to guide decisions about accommodations are shown in Figure 1-1. The use of accommodations in instruction is the most frequently cited criterion by states, followed by meeting individual student needs and maintaining the validity of the test. States using length of time as a criterion (Alabama, Alaska, Colorado, Georgia, New Mexico, and Wyoming) are referring to the length of time that the accommodation has been used in instruction prior to testing—the justification being that it is not appropriate to introduce an accommodation a day or two before testing just so that it can be used during the assessment.

Other criteria include a range of topics, but most often include a concern that the accommodations actually be documented in the IEP or 504 plan. Other criteria include that parents provide input, and that the student show skill in using the accommodation.

States also have identified factors that they do not want to see included as a basis for decisions that are made about accommodations. For example, the nature of the disability is not supposed to determine the accommodations used—this is a reaction to early accommodation policies that indicated that if a child had a learning disability, the accommodations to be used were X, Y, and Z. But, as shown in Figure 1-2, there are other factors that states have identified as ones that they do not want to see as the basis for decisions, such as administrative convenience or the percentage of time that the student receives services.

When specific accommodations that may be needed are not listed, the majority of states require that approval for their use dur-

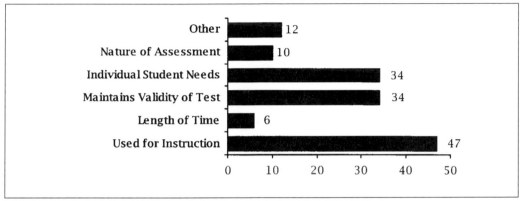

FIGURE 1-1

Numbers of States Citing Specific Criteria to Guide Accommodation Decisions

Note. Based on preliminary version of *2005 state policies on assessment participation and accommodations for students with disabilities* (p. 11) by S. S. Lazarus, M. L. Thurlow, K. E. Lail, K. D. Eisenbraun, & K. Kato, 2006. Minneapolis, MN: University of Minnesota, National Center on Educational Outcomes.

ing the state test is sought. Data are not really kept about these kinds of approvals. How often do they occur? When they occur, how often is approval given? Are data kept on these accommodations? Better information about this particular policy avenue is needed.

ACCOMMODATION POLICIES ARE MUCH MORE COMPLICATED THAN THEY USED TO BE

When NCEO first started summarizing policies, accommodations were categorized as allowed, prohibited, and not mentioned. Since then, the terms accommodation and modification have been widely used to denote changes that do not alter the construct (accommodation) and those that do alter the construct (modification), but over time policies have become much more complicated. For this reason this chapter will define accommodations in the following way:

A   =   Allowed

A*   =   Allowed, but considered a nonstandard accommodation (no implications for scoring or aggregation)

AI   =   Allowed with implications for scoring and/or aggregation (i.e., score is reduced or eliminated from scoring or aggregation with other scores)

AC   =   Allowed in certain circumstances (e.g., allowed in math but not reading, or on one part of the test but not another)

P   =   Prohibited

Using these codes, NCEO researchers categorize policies and cluster accommodations into four general groups: presentation, response, timing, and setting. Recently we have also looked at those accommodations that are provided by humans and now refer to them as "access assistants."

Presentation Accommodations

The most frequently mentioned presentation accommodations are large print, Braille, and signing directions. This is the case even though these are not the most frequently requested or used accommodations.

Even though Braille is one of the more frequently allowed accommodations, it is not uniformly allowed without restrictions

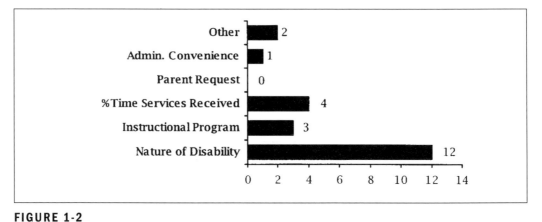

FIGURE 1-2

Numbers of States Citing Specific Criteria that Should Not be Used to Guide
Accommodation Decisions

Note. Based on preliminary version of 2005 *state policies on assessment participation and accommodations for students with disabilities* (p. 12) by S. S. Lazarus, M. L. Thurlow, K. E. Lail, K. D. Eisenbraun, & K. Kato, 2006. Minneapolis, MN: University of Minnesota, National Center on educational Outcomes.

across the states (Clapper, Morse, Lazarus, Thompson, & Thurlow, 2005). A couple of the more controversial presentation accommodations are sign language interpretation of the questions and reading aloud the questions. It is interesting that signing of questions is, in general, more often allowed (8 states outright, 19 additional states under certain conditions, and 12 more under certain conditions and with implications for scoring, totaling 39 states). For reading aloud the questions, 2 states allow this outright; 6 states allow it but call it nonstandard, yet seem to have no consequences for scoring or aggregation (although they may put some notation on the student's record in certain circumstances—such as when the test was a reading test); 26 allow it in certain circumstances; and 11 allow it under certain circumstances and with implications for scoring (totally 45 states). The circumstances under which both signing and reading aloud are not allowed is almost always reading—these accommodations are not considered appropriate for the reading assessment, or for a certain part of the reading assessment.

Response Accommodations

In the accommodations referred to as response accommodations, there are several that are the source of controversy, and several that are interesting. The computer/machine accommodation is interesting because it seems to provide for accommodations that are not allowed through other avenues. The computer/machine is a general description in most states, and when there is an indication that it can be used under certain conditions, the condition usually refers to disabling spell checker and grammar devices.

In NCEO's recent analysis of accommodation policies (Lazarus, Thompson, & Thurlow, 2006), computer/machine accommodations are clearly separated from policies that identified the possibility of using a speech-to-text or text-to-speech device (including computers for this purpose). For the states that allowed these devices, most were allowing speech-to-text (Arizona, California, Connecticut, Michigan, North Dakota, Minnesota, South Carolina, Utah, and Vermont); some allowed text-to-speech

(Delaware, Florida, Indiana, Massachusetts, New York, Pennsylvania, Washington). Kentucky, North Carolina, and Wisconsin allowed both speech-to-text and text-to-speech. Few of these states were qualifying the use of these devices; Arizona indicated that speech-to-text is allowed under certain conditions and has implications for scoring, and Connecticut indicated that speech-to-text is allowed under certain conditions. The text-to-speech is an interesting addition to the read aloud accommodation. Although the read aloud accommodation is not allowed very often without qualification, it seems that the speech-to-text device may be allowed more often. More investigation is needed here.

Timing Accommodations

The most controversial timing accommodations are those dealing with multiple sessions or multiple days. When these accommodations are allowed under certain circumstances, the circumstances usually refer to restrictions (e.g., must occur within the testing window, or testing day for sessions), and only sometimes refer to specific tests. Most timing accommodations are allowed.

Setting Accommodations

Setting accommodations are also generally accepted across the states. The student's home is one of the less frequently approved accommodations; when it is mentioned it is often listed as allowed under certain circumstances.

Access Assistants

In 2005, NCEO examined the number of states that had guidelines for the individuals who were involved in accommodations, such as readers, sign language interpreters, and scribes. For the 2005 policies, the numbers of states with policies were: 26 for readers, 20 for sign language interpreter, and 33 for scribe; 10 states had no guidelines at all. A study conducted on the 2003 guidelines (Clapper et al., 2005) showed that the guidelines specified what the access assistants could and could not do, detailed the qualifications that the individuals needed, and the nature of the training that the individuals needed to have or that needed to be provided. It was obvious in the guidelines that were included in that report that the requirements were different, and that sometimes the implications of having an access assistant were different from those of accommodations that were similar but without the human element. For example, guidelines for scribes often have instructions about spelling. In one state, students were allowed to see correctly spelled words when they had a scribe, even though they could not do so when a computer was used.

These kinds of inconsistencies become evident when examining many of the state policies related to text-to-speech technology and access assistants. Consistency in accommodations is probably one of the criteria that needs to be attained in order for educators to feel confident about how tests are administered. Consistency is also a critical element of the validity of the assessments where accommodations are used. This is the first of many issues that emerge related to accommodations.

ISSUES AND IMPLICATIONS

There are many issues and implications that emerge from state policies on accommodations. Three of these issues are addressed in the following sections.

Accommodation Decision Making

Research-based decision-making practice in which accommodation issues are identified by a state and then researched through randomized trial designs to produce a decision about accommodation policy may have to remain an ideal. Perhaps it is possible to conduct studies in large states where sufficient numbers of students are available to support such designs, and where there is confidence that the students who need the accommodations are the ones included in the research, but this may not be possible in most states. It is important for researchers to continue to conduct accommodations research, making all of their assumptions and decisions very clear, so that the applicability to states can be judged by the states themselves.

Research, however, is never going to answer all the questions that states face related to accommodations decisions. Reasoned judgment is going to have to take a role in these decisions. It is important that those making the reasoned judgments have a good basis for those judgments and are making them as a total team: A team comprised of assessment, special education, and curriculum who know about the constructs to be measured, current and future life functioning, and probably other factors as well.

There is a tremendous need for better decision making about specific accommodations that individual students need. General characteristics of students, not their categories, have been used to help determine what accommodations students need. Still, there is nothing like data-based decision making to determine which accommodations are useful to students and which they will actually use. Yet, educators seem to be reluctant to use these techniques to determine needed accommodations. This is true for instruction, which should be the basis for determining accommodations for assessment.

The most important way to improve the decision-making process is to allow educators to bring knowledge based on successful use in the classroom, to the IEP team. Yet there is little research on this approach. If the decisions about who needs what accommoda-

tions are faulty, then how can the assessment itself be considered valid?

Concerns about accommodations that produced invalid results were somewhat of a hidden issue in the past. Those accommodations were used by students, but they were given a zero score. The issues are no longer so hidden. States and schools really cannot afford to be giving students scores of zero when they have performed on a test and demonstrated knowledge against standards. Solutions other than giving zero scores have to be found, such as looking at what the constructs are—what is really being measured. One solution may involve breaking the components of a test apart when giving scores, and then adding them back together. For example, only the items that truly measure decoding would get a zero on a test that is read to a student, but for the component that measures understanding of information, the earned scores would be recorded. These approaches need us to have some highly controversial discussions until we reach some agreement on solutions.

K-12 Versus Postsecondary Accommodations

As more and more students move through a K–12 system in which they are allowed to use a range of accommodations, what will happen as they enter the postsecondary system? Will there be greater flexibility there, or are students being set up for failure in a system where they will not have access to the same accommodations, or where accommodations will not be provided to them without special requests? Are students being adequately prepared for the postsecondary scene when accommodations are provided relatively liberally during both assessment and instruction in the K–12 system? There is little evidence that states have tried to tie their accommodations policies to testing that occurs after K–12 education.

Future of Accommodations and Related Areas

Accommodations have produced several related areas of study that are pushing innovative ideas in the area of assessment. One of them is universal design applied to assessment. Universal design has had many positive effects, yet recently has also been the subject of backlash. There have been questions such as, "What is it really?" "Is it too costly (for test publishers)?" One wonders why is seems easier to push costs to the field in the form of accommodations than from the beginning for everyone in the form of universally designed assessments.

Work in the area of accessible reading assessments shows that a whole area such as this can also get very political—with different agendas pushing and pulling away from the goal of targeting the issues and trying to ensure that students show what they know and can do in the area of reading.

CONCLUSIONS

Accommodations are at the forefront of the assessment frontier that has to be addressed if all students are going to be included. States worked on their accommodations policies in earnest in the mid-1990s, and then have moved along refining this and that since then. Lately states have devoted considerable energy to alternate assessments, and rightly so. But as that occurred, the use of accommodations has burgeoned. On the one hand, this is good. Educators and students are more aware of them and are asking for them. On the other hand, we need to get a handle on what is going on. Following are a few of these implications that require additional work.

1. Researchers and educators need to think about new ways to conduct research in this area. Isolating one accommodation at a time has problems because few students need only one accommodation. As

soon as we limit, we have produced an invalid situation for most students. Perhaps looking at the effects of various accommodations by item is the next step in approaches that have been taken. There is some reason to believe that accommodations do not work at the test level, but rather at the item level. Lynn Fuchs and Jerry Tindal and their colleagues have suggested this, and continued exploration is definitely warranted.

2. Professional development is a must. We have had repeated evidence that even though states are more savvy about accommodations and are producing better policies and guidelines, those individuals who make decisions may not be aware of their own state policies. This does not mean that they should start from the policies in making their decisions, but they certainly should know them. They should know that if they allow a certain accommodation, it might result in the student not receiving a score. A study a couple years ago showed that a significant percentage of teachers on IEP teams did not know which accommodations in their state would produce this type of outcome for a student's test results (Lazarus et al., 2006).

3. States and districts need to keep track of what is happening with accommodations. They need to have some process to check whether students are getting the accommodations they are supposed to be getting, getting accommodations other than what they are supposed to be getting, or perhaps, not getting the accommodations that they should be getting. They need to keep track of whether accommodations are being bundled for the sake of ease, an approach that can result in lowering the scores of some students.

4. There must be continued improvement of assessments. Whether we call it striv-

ing to make assessments more accessible or more universally designed, there are still things that can be done to improve assessments. We need to address the concerns of both testing companies and states.

Accommodations are going to continue to be an important part of assessments for students with disabilities. It is important for us to learn as much as we can about what works—and what we need to do to make what works really work.

REFERENCES

Clapper, A. T., Morse, A. B., Lazarus, S. S., Thompson, S. J., & Thurlow, M. L. (2005). *2003 state policies on assessment participation and accommodations for students with disabilities* (Synthesis Report 56). Minneapolis, MN: University of Minnesota, National Center on Educational Outcomes.

Clapper, A. T., Morse, A. B., Thompson, S. J., & Thurlow, M. L. (2005). *Access assistants for state assessments: A study of state guidelines for scribes, readers, and sign language interpreters* (Synthesis Report 58). Minneapolis, MN: University of Minnesota, National Center on Educational Outcomes.

Lazarus, S. S., Thompson, S. J., & Thurlow, M. L. (2006). *How students access accommodations in assessment and instruction: Results of a survey of special education teachers* (EPRRI Issue Brief Seven). College Park, MD: University of Maryland, Educational Policy Reform Research Institute.

Lazarus, S. S., Thurlow, M. L., Lail, K. E., Eisenbraun, K. D., & Kato, K. (2006). *2005 state policies on assessment participation and accommodations for students with disabilities.* (Synthesis Report 64). Minneapolis, MN: University of Minnesota, National Center on Educational Outcomes. Retrieved from the World Wide Web: http://education.umn. edu/NCEO/OnlinePubs/Synthesis64/

Rivera, C., Collum, E., Willner, L. S., & Sia, J. K. (2006). Study 1: An analysis of state assessment policies regarding the accommodation of English language learners. In C. Rivera &

E. Collum (Eds.), *State assessment policy and practice for English language learners: A national perspective* (pp. 1–173). Mahwah, NJ: Lawrence Erlbaum.

Sireci, S. G., Scarpati, S. E., & Li, S. (2005). Test accommodations for students with disabilities: An analysis of the interaction hypothesis. *Review of Educational Research, 75*(4), 457–490.

Thompson, S. J., Johnstone, C. J., Thurlow, M. L., & Altman, J. R. (2005). *2005 State special education outcomes: Steps forward in a decade of change.* Minneapolis, MN: University of Minnesota, National Center on Educational Outcomes.

Thompson, S. J., & Thurlow, M. L. (1999). *1999 State special education outcomes: A report on state activities at the end of the century.* Minneapolis, MN: University of Minnesota, National Center on Educational Outcomes.

Thurlow, M. (2001). *Use of accommodations in state assessments: What databases tell us about differential levels of use and how to document the use of accommodations* (Technical Report 30). Minneapolis, MN: University of Minnesota, National Center on Educational Outcomes.

Thurlow, M. L., Moen, R., & Altman, J. (2006). *Annual performance reports: 2003–2004 state assessment data.* (Available from the NCEO Web site at http://www.education.umn.edu/ nceo/OnlinePubs/APRsummary2006.pdf). Minneapolis, MN: University of Minnesota, National Center on Educational Outcomes.

Thurlow, M. L., Ysseldyke, J. E., & Silverstein, B. (March, 1993). *Testing accommodations for students with disabilities: A review of the literature* (Synthesis Report 4). Minneapolis, MN: University of Minnesota, National Center on Educational Outcomes.

Thurlow, M. L., Ysseldyke, J. E., & Silverstein, B. (1995). Testing accommodations for students with disabilities. *Remedial and Special Education, 16*(5), 260–270.

Tindal, G., & Fuchs, L. S. (1999). *A summary of research on test changes: An empirical basis for defining accommodations.* Lexington, KY: University of Kentucky, Mid-South Research Resource Center.

English Language Learners With Disabilities

JAMAL ABEDI

University of California, Davis

Although the No Child Left Behind Act of 2001 (NCLB) has placed substantial focus on accountability for both students with disabilities (SWD) and English language learners (ELL), limited information on numbers, demographic background, educational settings, and performance has been gathered for English language learners with disabilities (ELLWD). ELLs represent a significant and growing segment of students in special education. The U.S. Department of Education's Office of English Language Acquisition estimates the number of ELLWD in Grades K to 12 in U.S. public schools to be around 357,300 students during the 2001 to 2002 school year, which represents 9% of the total ELL student population, and 8% of all children in special education (National Symposium on Learning Disabilities in English Language Learners, 2003). This estimate is similar to those provided by researchers based on surveys from local educational agencies (Zehler, Fleischman, Hopstock, Pendzick, & Stephenson, 2003). A serious concern regarding ELL students is the sub-

stantial achievement gap between them and other students.

This chapter provides an overview of the performance of ELLWD on state assessments and outlines three areas or critical points of interaction that influence performance outcomes for these students: classification, accommodations, and assessment.

PERFORMANCE GAP

Research studies reported in the literature show a substantial performance gap between ELL and non-ELL students (see, e.g., Abedi, 2004; Abedi, Hofstetter, & Lord, 2004; Abedi, Leon, & Mirocha, 2003). Many different factors contribute to a performance gap, including those related to instruction and assessment. Our focus is on factors related to assessment, in particular, linguistic factors of test items. The linguistic complexity of test items makes them more difficult for ELL students to comprehend, and can contribute to the performance gap between ELL and non-ELL students (Abedi, 2006a). Recently reported studies also document a major performance gap between students with disabilities and students without disabilities. As a result of facing the dual challenges of both language limitations and a disability, the academic performance of ELL students with disabilities is projected to fall behind both students with disabilities and ELL students (Abedi, 2006c).

The information provided in Tables 2-1 and 2-2 compares performance on a variety of Grade K to 12 assessments across four subgroups: English language learners with disabilities (ELLWD), English language learners without disabilities (ELL), non-ELL students with a disability (SWD), and the non-ELL students without a disability (reference group). Data for this study come from two sites, called Sites 1 and 2 to assure anonymity. Site 1 represents an urban public school district. Site 2 represents a large state (unrelated to Site 1). The data include assessment outcomes and student background variables. The background variables include gender, ethnicity, free/reduced price lunch participation, parent education, student limited English proficiency (LEP) status, and student disability status. Item-level standardized achievement test data were also obtained. However, the sites differed in the standardized tests used, the type of language proficiency index used, and the type of background variables provided. (For a complete description of the data sites and analyses of data, see Abedi, Leon, & Mirocha, 2003.)

Descriptive statistics including mean, standard deviation, and number of students are reported for each group. In addition, performance differences between subgroups were also estimated in terms of effect sizes (Cohen, 1988; Kirk, 1995). The effect sizes are reported in two columns, the *partial effect*, which are effect sizes comparing each subgroup with the reference group, and the *group effect*, which compares the average performance of the three groups (ELL, SWD, and ELLWD) with the reference group.

Tables 2-1 and 2-2 show descriptive statistics and effect sizes for Grade 9 students and Grade 3 students, respectively.

Findings reported in Tables 2-1 and 2-2 are consistent and suggest that ELLWD students show the lowest performance when compared with other students, including ELL students and SWD. For example, in Grade 9 reading the performance gap between ELLWD students and the reference group is about 31 points, with smaller gaps when the reference group is compared to SWD (21 points) or ELL students (23 points). For math, the performance gaps are approximately 23, 19, and 15 points for these three groups respectively, and for science the respective performance gaps with the comparison groups are approximately 20, 15, and 15. A similar trend can be observed in Table 2-2 in which a summary of data analyses is reported for Grade 3 in reading and math. These large performance gaps between ELLWD and the comparison groups are partially due to the dual challenges these students face. However, these performance gaps may be reduced by drawing attention to the three previously mentioned critical points of interaction: classification, accommodation, and assessment.

CRITICAL POINTS OF INTERACTION: CLASSIFICATION, ACCOMMODATIONS, AND ASSESSMENT

It is clear that ELLWD students are faced with particular academic challenges and that these challenges persist across different grades and content areas. Although the observed performance gaps are credible, some of the differences between ELLWD scores and the scores of the other groups may result from other factors such as classification criteria, assessment characteristics, and accommodation policies rather than pure achievement differences. Figure 2-1 illustrates a model for the interaction between classification, assessment, and accommodations for ELLWD stu-

TABLE 2-1

Descriptive Statistics and Effect Sizes for Grade 9 Students in Reading, Math, and Science

					Effect Size	
Subgroups	M	SD	N	Gap	*Partial*	*Group*
Grade 9: Reading						
ELLWD	16.24	9.87	3635	30.67	.042	
ELL only	24.20	12.50	46532	22.71	.203	
SWD only	25.53	16.11	15142	21.38	.078	
Reference	46.91	18.15	196906			
Total	41.22	19.75	262215			.253
Grade 9: Math						
ELLWD	30.95	10.82	3635	23.37		.022
ELL only	38.89	15.04	46532	15.43	.092	
SWD only	35.32	14.61	15142	19.00	.055	
Reference	54.32	19.37	196906			
Total	50.16	19.73	262215			.137
Grade 9: Science						
ELLWD	30.09	11.51	3635	19.97	.022	
ELL only	35.48	12.57	46532	14.58	.113	
SWD only	35.41	14.58	15142	14.65	.046	
Reference	50.06	16.16	196906			
Total	46.35	16.74	262215			.149

Note. Data provided from 1998–1999 from Site 1.

dents. This model suggests that decisions for selecting accommodations for ELLWD and the performance outcomes of their accommodated assessments can be influenced by issues concerning classification and assessment. The selected accommodations can then impact both classification and assessment outcomes. All these factors can then determine the validity of assessment outcomes. A comprehensive view of any of these three components requires knowledge of the other two components.

Issues in Classification

This section of the chapter focuses on three areas of classifying ELLs. The first focus is on factors that impact classifying students as ELL with no disabilities, followed by classifying ELL students with disabilities (ELLWD),

and finally reclassifying ELLWD students to students with disabilities (SWD).

Classifying Students as ELL With No Disabilities. A number of researchers have raised concerns over the validity of criteria used for classifying ELLs. For example, according to recent research findings, there is not a strong relationship between students' ELL classification status (ELL/non-ELL) and their English language proficiency test scores. Studies found that only between 5% and 10% of the variance of ELL classifications can be explained by language proficiency test scores (see, e.g., Abedi, Leon, & Mirocha, 2003). This finding seems counterintuitive because a common characteristic of ELL students is their limited proficiency in the English language. If these students become proficient in English, they should be

TABLE 2-2

Descriptive Statistics and Effect Sizes for Grade 3 Students in Reading, Math, and Science

Subgroups	M	SD	N	Gap	Effect Size Partial	Effect Size Group
Grade 3: Reading						
ELLWD	19.15	13.76	5244	29.74	.032	
ELL only	27.97	15.82	97927	20.92	.184	
SWD only	31.61	20.82	19873	17.28	.039	
Reference	48.89	20.44	243817			
Total	41.95	21.64	366861			.208
Grade 3: Math						
ELLWD	25.07	16.63	5244	25.38	.021	
ELL only	37.00	18.16	97927	13.45	.077	
SWD only	34.64	20.94	19873	15.81	.029	
Reference	50.45	21.18	243817			
Total	45.64	21.49	366861			.104

Note. Data provided from 1998–1999 from Site 1.

reclassified as fluent English proficient. Therefore, scores of English language proficiency should be the sole or the major determinant of the ELL classification.

Results of studies published in the research literature have shown that in addition to students' level of English proficiency other factors may also influence decisions on ELL classification. Grissom (2004) and Abedi (2004) both found that variables such as gender, socioeconomic status (SES; as measured by free/reduced price lunch), ethnicity, and parent education are powerful predictors of ELL classification/reclassification. For example, Grissom indicated that in California, multiple criteria are used for classifying from ELL to redesignated fluent English proficient (RFEP). These criteria, according to Grissom include: (a) assessment of English language proficiency; (b) teacher evaluation; (c) parent opinion and consultation; and (d) performance in basic skills.

Classification of ELL as ELLWLD. In addition to issues in classifying ELLs, there are even greater issues in determining if an ELL also has a disability (particularly a learn-

ing disability or speech and language impairment). Problems associated with identifying these students require special attention. If these students are not identified as having a disability, then they may receive inappropriate instruction, assessments, and accommodations. ELLWD may not be properly identified if their disability is masked by their limited English proficiency, or their limited English proficiency may be inaccurately diagnosed as a disability. Literature shows ELL students with lower proficiency levels in their primary and secondary languages have the highest rate of identification in the special education categories. In addition, more ELL students tend to be placed in the "learning disability" category than in the "language and speech impairment" category (Artiles, Rueda, Salazar, & Higareda, 2005).

Similarly, Artiles, and Ortiz (2002) found a differential rate of overrepresentation of ELL students in special education programs in some states. For example, based on their data, 26.5% of ELLs in Massachusetts, 25.3% in South Dakota, and 20.1% in New Mexico were placed in special education programs,

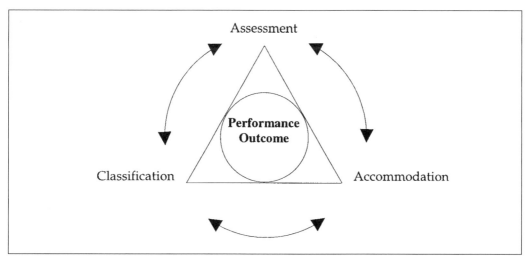

FIGURE 2-1

Interaction Between Classification, Assessment, and Accommodations for ELLWD

whereas less than 1% of ELLs in Colorado, Maryland, and North Carolina were placed in similar programs. Rueda, Artiles, Salazar, and Higareda (2002) reported that over a 5-year period (1993–1994 to 1998–1999), the placement rate of Latino ELLs in special education programs increased by 345% while their overall population in the district increased by only 12% during this period of time. Ortiz and Yates (2001) indicated that the overrepresentation of ELLs in special education classes may be due to the difficulty distinguishing students who truly have learning disabilities from other students, such as ELL students at the lower end of the English language proficiency distribution. Therefore, it is imperative that ELL students without disabilities are properly distinguished from ELL students with disabilities so that both groups can receive accommodations for both testing and instruction that is appropriate to their respective needs.

Reclassification of ELLWD to SWD. To examine the impact of variables that are unrelated to students' language background on the ELL classification system, a cohort of 1993–1994 Grade 7 students (*n* = 23,856) was created and followed for a period of 6 years (12 semesters, Fall 1993 to Spring 1999). An event history analysis (also referred to as a *survival analysis* approach, see Miller & Zhou, 1997) was conducted. Results of the event history analyses, which are presented in Table 2-3, indicated that in addition to the students' level of language proficiency, their family SES and their background variables (such as ethnicity) appear to correlate with their reclassification. In fact, this research showed that it took almost 10 semesters for Hispanic students to be reclassified from LEP to RFEP while it took half as much time for Asian and Caucasian students to be reclassified.

Due to lower performance of ELLWD students on assessments, one would expect the reclassification process to take longer. To have some understanding of the reclassification trend of ELLWD students, an event history analyses was conducted on a cohort of ELLWD students. Table 2-4 present results of these analyses. The data in Table 2-4 show a substantial increase in time to reclassify ELLWD as compared with the time to reclassify ELL students included in Table 2-3. In all categories of all variables used in this study, it took over 12 semesters for ELLWD to be

TABLE 2-3

Site 2 Grade 7 1993–1994 Cohort ELL Event History Analysis by Student Background Variables

Subgroup	Number ELL at Start	% RFEP Within 0–6 Years	% RFEP Within 7–12 Years	Mdn Time in ELL Status
Gender				
Female	11,763	27	62	9.08
Male	12,093	23	53	9.98
Ethnicity				
Asian	1,246	55	77	5.45
Hispanic	21,167	21	57	9.91
Caucasian	1,019	55	68	5.49
Free Lunch				
Free/Reduced	19,099	24	59	9.52
Nonparticipant	4,757	29	50	9.55
Title I				
Title I	14,166	18	56	10.13
Non-Title I	9,690	34	60	8.45
93–94 SAT9 Reading Test				
Not tested	10,465	18	38	>12.00
Percentile 1–15	3,835	08	42	>12.00
Percentile 16–36	5,704	23	75	8.83
Percentile 37+	3,852	59	94	5.07
96–97 SAT9 Reading Test				
Not tested	10,980	17	38	>12.00
Percentile 1–15	6,141	15	52	10.80
Percentile 16–36	3,747	32	84	7.89
Percentile 37+	2,988	58	94	5.13

Note. Students with missing data were deleted, therefore, totals are slightly different across different groups.
Source: Data provided from 1993–94 from Site 1.

reclassified to the fluent English proficiency category. Since the data is limited to 12 semesters, we are unable to determine how much beyond 12 semesters it took to reclassify these students, if at all.

Minnema, Thurlow, Anderson, and Stone (2005) stated, "The classification of an English language learner with disabilities remains elusive in part due to the lack of consensus in the field on who an English language learner actually is and how to refer to these students" (p. 10). The authors noted that "a major concern rests on English language proficiency measures and definitions of language proficiency, which is confounded even more when paired with a disability" (p. 10).

Issues in Assessment

Prior research on the technical adequacy of state assessments for ELLs shows a substantial

TABLE 2-4

Site 2 Grade 7 1993–1994 Cohort ELL/SD Event History Analysis by Student Background Variables

Subgroup	Number ELL & SD at Start	% RFEP Within 0–6 Years	% RFEP Within 7–12 Years	Mdn Time in ELL Status
Gender				
Female	239	1	6	>12.0
Male	495	5	5	>12.0
Ethnicity				
Asian	Below 30			
Hispanic	687	4	5	>12.0
Caucasian	Below 30			
Free Lunch				
Free/Reduced	569	4	4	>12.0
Nonparticipant	165	3	10	>12.0
Title I				
Title I	323	4	5	>12.0
Non-Title I	411	3	5	>12.0
93–94 SAT9 Reading Test				
Not Tested	688	4	4	>12.00
Percentile 1–15	34	6	9	>12.00
Percentile 16–36	Below 30			
Percentile 37+	Below 30			
96–97 SAT9 Reading Test				
Not Tested	481	3	2	>12.00
Percentile 1–15	238	4	8	>12.00
Percentile 16–36	Below 30			
Percentile 37+	Below 30			

Note. Students with missing data were deleted, therefore, totals are slightly different across different groups.
Source: Data provided from 1993–94 from Site 1.

gap in reliability (internal consistency) and validity (concurrent validity) between ELL and non-ELL students on test items with substantial language demand (Abedi, 2006a; Abedi, Leon, et al. 2003). This gap in reliability and validity coefficients reduces as the assessment's language demand level decreases. For example, the results of analyses for an existing state assessment showed that the reliability coefficients (alpha) for English-only students ranged from .898 for math to .805 for both science and social science. For ELL students, however, alpha coefficients differed considerably across the content areas. In math, where language factors might have less influence on performance, the alpha coefficient for ELL students (.802) was slightly lower than the alpha for English-only students (.898). In language, science, and social science, however, the gap in alpha between English-only and ELL students was large. Averaging over language, science, and social science results, the alpha for English-only was .808 as compared to an average alpha of .603 for ELL students. These results suggest that language factors introduce a source of measurement error for ELL student test outcomes. Studies in which the linguistic complexity levels were reduced for science and social science items showed the gap in the reliability coefficient between ELL and non-ELL students was reduced substantially. (For a more detailed description, see Abedi, 2006a; Abedi, Leon, & Mirocha, 2003.)

For ELLWD students, the technical quality of an assessment is even more alarming. The information shown in Table 2-5 compares internal consistency coefficients for ELL, SWD and ELLWD students with the reference group (non-ELL/non-SWD) in Grade 9 reading, math, and science. As the data in Table 2-5 show, the internal consistency coefficients for SWD and ELL students were lower than the coefficients for the reference group. For the ELLWD this gap was even larger. For example, the internal consistency coefficient for reading was .833 for ELL students, .887 for SWD, and .731 for ELLWD (which is substantially lower than the coefficient for either SWD or ELL students). In math problem solving where test items may be linguistically complex, the internal consistency coefficient was .807 for ELL students, .789 for SWD, and .591 for ELLWD, as compared with a coefficient of .895 for the reference group. A similar pattern can be seen in science assessments. The coefficient was .633 for ELL students, .728 for SWD, and .537 for ELLWD, as compared with a coefficient of .799 for the reference group.

It is likely that the poor internal consistency for ELLWD students is due to a variety of factors. When considering just the assessments, it could be that ELLWD students have trouble with the difficulty of test items specifically related to the language load.

These language-related factors could be addressed and reduced with appropriate testing accommodations and assessments that are more universally designed. In addition, more explicit instruction in academic language may alleviate this issue.

Issues in Accommodations for ELLWD

Assessment issues also greatly impact decisions regarding the type of accommodations and the outcome of these accommodated assessments for ELLWD students. Literature has clearly demonstrated the impact of language factors on the assessment of ELL students. For example, Abedi, Lord, and Plummer (1997) showed that ELL students had more difficulty with linguistically complex test items regardless of the items' content difficulty. This same study found that ELL students also had a substantially higher number of omitted/not reached items due to difficulty understanding the test items (see also Abedi, 2004; Abedi et al., 2004). Appropriate accommodations to help these students overcome language challenges must be provided. Unfortunately, many of the accommodations used for ELL students do not have sufficient value for them. The strategy of test accommodations for ELL students originates in testing students with disabilities. Because of this, many forms of accommodations used for ELL students were created for SWD and may not be appropriate for ELL students. For example, in examining 73 accommodations used for ELL students across the nation (Rivera, 2003), only 11 (or 15%) of them were found to be relevant for ELL students (Abedi, 2006b). In making this determination, accommodations that directly address language needs were identified as being relevant for ELL students.

As states try to achieve greater inclusion of these students in their content-based assessments, multiple testing accommodations have been implemented. These accom-

TABLE 2-5

Internal Consistency for Grade 9 Students and Reading, Math, and Science

Subgroup	Cronbach's Alpha	N of Subjects	N of Items
Grade 9: Reading Reliability			
ELL only	.833	48801	54
SWD only	.887	16171	54
ELLWD	.731	3919	54
Reference	.907	202907	54
Grade 9: Math Reliability			
ELL only	.807	50666	48
SWD only	.789	16772	48
ELLWD	.591	4149	48
Reference	.895	204819	48
Grade 9: Science Reliability			
ELL only	.633	50179	40
SWD only	.728	16734	40
ELLWD	.537	4108	40
Reference	.799	204050	40

Note. Data provided from 1998–1999 from Site 1.

modations are provided to help ELLWD overcome challenges due to language acquisition and their disabilities. However, these accommodations have not been sufficiently evaluated (Rivera, Collum, Shafer, & Sia, 2004). Thus, literature on assessment and accommodations of ELL students with disabilities is scarce. Minnema et al. (2005) reviewed literature regarding ELLWD and large-scale assessments. They found only 10 articles related to all three of these criteria (ELLs, disabilities, and assessments) from the mid-1960s to 2004 (see also Thurlow & Liu, 2001).

Minnema et al.'s (2005) review of literature did not find any research studies that specifically addressed accommodations used during testing for ELLWD. The challenge is finding appropriate accommodations for ELLWD. State representatives that were interviewed by Anderson, Minnema, Thurlow, and Hall-Lande (2005) reported having separate accommodation policies for ELLs and SWDs. In these cases, a collaborative effort is needed to ensure that students are receiving accommodations that address both their linguistic and disability needs.

To better understand accommodations, one must view them within the entire academic system. That is, major factors that influence the selection of accommodations and affect the outcome of accommodated assessments must be carefully examined. For example, the validity of the accommodated assessments for ELLWD students is greatly influenced by factors affecting identification, classification, and assessment of these students.

DISCUSSION

ELLWD students face many challenges in their academic career. They must deal with their limited English proficiency (i.e., learning a new language) and coping with their disabilities, all factors that create obstacles in their academic progress. To help these students reach their highest educational attainment, as with any other students, different forms of assessment accommodations have been proposed. However, due to an extremely complex situation, these accommodations are often not effective and may even impact the validity of scores on the assessment. There are many factors affecting the selection of accommodations and the outcome of accommodated assessments. Among these factors are issues concerning properly identifying and classifying these students, along with the technical quality of assessments. Inappropriate placement of students (or lack of placement) in the ELLWD category can seriously affect decisions on selecting accommodations for these students and the accommodated assessment outcomes.

Discussing the pertinent issues related to identifying and assessing ELL and ELLWD students helps us to understand the complexity inherent in accommodation theory and practice for ELLWD students. Because these students are at a disadvantage from two aspects (language and disability issues), they should be accommodated for both their language needs as well as for their disabilities. Therefore, in many cases a combination of accommodations should be provided.

For the language aspect, their language background variables must be reviewed and accommodations that are relevant to their language background must be provided to them. For ELL students, the most common accommodations currently used by states are: use of extended time (42 of 48 states), use of a glossary (26 states), use of an English dictionary (33 states), use of a bilingual dictionary (22 states), and linguistically-simplified test items (12 states). Rivera (2003) presented a list of commonly used accommodations for ELL students. This list includes 73 accommodations, many of which may not be relevant for these students (Abedi, 2006b).

Research-based recommendations can be provided for some accommodations that can help these students with their language needs. For example, depending on their level of English language proficiency, accommodations such as linguistically modified tests (Abedi, 2006a); customized English and bilingual dictionaries (Abedi et al., 2004; Sireci, Li, & Scarpati, 2003) or native language or bilingual test booklets (Abedi, Lord, Hofstetter, & Baker, 2000; Sireci et al.); and computer-based testing would be relevant.

To assist ELLWD students with their disabilities, recommendations should be made based on several factors. First, the accommodations must be consistent with the IEP. Second, there must be some research evidence on the validity and effectiveness of accommodations to justify their use. According to a study by Thurlow et al. (2000), the most commonly permitted accommodations for students with disabilities were: Braille (allowed by 33 of the 48 states studied); computerized assessment (34 states); dictation of responses to a scribe (32 states); extended time (37 states); translation of instructions (40 states); allowance for marking answers in the test booklets (33 states); test items read aloud (34 states), or simplified test directions (31 states); and test breaks (33 states). Unfortunately, there is not sufficient research evidence to support the effectiveness or validity of many of these accommodations (Thurlow et al., 2000).

Providing valid, effective, and appropriate accommodations for ELLWD is based on a valid classification system for these students and high quality assessment instruments. If students are not correctly identified as ELLWD, then accommodations provided for these students may not work no matter how valid and effective they are. This is particularly important for ELLWD because improper classification may have even greater effects. Unfortunately, due to major limitations, existing data may not provide the evidence needed to examine the effect of misclassification and assessment issues on the provision, effectiveness, and validity of accommodations used for these students. This is an area of research that should be a high priority on the national agenda.

IMPLICATIONS

Implications for Policy Makers

Classification, assessment, and accommodations for ELLWD have major implications for policy makers because these students are faced with challenging tasks in their educational career. The main concern is the possibility of improper classification of ELL students as students with learning disabilities, particularly with the ELL students at the lowest level of English proficiency. Research has demonstrated that it takes a relatively long time (between 5–7 years) for these students to become proficient enough in English to participate and to benefit from instruction in English and also to understand assessment questions in English (see, for example, Hakuta, Butler, & Witt, 2000). During this transition period, they might be at risk of being misclassified as ELLs with learning disabilities. It is important for policy makers to be aware of the limitations of existing content-based assessments for ELL students in general and ELLWD students in particular. Earlier in this chapter we indicated that language factors have a more profound impact on the achievement outcomes of these students than any other group; therefore, to provide a fair assessment for these students, the impact of unnecessary linguistic complexity must be controlled for this group of students who are most affected by such factors. Even more importantly, policy makers should be aware of the technical issues in the selection and use of accommodations for these students. Appropriateness, effectiveness, and validity of the accommodations for these students should be clearly examined before using any accommodations for these students.

Implications for Researchers

Examining issues concerning classification, assessment, and accommodations for ELLWD students requires a more sophisticated research design and more attention because many different variables influence performance outcomes for these students. If researchers can understand the complexity inherent in the design of research for this group, they can first try to identify factors that influence performance of these students. Due to the dual challenges these students face, they may need more than one accommodation. Researchers are posed with the challenge to examine the effectiveness and validity of multiple accommodations for these students. On the other hand, issues concerning classification of these students may add to the complexity of the design for investigating the performance gap between ELLWD students and other students. This chapter may help researchers to include variables that are important to consider when dealing with the assessment of ELLWD students.

Implications for Practitioners

Educational practitioners can plan for more effective instruction and assessment systems for these students when they understand the issues involved in the assessment of ELLWD. According to the data presented previously, this subgroup had the lowest level of performance among any other subgroup of students. At least part of this achievement gap can be explained by nuisance variables that affect instructional and assessment systems for these students. Therefore, by gaining knowledge about these issues, teachers and other school officials could help schools provide more accessible instruction and assessments for ELLWD students which would provide more accurate information about what these students know.

REFERENCES

Abedi, J. (2004). The No Child Left Behind Act and English language learners: Assessment and accountability issues. *Educational Researcher, 33*(1), 4–14.

Abedi, J. (2006a). Language issues in item-development. In S. M. Downing & T. M. Haladyna (Eds.), *Handbook of Test Development* (pp. 377–398). Mahwah, NJ: Erlbaum.

Abedi, J. (2006b, April). *Are Accommodations Used for ELL Students Valid?* Paper presented at the 2006 annual meeting of the American Educational Research Association in San Francisco.

Abedi, J. (2006c). Psychometric Issues in the ELL Assessment and Special Education Eligibility. *Teacher's College Record 108*(11), 2282–2303.

Abedi, J., Hofstetter, C., & Lord, C. (2004). Assessment accommodations for English language learners: Implications for policy-based empirical research. *Review of Educational Research, 74*(1), 1–28.

Abedi, J., Leon, S., & Mirocha, J. (2003). *Impact of student language background on content-based performance: Analyses of extant data* (CSE Tech. Rep. No. 603). Los Angeles: University of California, National Center for Research on Evaluation, Standards, and Student Testing.

Abedi, J., Lord, C., Hofstetter, C., & Baker, E. (2000). Impact of accommodation strategies on English language learners' test performance. *Educational Measurement: Issues and Practice, 19*(3), 16–26.

Abedi, J., Lord, C., & Plummer, J. (1997). *Language background as a variable in NAEP mathematics performance* (CSE Tech. Rep. No. 429). Los Angeles: University of California, National Center for Research on Evaluation, Standards, and Student Testing.

Anderson, M., Minnema, J., Thurlow, M., & Hall-Lande, J. (2005). *Confronting the unique challenges of including English language learners with disabilities in statewide assessments* (ELLs with Disabilities Report 9). Minneapolis, MN: University of Minnesota, National Center on Educational Outcomes.

Artiles, A. J., & Ortiz, A. A. (Eds.). (2002). *English language learners with special education needs: Identification, assessment, and instruction.* Washington, DC: Center for Applied Linguistics.

Artiles, A. J., Rueda, R., Salazar, J., & Higareda, I. (2005). Within-group diversity in minority disproportionate representation: English Language Learners in urban school districts. *Exceptional Children, 71,* 283–300.

Cohen, J. (1988). *Statistical power analysis for the behavioral sciences* (2nd ed.). Hillsdale, NJ: Erlbaum.

Grissom, J. B. (2004). Reclassification of English language learners. *Education Policy Analysis Archives, 12*(36). Retrieved September 3, 2004, from http://epaa.asu.edu/epaa/v12n36/

Hakuta, K., Butler, Y., & Witt, D. (2000). *How long does it take English learners to attain proficiency?* (Policy Report 2000-1). University of California: Linguistic Minority Research Institute.

Kirk, R. E. (1995). *Experimental design: Procedures for the behavioral sciences* (2nd ed.). Pacific Grove, CA: Brooks/Cole.

Miller, R. A., & Zhou, X. (1997). *Survival analysis with long-term survivors.* New York: John Wiley & Sons.

Minnema, J., Thurlow, M., Anderson, M., & Stone, K. (2005). *English language learners with disabilities and large-scale assessments: What the literature can tell us* (ELLs with Disabilities Report 6). Minneapolis, MN: University of Minnesota, National Center on Educational Outcomes.

National Symposium on Learning Disabilities in English Language Learners. (2003). Washington, DC: U.S. Department of Education. Office of Special Education and Rehabilitative Services, Office of English Language Acquisition.

Ortiz, A. A., & Yates, J. R. (2001). A framework of serving English language learners with disabilities. *Journal of Special Education Leadership, 14*(2), 72–80.

Rivera, C. (2003, June). *State assessment policies for English language learners.* Paper presented at the annual Council of Chief State School Officers National Large-Scale Assessment Conference, San Antonio, TX.

Rivera, C., Collum, E., Shafer, L., & Sia, J. K. (2004). *Analysis of state assessment policies regarding the accommodation of English language learners, SY 2000–2001.* Arlington, VA: George Washington University, Center for Equity and Excellence in Education.

Rueda, A., Artiles, A. J., Salazar, J., & Higareda, I. (2002). An analysis of special education as a response to the diminished academic achievement of Chicano/Latino students: An update. In R. R. Valenica (Ed.), *Chicano school failure and success: Past, present, and future* (2nd ed., pp. 310–332). London: Routledge/Palmer.

Sireci, S. G., Li, S., & Scarpati, S. (2003). *The effects of test accommodation on test performance: A review of the literature* (Center for Educational Assessment Research Report No. 485). Amherst, MA: School of Education, University of Massachusetts, Amherst.

Thurlow, M., & Liu, K. (2001). *State and district assessments as an avenue to equity and excellence for English language learners with disabili-*ties (LEP Projects Report 2). Minneapolis, MN: University of Minnesota, National Center on Educational Outcomes.

Thurlow, M. L., McGrew, K. S., Tindal, G., Thompson, S. J., Ysseldyke, J. E., Elliott, J. L. (2000). *Assessment accommodations research: Considerations for design and analysis* (Tech. Rep. No. 26). Minneapolis, MN: University of Minnesota, National Center on Educational Outcomes.

Zehler, A. M., Fleischman, H. L., Hopstock, P. J., Pendzick, M. L., & Stephenson, T. G. (2003). *Descriptive study of services to LEP students and LEP students with disabilities* (Special Topic Report No. 4: Findings on Special Education LEP Students). Arlington, VA: Development Associates.

Author Note: The author acknowledges the valuable contribution of colleagues in preparation of this manuscript. Lisa Sullivan and Jenny Kao contributed substantially with comments and assistance in structuring and revising the paper. Seth Leon provided valuable assistance with the data analyses.

CHAPTER 3

Accommodations in Testing: Law, Policy, and Practice

DIANA PULLIN
Boston College

With high-stakes testing playing an increasing role in local schools and in public accountability, the participation of students with disabilities also takes on increasing importance. However, the inclusion of students with disabilities in state or local standardized testing includes a number of challenges for local educators, students and parents, and public officials. This chapter provides a framework for considering the legal, public policy, and educational issues associated with accommodations in testing for students with disabilities.

Three key issues in considering accommodations in testing for students with disabilities include:

- What are the public policy goals for current education reform initiatives? For educating students with disabilities?

- What are the consequences of including students with disabilities in general education reform initiatives?

- What are the legal and technical requirements concerning students with

disabilities and education reform initiatives?

The last issue will be the focus of this chapter, but this it cannot be fully understood without considering the two previous issues.

There are several competing public policy goals and aspirations associated with the inclusion of students with disabilities in current education reform initiatives, particularly the use of standardized tests to make high-stakes decisions about students, schools and school systems, and educators. Current efforts to implement the No Child Left Behind Act of 2001 (NCLB) and many state education reform laws are based on decisions that the greater good (for *all* students and for society) is enhanced (a) when common content standards are articulated for all students and (b) when standardized tests are used to both drive instruction and to determine accountability for educational achievement.

These public policy choices about education reform and how all students should be educated have been accompanied by decisions to include students with disabilities in the new initiatives. However, education reforms based on the premise that (a) all students should be exposed to common curriculum content and (b) curriculum achievement should be assessed by standardized tests occur in a context in which the nation's schools have been operating for over a quarter of a century under a set of legal provisions requiring *individualized approaches* to the education of students with disabilities. As a result, the inclusion of students with disabilities in test-based education reform presents a series of public policy, legal, and practical challenges for educators.

There are tensions among standardization, individualization, and accountability when students with disabilities participate in current education reform efforts. Educators, testing organizations, and public policy makers must try to ensure individual opportunity to learn for students with disabilities while also trying to avoid disability-based discrimination.

These policy and practical problems present a challenging, but surmountable, set of pedagogic and psychometric issues that continue to evolve as the implications of current accountability efforts become clearer. And, while the basic legal provisions concerning these initiatives remain unchanged, the U.S. Department of Education and most state education agencies have changed their policies and regulations several times as implementation challenges become more evident. As a result, the legal requirements continue to evolve and practitioners are required to continually check these provisions to determine compliance requirements.

This chapter addresses one particular set of issues concerning the participation of students with disabilities in test-based, standards-driven education reform: accommodations in testing.

THE IMPACT OF EDUCATION REFORM ON STUDENTS WITH DISABILITIES

Many advocates for students with disabilities applaud the inclusion of this student population in current education reform initiatives. From their perspective, the initiatives continue the movement for full inclusion in education, while at the same time enhancing accountability for improved educational outcomes for the population. In reality, there is good news and bad news associated with the participation of students with disabilities in current education reform initiatives. The good news is that more students with disabilities are participating in education reform and accountability systems. The bad news is that more and more frequently, students with disabilities are the low-performing subgroup causing otherwise high performing schools and districts to fail to meet measures of adequate yearly progress (AYP; Pullin, 2005). This places pressure on educators, and on students, to enhance test scores among this population. It also presents educational challenges, and sometimes ethical challenges, as choices must be made about where to focus limited educational resources and whether there are means to increase scores readily. Also, there are more and more technical challenges associated with determining how to educate and how to validly and reliably test students with disabilities.

There are increasing levels of proficiency among students with disabilities, which many state-level officials attribute to, among other things:

- Better alignment of students' IEPs with state standards.
- Increased access to standards-based instruction.
- Improved professional development.
- The development and implementation of accommodations.
- Guidelines and training (Thompson, Johnstone, Thurlow, & Altman, 2005).

There is evidence of wide variation in accommodations approaches and in levels of specificity of state policies on accommodations (Thompson, Johnstone, Thurlow, & Altman, 2005). And, there is still a great deal to be learned, as discussed elsewhere in this book, about the technical and pedagogic issues associated with accommodations in testing. A brief overview of some of the legal and technical issues follows.

LEGAL REQUIREMENTS CONCERNING PARTICIPATION IN TESTING

There are several sources of federal law impacting the testing of students with disabilities and their participation in state and national education reform initiatives. The most recent provisions of the Individuals With Disabilities Education Act (IDEA), the Individuals With Disabilities Education Improvement Act of 2004, call on states to include students with disabilities in state education reform initiatives, while at the same time requiring compliance with long-standing requirements for individualized educational opportunities for this population. NCLB reinforces the importance of the participation of students with disabilities in standards-based education reform and, among other things, requires that test results for these students be included in accountability reports and, as well, reported as a disaggregated subgroup in determining the AYP of schools so that there is specific accountability for educating this population.

In addition to the provisions of federal law specifying the educational opportunities and accountability to be afforded for students with disabilities, there are also some applicable civil rights statutes. Two federal laws bar discrimination on the basis of disability status: Section 504 of the Rehabilitation Act of 1973 and the Americans With Disabilities Act of 1990 (ADA). In addition, federal civil rights provisions barring discrimination against racial and language minorities (Title VI of the Civil Rights Act of 1964) are also applicable for some of these students.

Section 504 requires that:

> No otherwise qualified individual with a disability . . . shall, solely by reason of his or her disability, be excluded from the participation in, be denied the benefits of, or be subjected to discrimination under any program or activity receiving Federal financial assistance. 29 U.S.C. § 794(a)

Under the regulations for Section 504, schools receiving federal funding may not, on the basis of disability:

> (i) [d]eny a qualified handicapped person the opportunity to participate in or benefit from . . . [an] aid, benefit or service; (ii) [a]fford a qualified handicapped person an opportunity to participate in or benefit from . . . [an] aid, benefit, or service that is not equal to that afforded others; (iii) [p]rovide a qualified handicapped person with an aid, benefit or service that is not as effective as that provided to others; [or] (iv) [p]rovide different or separate aid, benefits or services to any handicapped person or to any class of handicapped person unless such action is necessary to provide qualified handicapped persons with aid, benefits, or services that are as effective as those provided to others. (34 C.F.R. § 104.4(b)(1))

The Section 504 regulations also require that programs and services for persons with disabilities be equally effective compared to those received by others and that an aid, benefit or service "must . . . afford [disabled] persons equal opportunity to obtain the same result, to gain the same benefit, or to reach the same level of achievement" (34 C.F.R. § 104.4(b)(2)). Given the provisions of NCLB, full and effective participation of students with disabilities in standards-based education reform initiatives would be the type of "benefit" called for by Section 504.

ADA expressly prohibits public entities and public and private employers and schools from discrimination on the basis of disability, from "[p]rovid[ing] different or separate aids, benefits or services [to persons with disabilities] that are not as effective as those provided to others" (42 U.S.C. § 12101 *et seq.*). Title II of the ADA prohibits any State, school district or school from excluding from participation, denying benefits, aids, or services, or otherwise discriminating against a qualified individual with a disability, on the basis of his or her disability (42 U.S.C. § 12131 *et seq.*). Title III of the law bars disability-based discrimination in "public accommodations and services operated by private entities" (42 U.S.C. 12181-12189). As a result of these provisions both public and private schools are covered by the ADA and its nondiscrimination requirements.

The ADA includes a specific provision governing examinations:

> Any person that offers examinations or courses related to applications, licensing, certification, or credentialing for secondary or post-secondary education, professional, or trade purposes shall offer such examinations or courses in a place and manner accessible to persons with disabilities or offer alternative accessible arrangements for such individuals. (42 U.S.C. 12189)

Associated with this statutory requirement are regulations requiring that testing sites be physically accessible and that the test formats used be the most effective manner for persons with disabilities to demonstrate that they possess the required skills and knowledge being tested.

In addition to these requirements coming from federal statutes, there are some provisions of the United States Constitution that apply to testing students with disabilities and, in fact, apply to all students. Courts have previously stated that when there are high stakes associated with testing, like the award of high school diplomas, the Equal Protection and Due Process Clauses of the Fourteenth Amendment require that the tests be valid and reliable and that students have a fair opportunity to learn the content covered on the tests (*Debra P. v. Turlington*, 1979/1984). This approach has been included in IDEA's statutory provisions now as well, with the mandate that IEP teams address the participation of a student with disabilities in a testing program.

There are also provisions in state laws that may be relevant. Whereas in most instances state laws are consistent with federal provisions, some state laws may provide more protections for individuals with disabilities than the federal laws provide. It is important, therefore, to check these sources: state laws on special education; state laws barring discrimination on basis of disability; state education reform laws; state civil rights provisions protecting racial and language minorities; and state constitutional provisions, which in some states give students the right to receive an adequate education. In about half the states, state courts have determined that there are state constitutional rights obligating public officials to provide adequate education for all students, requiring the elimination of funding disparities between districts, ensuring teacher quality, requiring early childhood education and the like. Some of these cases find particular constitutional obligations to adequately educate students with disabilities.

DEFINING AND DOCUMENTING DISABILITY

Accommodations decisions must first begin with a determination of whether or not the individual seeking an accommodation has a disability covered by the legal protection of the ADA and Section 504 or IDEA. The first step in making any accommodations decision is to have a clear diagnosis of an individual's disability and an understanding of the characteristics of the disability condition. The relevant federal laws each have their own definitions of the categories of individuals covered by the law, with the definitions under the ADA and 504 being the same.

To be covered by IDEA, a student must both have a disability and be in need of special education. The statute and regulations set out the disability conditions covered. The IDEA and its implementing regulations define the disability categories covered by the law, and many state laws provide definitions as well. The IDEA categories are: mental retardation, hearing impairments (including deafness), speech or language impairments, visual impairments (including blindness), serious emotional disturbance, orthopedic impairments, autism, traumatic brain injury, other health impairments (which the U.S. Department of Education has said includes attention deficit/hyperactivity disorder), or specific learning disabilities. The existence of one of these listed conditions, however, is not sufficient to make a student eligible for IDEA provisions. The student must have one of the listed conditions and be in need of special education.

All IDEA students, because they have disabilities, are a subset of the larger group of students covered by ADA and Section 504. In addition to IDEA students who might need testing accommodations, there is a large group of students who have disabilities, but do not need special education. These are the students who could assert 504 or ADA provisions in seeking testing accommodations. The definition of students covered by ADA and Section 504 is more subtle and complicated. These statutes protect individuals who have a disability that limits participation in major life activities, who are perceived as having a disability, or who have a record of having had a disability. Probably the latter two categories don't come into play regarding testing accommodations, but

there is really not any case law to address this problem as yet.

Recent court decisions in this area have resulted in changes in the federal law and although these decisions have not been about elementary and secondary education, the cases may have ramifications for schools. It is important to note, however, that in cases involving disputes outside of education, the U.S. Supreme Court, while emphasizing that determinations under the nondiscrimination laws must be made on an individualized basis, has also determined that the disabilities covered under the law must be substantial and do not include those in which there are measures for mitigating the impact of the disability, such as such as wearing eyeglasses or contact lenses, or taking medication. The Court has also narrowed the number of individuals protected by the laws by requiring evidence of a disability's impact on a major life activity. Because learning and/or participating in elementary and secondary education are major life activities, presumably a disability impacting participation in school would be a disability covered by ADA and Section 504.

It is necessary to establish the existence of a disability and the characteristics of the individual student's disability in order to make individual educational decisions and appropriate accommodations decisions. Documentation must include not only characteristics that impact learning, but also characteristics that might impact participation in testing.

APPROPRIATENESS AND INDIVIDUALIZATION REQUIREMENTS

At the cornerstone of the IDEA is the requirement that all IDEA students receive an appropriate education, individually determined according to the student's individualized education program (IEP). (Note that the U.S. Department of Education has just issued its new regulations for the implementation of IDEA 2004; U.S. Department of Education, 2006b.) Under the regulations for Section 504, students covered by that law are also entitled to an appropriate, individually determined education. For Section 504 students, many schools create a "504 Plan" that is very similar to an IEP. Under the provisions set forth for individual planning for students, the IEP or 504 team decides participation, individual accommodations, and modifications in state testing programs that are consistent with state rules for making assessments valid, reliable, and consistent with professional and technical standards. A discussion about this follows. In many respects, issues concerning 504 students and IDEA students' participation in accommodated testing are the same. The U.S. Department of Education suggests that schools treat 504 students the same way they treat IDEA students in terms of teams, individuals' plans, and accommodations in testing.

How a student should participate in accountability testing requires a determination of the appropriate testing method for the individual. The general presumption is that students will participate in the general testing program, with no accommodations. The four other alternatives include: testing with accommodations, alternate testing, testing on modified achievement standards, and alternate assessment based on alternate achievement standards—all which require a decision appropriate for an individual student with disabilities (Spellings, 2005; U.S. Department of Education, 2006a, 2006b).

After determining the existence of a disability and the impact that disability has on an individual's participation in testing, if it is determined that an individual needs accommodations in testing in order to participate, then the next consideration is how to determine which accommodations are reasonable for that student.

DETERMINING REASONABLE ACCOMMODATIONS IN TESTING

The United States Supreme Court has stated that a person with a disability:

> [M]ust be provided with meaningful access to the benefit that [a program] offers. The benefit itself, of course, cannot be defined in a way that effectively denies otherwise qualified handicapped individuals the meaningful access to which they are entitled; to assure meaningful access, reasonable accommodations in the . . . program or benefit may have to be made. (*Alexander v. Choate*, 1985, p. 301)

See also *Smiley v. California Department of Education* (2002).

Some commentators have asserted that fairness is the critical issue in determining accommodations (Fuchs & Fuchs, 1999; Thompson, Morse, Sharpe, & Hall, 2005; Thurlow, Elliott, & Ysseldyke, 2003). Fairness is certainly an important consideration. "Leveling the playing field" has also been described as the focus of an accommodations determination (Salvia, Ysseldyke, & Bolt, 2007). From the perspective of the legal requirements concerning disability testing, the specific inquiry about an accommodation is: What is "reasonable" or what approach would provide "meaningful access" to allow a student to participate in a testing program? There have been a few cases involving licensure testing and a very few concerning accommodations in testing in elementary and secondary education, but we can derive some guidance from these.

There is useful guidance from the statutes and regulations concerning the reasonableness of accommodations. For example, the Section 504 regulations on admissions testing have provisions requiring that:

> (i) admissions tests are selected and administered so as best to ensure that,

when a test is administered to an applicant who has a handicap that impairs sensory, manual, or speaking skills, the test results accurately reflect the applicant's aptitude or achievement level or whatever other factor the test purports to measure, rather than reflecting the applicant's impaired sensory, manual, or speaking skills (except where those skills are the factors that the test purports to measure); (ii) admissions tests that are designed for persons with impaired sensory, manual, or speaking skills are offered as often and in as timely a manner as are other admissions tests; and (iii) admissions tests are administered in facilities that, on the whole, are accessible to handicapped persons. (34 CFR 104.42 (b)(3), 2006)

The regulations under the ADA offer even more detailed provisions that include, among other things, provisions that:

Any private entity that offers examinations or courses related to applications, licensing, certification, or credentialing for secondary or postsecondary education. . . shall offer such examinations or courses in a place and manner accessible to persons with disabilities or offer alternative accessible arrangements for such individuals. . . [assuring that] . . .

The examination is selected and administered so as to best ensure that, when the examination is administered to an individual with a disability that impairs sensory, manual, or speaking skills, the examination results accurately reflect the individual's aptitude or achievement level or whatever other factor the examination purports to measure, rather than reflecting the individual's impaired sensory, manual, or speaking skills (except where those skills are the factors that the examination purports to measure);

An examination that is designed for individuals with impaired sensory, manual, or speaking skills is offered at equally convenient locations, as often,

and in as timely a manner as are other examinations; and

The examination is administered in facilities that are accessible to individuals with disabilities or alternative accessible arrangements are made.

Required modifications to an examination may include changes in the length of time permitted for completion of the examination and adaptation of the manner in which the examination is given.

A private entity offering an examination covered by this section shall provide appropriate auxiliary aids for persons with impaired sensory, manual, or speaking skills, unless that private entity can demonstrate that offering a particular auxiliary aid would fundamentally alter the measurement of the skills or knowledge the examination is intended to test or would result in an undue burden. Auxiliary aids and services required by this section may include taped examinations, interpreters or other effective methods of making orally delivered materials available to individuals with hearing impairments, Brailled or large print examinations and answer sheets or qualified readers for individuals with visual impairments or learning disabilities, transcribers for individuals with manual impairments, and other similar services and actions.

Alternative accessible arrangements may include, for example, provision of an examination at an individual's home with a proctor if accessible facilities or equipment are unavailable. Alternative arrangements must provide comparable conditions to those provided for nondisabled individuals. (28 C.F.R. 36.309, 2006)

One court has interpreted the requirement in the ADA provisions that testing be "accessible" as best understood to mean "not exactly comparable." According to that court, the statute does not mandate that examinations be provided to students with disabilities that yield technically equal results, but mandates alternative accessible arrangements, so that students with disabilities who are disadvantaged by certain features of standardized examinations may take the examinations without those features that disadvantage them (*Doe v. National Bd. of Medical Examiners*, 1999).

For the vast majority of accommodations decisions, the test publisher or the state or school district should specify which accommodations are appropriate for a particular test. These guidelines should be based upon an understanding of the content or construct being assessed, the appropriate modality to assess those competencies, and the impact on test validity and reliability as a result of particular accommodations. Departure from these guidelines should only occur when there has been full consideration of all of the factors discussed here concerning the reasonableness of a proposed accommodation.

One court has indicated that the decisions concerning accommodations reflected in an IEP or a 504 plan should be given deference by state officials (*Chapman v. California Department of Education*, 2002).

The most common type of accommodation is extended time. As a result, it is worth considering whether timed test administrations for any examinee are an important factor in assessing the construct or content a test is designed to measure. The availability of untimed tests, as a type of universal design approach, could eliminate many accommodations issues. If the ability to perform under time constraints is a relevant variable to the construct being tested, then untimed testing would not be appropriate. But, if refusal to provide untimed tests is simply an administrative convenience, then it is worth considering further whether the timing factor is in fact defensible.

Courts have interpreted both the ADA and Section 504 as allowing refusal to provide an accommodation that would cause "undue hardship." Although this standard has never been applied in a testing context, in other settings, "undue hardship" has been defined as an action requiring significant difficulty or expense considered in light of the nature and cost of the accommodation, the overall size, nature, and financial resources of the entity being asked for an accommodation, and the type of program involved. Given the wide range of obligations to provide special services to elementary and secondary students with disabilities, it is not clear that this hardship standard could apply to testing accommodations, because most expensive accommodations are ordinarily already being provided.

It is fair to summarize the considerations for a "reasonable accommodation" in a testing program as one that:

1. Is determined by an IEP or 504 team to be needed by an individual child to measure academic achievement and functional performance, and

2. Maintains validity of inferences from test.

A discussion of the technical issues associated with accommodations decisions follows.

VALIDITY, RELIABILITY AND TEST ACCOMMODATIONS

Although one court has stated that tests don't have to be exactly comparable, the technical quality of a test, as well as the quality of a test administered with accommodations, is always of critical importance. This is particularly true when the test's scores might be used for some high-stakes purpose, such as determining the award of a high school diploma, grade-to-grade promotion, or the determination of a school's AYP (Baker & Linn, 2004). The benchmarks for the technical quality of a test, including an accommodated test, are the validity and reliability of the test and the inferences that can be made on the basis of a test score (Pitoniak &

Royer, 2001). *Test validity* is a reflection of the degree to which sufficient evidence and theory support the inferences that can be made based upon a test score. *Test reliability* is a reflection of the degree to which test scores are consistent over repeated testing and are therefore dependable and free of errors of measurement. The validity and reliability of a test, as well as the validity and reliability of an accommodated administration of a test, must both be assessed. The recent *Toolkit* on testing students with disabilities from the U.S. Department of Education is a good resource for understanding these technical issues (U.S. Department of Education, 2006a).

There are professional standards of practice for testing that set forth the applicable technical requirements (American Educational Research Association, AERA, 2000) that NCLB incorporates. The most recent 1999 version of the *Standards for Educational and Psychological Testing* developed by the American Educational Research Association (AERA), the American Psychological Association (APA), and the National Council on Measurement in Education (NCME) offers some provisions concerning the testing and assessment of individuals with disabilities (AERA, APA, & NCME, 1999). The document recognizes that there is a far from perfect match between the current technical capabilities of the measurement community and the social policy and legal goals that have been embraced concerning the interests of individuals with disabilities. The chapter on testing individuals with disabilities calls for careful attention to the validity of inferences drawn from tests of individuals, careful utilization of knowledge concerning the impact of disabilities on test performance, and special attention to the development and impact of accommodations in testing. The chapter also calls for greater emphasis on the collection and analysis of data from modified administrations of tests to study the impact of modification practices, particularly on validity and other technical characteristics of a test.

For accommodated administrations of tests, judgments about technical quality require careful consideration of the content or construct the original, unaccommodated test was designed to assess. The first consideration of the appropriateness of a potential accommodation requires a specific definition of this original content or construct the unaccommodated test was targeting. Judgments about the appropriateness of any possible accommodation will require decisions about the extent to which that accommodation might diminish the validity or reliability of the assessment of the underlying original content or construct. This requires some precision. So, for example, decision makers trying to assess the appropriateness of a reading test need to know more than simply the fact that the target test measures reading proficiency. They need to know more precisely what about reading the original test sought to assess; for example, comprehension or decoding are two types of reading skills, the testing of which might tolerate very different types of legitimate accommodations. The goal for determining the technical appropriateness of an accommodation is to allow assessment as validly and reliably as possible of the target content or construct while limiting as much as possible variance not related to that target.

Many testing programs could more thoroughly "standardize" the provision of assessments, particularly concerning the use of "access assistants," the qualifications and training and guidelines for them (especially for those who become more involved with students around the content of the tests like scribes, readers, and sign language interpreters). The failure to standardize the use of access assistants as much as possible leads to the introduction of construct-irrelevant variance that might create validity challenges (Clapper, Morse, Thompson, & Thurlow, 2005).

Because of the importance of judging the appropriateness of a proposed accommodation in light of the particular content or construct being assessed, the provision of an accommodation in one context doesn't necessarily mean it is appropriate in another. Certainly, the provision of a classroom accommodation called for by an IEP or a 504 Plan is a good basis for beginning an accommodation consideration. However, an accommodation in a classroom or on one test doesn't necessarily mean it is appropriate to afford an accommodation (or the same accommodation) on another test (SAT, ACT, NAEP, AP, or other state test). The underlying construct for each test, subtest, or item is the critical issue in determining the nature of appropriate accommodations that would interfere as little as possible with the assessment of the target construct and reduce as little as possible validity and reliability.

The U.S. Department of Education (2006b) has noted in its most recent rules that in reporting on AYP, states and local schools should report only on accommodations that don't invalidate the score. The Department described what it characterized as an affirmative duty on the part of states to identify accommodations that don't diminish validity.

Many accommodation needs could be addressed by changing standardization approaches. Given that the most widely used accommodation is extended time (Thompson, Johnstone, Thurlow, & Altman, 2005), using untimed testing could enhance opportunities for all types of students, not just those with disabilities. For most elementary and secondary school content, the speed of responses are not really a part of the construct being assessed, thus it is appropriate to consider if administrative efficiency is the primary factor motivating timed testing. Many states do not time their state tests at all. Most states are in some form pursuing "universally designed assessments" (assessments designed from the beginning to be accessible and valid for the widest possible range of students, including those with disabilities and those who are English language learners, ELLs; Thompson, Johnstone, Thurlow, & Altman, 2005). There are some closely associated issues concerning accommodations in testing ELLs and also some conclusions, based on that literature, that some modifications or standardization approaches could benefit all students, not just ELL students (Abedi, Hofstetter, & Lord, 2004).

Technical issues associated with disability accommodations are considerable. There is little high-quality research available to determine the impact of accommodations on the validity and reliability of test scores and the inferences drawn from those scores. For this reason it is incumbent on test publishers and states to provide local users with information to assist them in making reasonable accommodations decisions. A summary of prior research and research designs for future studies are included in Section II of this book.

IMPLICATIONS FOR SCHOOL-BASED DECISION MAKING

Given these legal and technical considerations, there are some guidelines that can be offered for school-based practice concerning accommodations in testing. The paramount issue is probably the need to enhance knowledge on the part of all involved in making accommodations decisions and in utilizing data that includes accommodated tests. There is a need for professional development for IEP team members, administrators, and other educators. In addition, there is a need for better parent information concerning appropriate accommodations in testing.

Some specific guidelines for IEP and 504 teams concerning accommodations in testing should be provided to all who participate in these decisions. In its recent *Toolkit* for testing individuals with disabilities, the U.S.

Department of Education (2006a) points out that all students must participate in statewide assessments in one modality or another, unless a parent raises one of the limited number of legitimate objections to testing participation, such as content on the test that violates religious belief. Even this objection would probably require a type of accommodated testing, with the objectionable content removed from the test, with the rest of the test being utilized.

The U.S. Department of Education *Toolkit* also advises that it is appropriate for an IEP or 504 team to take into account the impact of a participation method on high school graduation. The Department calls for state test guidelines to specify the graduation consequences for each type of test participation.

In formulating the content of an IEP or a Section 504 plan for a student with a disability, the accommodations decision making is addressed in several different ways. The mandated content of an IEP relevant to accommodations should address, among other things:

- A statement of how the child's disability affects the child's involvement and progress in the general curriculum (i.e., the same curriculum as for children without disabilities).

- A statement of any individual modifications in the administration of State or districtwide assessments of student achievement that are needed in order for the child to participate in the assessment.

- A statement of how the student's progress in the general education curriculum will be assessed.

- A statement of how the student will participate in school or state accountability systems. (IDEA, 2004; see also U.S. Department of Education, 2006b).

As one court pointed out, the right to participate meaningfully in assessment is the goal called for under the nondiscrimination requirements of the ADA and Section 504 and is the goal for all the team decisions about the student (*Chapman v. California Department of Education*, 2002).

To facilitate accommodation decisions and other participation decisions for each student with a disability, the membership of an IEP team is required to include individuals with general curriculum expertise. A special educator or another individual familiar with disability needs should also participate in accommodations decision making. It is probably best to treat 504 and IDEA students the same when it comes to these types of decision-making processes (Spellings, 2005). The court cases concerning previous disputes over the participation of individuals with disabilities in other types of testing programs suggest that it is most important that the decision makers involved can demonstrate that their choices were the product of orderly and logical deductive processes (*Petition of Rubenstein*, 1994). Also, the decision makers need to be able to relate the accommodations decision to the content or constructs being assessed on the test (*Wynne v. Tufts University*, 1991).

Another responsibility of local educators is to promote parent understanding of accommodations decision making. Parents naturally want their children to do well on tests and ordinarily expect that an accommodation will increase a test score. Many students, parents, and educators don't understand why the need for an accommodation isn't universal. They may not necessarily understand that the reasonableness of an accommodations decision must be related closely to the content or construct being assessed.

There is no doubt that there will be pressure to consider the accommodations issue and its consequences for both the individual and for the school or district participating in the state or NCLB accountability system. Many times, it will be the scores of students with disabilities that will be the sole factor in determining whether a school or district meets its AYP goals (Pullin, 2005). There is undoubtedly pressure on local schools and educators to be influenced by the need to promote increases in the AYP index for the school and district. This could sometimes lead to the temptation to be influenced in an accommodation decision by the urge to focus more on institutional rather than individual accountability. However, all the provisions of the federal laws make clear that the most important consideration is the individual's interest unless the accommodation would violate the "reasonableness" standards discussed previously.

Local educators and parents should also study or closely watch the consequences of accommodations choices to help refine further our understanding of accommodations and their consequences. Also, it is incumbent on all to track how legal requirements in this area continue to evolve. Practitioners are obligated to continually check these provisions to determine compliance requirements

IMPLICATIONS FOR POLICY MAKERS

Policy makers at the state, federal, and local levels also need to increase their understanding of the technical and legal issues associated with accommodations in testing. At present, our public policy goals for the inclusion of students with disabilities in standards-based, test-driven education reform are not necessarily consistent with our technical capabilities to deliver the tests or the educational opportunities required to meet our goals.

Policy makers need to create processes and goals that allow test developers and users the time and the guidance to address the issues described in this chapter. Policy makers need to clarify the constructs and content

they seek to teach and to assess. They need to require test developers and publishers and state officials to specify appropriate accommodations practices. The U.S. Department of Education (Spellings, 2005) has recently emphasized the importance of high technical quality, validity, and reliability of tests. Policy makers need to ensure full compliance with professional standards and legal requirements regarding testing, including requirements for complete technical manuals on tests, including evidence on accommodations practices. And, they need to be cautious in the use of accommodated test scores in making accountability decisions if validity and reliability data are weak.

Finally, policy makers need to take a long view about solving the challenges associated with high-stakes testing. They need to fund more research and development on testing and accommodated testing. And, because there is a critical shortage of well-qualified individuals to do this work, policy makers need to fund training grants to prepare more psychometricians and other professionals well versed in testing and disability issues in the content areas being tested.

IMPLICATIONS FOR FURTHER RESEARCH/TEST DEVELOPMENT

In light of the limited research evidence now available on accommodations for disabilities in testing, much more research is needed on the means for determining reasonable and appropriate accommodations. When accommodations are reasonably offered, there is a need for additional research to consider the impact of accommodations on validity and reliability. To conduct this research, content specialists and test developers need to work closely together and to pay closer attention to construct clarity and fidelity between items and constructs.

Given the weighty consequences for institutions associated with the requirements for progress on AYP indexes to full proficiency by 2014 as required by NCLB, there is also a need for research on the impact of testing requirements on practices with unintended consequences, such as those that might force more students out of school or out of programs appropriate for their individual needs.

CONCLUSION

The full inclusion of individuals with disabilities in society is an important public policy goal, as is the goal of increasing educational attainment for all students. When full and fair participation for students with disabilities requires accommodations in testing, the provision of reasonable accommodations is our obligation. The quest for technical quality in testing is also a part of our obligation to these students. The legal requirements described in this chapter address these goals and call for our efforts to meet the challenges associated with disability accommodations in testing.

REFERENCES

Abedi, J., Hofstetter, C. H., & Lord, C. (2004). *Assessment accommodations for English language learners: Implications for policy-based empirical research.* Los Angeles: University of California, Center for the Study of Evaluation.

Alexander v. Choate, 469 U.S. 287 (1985).

American Educational Research Association, American Psychological Association, & National Council on Measurement in Education. (1999). *Standards for educational and psychological testing.* Washington, DC: American Educational Research Association.

American Educational Research Association. (2000). *AERA position statement on high-stakes testing in preK–12 education.* Washington, DC: American Educational Research Association.

Americans with Disabilities Act (1990), 42 U.S.C. 12101 *et seq.*

Baker, E., & Linn, R. (2004). Validity issues for accountability systems. In S. Fuhrman & R. Elmore (Eds.), *Redesigning accountability systems for education.* New York: Teachers College Press.

Chapman v. California Department of Education, 229 F. Supp. 2d 981 (N.D. Calif., 2002).

Clapper, A., Morse, A., Thompson, S., & Thurlow, M. (2005, December). *Access assistants for state assessments: A study of state guidelines for scribes, readers, and sign language interpreters.* Minneapolis, MN: National Center on Education Outcomes, University of Minnesota. Retrieved March 9, 2006 from http://education.umn.edu/nceo/OnlinePubs/Synthesis58.html

Debra P. v. Turlington, 474 F. Supp. 244 (M.D. Fla. 1979), *aff'd in part, rev'd in part,* 644 F.2d 397 (5th Cir. 1981), *on remand,* 564 F. Supp. 177 (M.D. Fla. 1983), *aff'd,* 730 F.2d 1405 (11th Cir. 1984).

Doe v. National Bd. of Medical Examiners, 199 F.3d 146 (3rd Cir. 1999).

Fuchs, L., & Fuchs, D. (1999, November). *Fair and unfair testing accommodations.* The School Administrator, pp. 24–29.

Individuals With Disabilities Education Act of 2004, Pub. L. 108–446, 20 U.S.C. 1400 *et seq.*

National Research Council. (1997). *Educating one and all: Students with disabilities and standards-based reform.* L. McDonnell, M. McLaughlin, and P. Morison, (Eds.). Washington, DC: National Academy Press.

No Child Left Behind Act of 2001, Pub. L. No. 107-110, 115 Stat. 1425 (2002).

Petition of Rubenstein, 637 A.2d 1131 (Del. Supr. Ct., 1994).

Pitoniak, M. J., & Royer, J. M. (2001, Spring). Testing accommodations for examinees with disabilities: A review of psychometric, legal, social, and policy issues. *Review of Educational Research 71*(1), 53–104.

Pullin, D. (2005). *When one size does not fit all—The special challenges of accountability testing for students with disabilities.* Uses and Misuses of Data for Educational Accountability and Improvement (E. Haertel & J. Herman, Eds.). Annual Yearbook of the National

Society for the Study of Education. 104:2, pp. 199–222.

Salvia, J., Ysseldyke, J., & Bolt, S. (2007). *Assessment in special and inclusive education*. Boston: Houghton Mifflin.

Section 504 of Rehabilitation Act 1973, 20 U.S.C. 794.

Smiley v. California Department of Education, 45 Fed. Appx. 780 (9th Cir. 2002).

Spellings, M. (2005, May 10). *Flexibility for states raising achievement for students with disabilities*. Letter to Chief State School Officers, U.S. Department of Education. Retrieved May 10, 2005, from http://www.ed.gov/policy/elsec/guid/secletter/050510.html

Thompson, S., Johnstone, C., Thurlow, M., & Altman, J. (2005). *2005 State special education outcomes: Steps forward in a decade of change*. Minneapolis, MN: University of Minnesota, National Center on Education Outcomes. Retrieved March 9, 2006, from http://www.education.umn.edu/nceo/OnlinePubs/2005StateReport.htm/

Thompson, S., Morse, A., Sharpe, M., & Hall, S. (2005, August). *Accommodations Manual: How to Select, Administer, and Evaluate Use of Accommodations for Instruction and Assessment of Students with Disabilities*. Second Edition. Washington, DC: Council of Chief State School Officers.

Thurlow, M., Elliott, J., & Ysseldyke, J. (2003). *Testing students with disabilities: Practical strategies for complying with district and state requirements* (2nd ed.). Thousand Oaks, California: Corwin Press.

U.S. Department of Education, Office of Special Education Programs (2006a). *Tool kit on teaching and assessing students with disabilities*. Retrieved July 20, 2006, from http:www.osepideasthatwork.org/toolkit

U.S. Department of Education, Office of Special Education Programs (2006b). Regulations for Assistance to States for the Education of Children With Disabilities and Preschool Grants for Children With Disabilities, 34 C.F. R. Parts 300 and 301.

Wynne v. Tufts University, 932 F. 2d 19 (1st Cir. 1991).

Research and Test Development

I n Section II of this book, Research and Test Development, the focus is on research that addresses the validity of test scores obtained under accommodated conditions and research that informs test development procedures that are designed to improve assessments for students with disabilities and English language learners (ELLs). In this section, the reader is provided with an overview of the existing research that has been carried out on accommodating students with disabilities on large-scale assessments. The chapters in this section also provide guidance on conducting future research, and advice for the types of research-based evidence that should be examined by practitioners and policy makers when interpreting test scores on assessments taken by students with disabilities and ELLs. The section concludes with a focus on the development of future assessments and how these assessments can combine Universal Design and digital technologies while ensuring standardization of the measurement of important constructs.

In the first chapter in this section, Chapter 4, Sireci and Pitoniak provide a detailed review of selected standards from the *Standards for Educational and Psychological Testing* (American Psychological Association, American Educational Research Association, & National Council on Measurement in Education, 1999), and use this review as a reference for a discussion of issues related to the need to balance fairness in testing examinees with disabilities with the possibility that the accommodations they receive may, in some instances, provide them with an unfair advantage on the test. In addition, this chapter provides the reader with an updated review of testing accommodation research. Detailed information is provided in the chapter on several of the most controversial accommodations (i.e., extra time, read aloud) as well as on new technology-based accommodations (e.g., dictation software). This chapter is particularly relevant for individuals who make decisions about which testing accommodation should (or should not) be allowed on a particular assessment or those individuals who interpret and use scores from accommodated assessments.

In Chapter 5 of this section, Cahalan Laitusis provides a review of different types of research that can be conducted to examine the impact of changes to a test on the validity of test scores and the accessibility of the assessment. The chapter includes a variety of research designs for both special data collections and for operational test data that can be used to document the validity of test scores. This chapter also provides useful information on minimum sample sizes and the advantages and disadvantages of using operational test data compared to collecting data for special studies. This chapter is most relevant for researchers and test developers, but has implications for policy makers and practitioners.

The final two chapters of this section show a progression from research on existing assessments to a focus on research for future assessments. In Chapter 6, Barton focuses on the building of valid assessment systems (VAS). She provides an overview of the type of validity evidence that should be included in technical reports for an assessment and encourages test developers to focus on VAS at the very beginning of the test development process by precisely defining the construct being measured and considering the impact of alternate presentation formats and response modes on the construct.

Section II of the book concludes with an overview by Dolan and Hall (Chapter 7) of the development of accessible and valid tests using both Universal Design and digital technologies. Dolan and Hall provide a background on current research focusing on Universal Design for Learning (UDL) and the application of UDL to assessments. In addition they discuss the research on and the practice of using universally designed assessments and assessments that include technology applications (e.g., keyboarding vs. handwriting to assess writing skills). Finally the authors discuss the implications of the fusion of universal design, technology, and assessment for practitioners, policy makers, and researchers.

CHAPTER 4

Assessment Accommodations: What Have We Learned From Research?

STEPHEN G. SIRECI
University of Massachusetts Amherst

MARY J. PITONIAK
Educational Testing Service

Test accommodations are provided to students with disabilities to give them the opportunity to demonstrate their knowledge, skills, and abilities in a manner that will improve the validity of interpretations that will be made from their scores. In this chapter, we focus on research that has investigated the validity of scores from accommodated tests. First, we review relevant validity-related concepts. Second, we discuss the most common test accommodations that are used to promote valid score interpretation. We then provide a review of research conducted on test accommodations for students with disabilities.

It is important to note that two terms are used to describe changes that are made to the test or testing situation for students with disabilities: modification and accommodation. The *Standards for Educational and Psychological Testing* (hereafter referred to as "the *Standards*;" American Educational Research Association, AERA, American Psychological Association, APA, & National Council on Measurement in Education, NCME, 1999) use the terms *modification* and

accommodation almost interchangeably, and use *accommodation* as "the general term for any action taken in response to a determination that an individual's disability requires a departure from standard testing protocol" (p. 101).

However, within the literature very different meanings are given to these terms, and this distinction is reflected in state policies as well. The term *accommodation* is used to refer to test or test administration changes that are not considered to alter the construct measured, and *modification* is used to refer to changes that are thought to alter the construct and thus would affect results for all students, not just those with disabilities (Hollenbeck, 2002).

Nonetheless, the distinction is not always easy to make, as changes thought by some to be accommodations may be viewed as others as modifications. Within this chapter, we will use the term accommodation to describe changes in testing conditions that are intended by most states to improve validity, although subsequent evidence might suggest the change may be better termed a modification.

VALIDITY ISSUES IN ACCOMMODATIONS

The *Standards* characterize *validity* as "the degree to which evidence and theory support the interpretations of test scores entailed by proposed uses of tests" (AERA, APA, & NCME, 1999, p. 9). Two concepts are key to any discussion of validity: (1) construct-irrelevant variance, and (2) construct representation (Messick, 1989).

Construct-irrelevant variance refers to the degree to which a student's test score is affected by factors that are not relevant to the construct (knowledge and skill domain) the test is intended to measure. The meaning and interpretation of the test scores may then be distorted by factors irrelevant to the construct. The *Standards* note that bias in tests may arise from either content-related or response-related sources. For example, if the response format of a test requires students to hand-write an essay, such a requirement will be difficult for students who have motor coordination problems, even though they are capable of demonstrating their writing ability using a head-stick and a computer keyboard.

Construct representation refers to the degree to which a test fully represents the construct tested. Construct underrepresentation arises when important parts of the construct that the test was designed to assess are not actually measured. As a result, the evidence provided by the test score is narrower than that implied by the testing purpose. In the area of testing accommodations, construct underrepresentation may be present when the accommodation involves omitting test content, such as when items involving graphs are omitted from a math test.

Construct representation can also suffer when a change to a test administration completely alters what is being measured. For example, some reading specialists claim

when a reading test is read aloud to students, the construct being measured changes from *reading comprehension* to *listening comprehension*. To evaluate the degree to which a change to standard administration affects construct representation, the construct measured must be clearly defined. If the test measures decoding, the accommodation may have a different effect on construct measurement than if the test is designed to assess comprehension.

As indicated previously, the purpose of test accommodations is to allow students to demonstrate their performance in a manner such that confounding factors related to their disability are minimized. Thus, test accommodations attempt to remove construct-irrelevant barriers to students' test performance while also maintaining construct representation.

An additional validity issue involves the comparability of scores obtained by students who receive accommodations and those who are tested under standard conditions. Standardization is a key concept in large-scale assessments, and refers to the degree to which administration and scoring of the assessment are conducted under uniform conditions (Sax, 1997). Such uniformity helps to ensure that test results are interpreted as being due to differences between individuals and not due to fluctuations in testing conditions. However, such standardization may introduce construct-irrelevant variance for students with disabilities. As such, the *Standards* acknowledge that standardization is not always a realistic goal:

> A standardized test that has been designed for use with the general population may be inappropriate for use for individuals with specific disabilities if the test requires the use of sensory, motor, language, or psychological skills that are affected by the disability and that are not relevant to the focal construct. (AERA, APA, & NCME, 1999, p. 101).

Thus, providing accommodations for standardized tests may be seen as the ultimate psychometric oxymoron (Sireci, 2005; Sireci, Scarpati, & Li, 2005). Standardized tests are designed to promote fairness in testing by keeping the exam content, administration, and scoring uniform for all examinees. However, not all test takers can display their true knowledge, skills, and abilities within the constraints of a standardized test administration. The need to promote fairness in testing must be balanced with the possibility that accommodations may provide an unfair advantage to some examinees. The *Standards* discussed in the next section, provide a reference for these issues; the issue of comparability is discussed further in a section on flagging.

RELEVANT STANDARDS

The *Standards* contain an entire chapter devoted to the discussion of testing individuals with disabilities. Although each of the 12 standards should be followed by those designing and administrating tests that will be taken by students with disabilities, the following standards are illustrative of the key concepts discussed.

Standard 10.1 states that "In testing individuals with disabilities, test developers, test administrators, and test users should take steps to ensure that the test score inferences accurately reflect the intended construct rather than any disabilities and their associated characteristics extraneous to the intent of the measurement" (AERA, APA, & NCME, 1999, p. 106).

Standard 10.4 stipulates that "If modifications are made or recommended by test developers . . . (unless) evidence of validity for a given inference has been established for individuals with the specific disabilities, test developers should issue cautionary statements in manuals or supplementary materials regarding confidence in interpretations based on such test scores" (AERA, APA, &

NCME, p. 106). As indicated earlier, the use of the term *modification* is not meant to imply a change in the construct, because the *Standards* use the terms *modification* and *accommodation* interchangeably.)

Additional standards relate to the need for those who make decisions about accommodations to base their actions on research in the field (10.2); the use of pilot tests to investigate the impact of accommodations on students with disabilities (10.3); the need for appropriate technical documentation (10.5); the use of empirical procedures to establish different time limits for students with disabilities (10.6); research on the validity of the interpretations made using the scores (10.7); the need for those making decision about test accommodations to obtain necessary information and inform students and others about the availability of accommodations (10.8); issues to be considered when making norm-referenced interpretations (10.9); the need to evaluate each individual student's situation in order to make an appropriate decision about accommodations (10.10); flagging of test scores when evidence about comparability is lacking (10.11); and the inadvisability of using a test score as the only indicator of a student's abilities (10.12).

Flagging

As just noted, Standard 10.11 addresses the flagging of test scores, which involves attaching an indicator to a test score to alert the user that the score was obtained under nonstandard conditions. If evidence exists that a score obtained by a student with disabilities under accommodated conditions has the same meaning as a score for a student without disabilities under standard conditions (i.e., that construct irrelevance has been removed, but construct underrepresentation has been prevented), then no flag need be attached. However, this determination is often difficult to make.

Sireci (2005) observed that the practice of flagging is a contentious issue. On one side are those who argue that a flagged test score alerts the score user to the fact that the student has a disability, which may then lead to discrimination against him or her. The *Standards* acknowledge this fact by noting "the inclusion of a flag on a test score where an accommodation for a disability was provided may conflict with legal and social policy goals promoting fairness in the treatment of individuals with disabilities" (AERA, APA, & NCME, 1999, p. 108). Where flagging is necessary, the *Standards* advise that no mention be made of the existence or type of disability, but instead that the nature of the accommodation be described.

The argument is also raised that it is not fair to students who took the test under standard conditions to have their scores compared to those who received accommodations, and that flagging will facilitate valid test score interpretations. Again, the *Standards* address this issue by stipulating that when evidence about score comparability is lacking, flagging should be done to assist users in interpreting scores appropriately.

However, evaluating the comparability of test scores is not an easy task. Sireci (2005) noted that most research in this area has focused on postsecondary and postgraduate admissions tests; in contrast, flagging of scores on large-scale Grade K to 12 assessments has not received as much attention. Later in this chapter, we review research on testing accommodations that can be used to evaluate the comparability of scores obtained under accommodated versus standard conditions.

Categories of Accommodations

The *Standards* describe six strategies for test accommodations; five of these (presentation, response, setting, timing, other) will be discussed in turn, with examples drawn from previous reviews of research (see Pitoniak &

Royer, 2001; Sireci, Li, & Scarpati, 2003; Thompson, Blount, & Thurlow, 2002). (The remaining type of accommodation described is that of using only portions of a test, which may be more relevant to clinical settings.) A more detailed description of each type of accommodation is provided in the Introduction to this book. Of these accommodation types presentation, response, and timing are usually the most controversial.

Presentation. Accommodations pertaining to presentation format aim to change the medium through which the test instructions and items are presented to the student. These include the use of large print and Braille tests for students with visual impairments, and written or signed test directions for examinees with hearing impairments. Other presentation accommodations are reading the test aloud, paraphrasing, simplified language, encouragement (redirecting), cueing, the use of computer administration, spelling assistance, and the use of manipulatives.

Response. Response accommodations are intended to take into account the preferred communication modality of students with disabilities. Technology may be used in the form of a tape recorder, word processing program, or Braille writer. Other options include the student's dictating a response to a scribe and indicating responses in the test booklet instead of the answer sheet.

Timing. The amount of time provided to students to take the test may also be changed. Accommodations include extending the amount of time allowed for the test, taking the test over multiple sessions and/or days, and taking frequent breaks. As the *Standards* note, this accommodation may be necessary in order to allow for the effective use of other accommodations such as Braille or read-aloud, since they may require additional time. However, timing accommodations are usually not as much of an issue on state standards-based assessments because most have generous time limits (vs. often-speeded tests used for admission or licen- sure).

Setting. Large-scale assessments are gen- erally administered to groups of students. Accommodations within the setting cate- gory are intended to remove sources of inter- ference that may arise from this group administration. Such accommodations may include individual or small-group adminis- tration in a separate room. Other possible changes to the test setting are the provision of tables or chairs that may better accommo- date a student with physical disabilities or a change in lighting for students with visual impairment.

Other Accommodations. The remaining accommodation categories reviewed by the *Standards* are less relevant to the purpose of the current review. The fifth type of accom- modation described is that of using only por- tions of a test, which may be more relevant to clinical settings. The sixth accommoda- tion category contains alternative assess- ments, used to evaluate the performance of students with significant cognitive or other disabilities who are unable to participate in general state assessments even with accom- modations; these assessments are beyond the scope of this chapter.

REVIEW OF RESEARCH

There have been several recent reviews of research related to test accommodations. Many have focused on validity issues in test accommodations and score interpretation (e.g., Pitoniak & Royer, 2001), while others have focused on the effects of test accommo- dations on students' performance (Bolt & Thurlow, 2004; Chiu & Pearson, 1999; Sireci, 2004; Sireci et al., 2005; Thompson, Blount, & Thurlow, 2002; Tindal & Fuchs, 2000). In this chapter, we focus on research evaluating the effects of test accommodation on students' performance. In doing so, we borrow from these reviews and discuss sev- eral recent studies in this area; the recent

studies reviewed are limited to those not dis- cussed in previous reviews of the literature in this area.

Conclusions From Previous Reviews

Sireci et al. (2005) reviewed 28 studies and found that the accommodations of extended time and oral administration were those most widely investigated. Based on their review, they concluded extended time gener- ally had a positive effect on test scores, par- ticularly for students with disabilities. The same conclusion was also reached in two pre- vious reviews of the literature (i.e., Chiu & Pearson, 1999; Thompson, Blount, & Thurlow, 2002). With respect to read-aloud (oral) accommodations, Sireci et al. con- cluded the effect for students with disabilities on math tests was generally positive (i.e., score gains under the accommodation condi- tion tended to be higher for students with disabilities than for their nondisabled peers), but that this finding did not generalize to other subject areas.

Sireci (2004) discussed three studies that evaluated the effects of an oral accommoda- tion on a reading test (also reviewed by Sireci et al., 2005). In one study (McKevitt & Elliot, 2003), there was no gain for stu- dents with or without disabilities when receiving an oral accommodation. In a sec- ond study (Meloy, Deville, & Frisbie, 2002), a gain was noted for both groups under the accommodation condition, but the gain for students with disabilities was not signifi- cantly larger than that observed for students without disabilities. The third study (Kosciolek & Ysseldyke, 2000), found a sim- ilar result. Although the gain under the oral accommodation for students with disabilities was larger than that observed for students without disabilities, there was no statistical significance for the differential gain. These results, coupled with the possibility that an oral accommodation may change the con- struct measured by reading tests, led Sireci

(2004) to conclude "there is little data to support oral accommodations on reading tests" (p. 23).

MORE RECENT STUDIES IN THIS AREA

The studies reviewed by Sireci et al. (2005) were all conducted before 2004, with most conducted before 2003. Since that review, several additional studies have been published. In this section, we review six of these more recent studies. One of the studies pertained to the accommodation of extended time; three pertained to oral accommodations; one pertained to a dictation accommodation; and one pertained to accommodations generally defined.

Extended Time

Cohen, Gregg, and Deng (2005) evaluated the effects of extended time on a statewide ninth-grade mathematics tests. They used sophisticated measurement models to investigate reasons why some items differed statistically across standard and extended time administrations. The data analyzed came from a 2003 ninth-grade math test that was part of the Florida Comprehensive Assessment Test. Two random samples of 1,250 students were drawn from the population of students who took the exam. One sample came from the group who had extended time on the test; the other came from the standard time group. There were three stages to their study. First, they conducted a differential item functioning (DIF) analysis to identify items that functioned differentially across the standard and extended time administrations. Of the 29 items investigated, 22 were flagged for DIF. In the second stage of their study, they applied a mixture item response theory model to the data to discover the types of students who best fit the two item response patterns predicted from the previous DIF analysis (one pattern based on standard time, and one based on extended time).

This model allowed for two patterns of item response: one consistent with no differential effect of extended time and one consistent with the full differential effect due to extended time. The mixture model then classified students into one of two groups according to how they responded to the items. Surprisingly, there was little relationship between whether students received extended time and the group into which they were classified. Cohen et al. concluded: "students' accommodation status is not a sufficiently useful explanatory variable for determining the cause of differential item performance" (pp. 228–299).

The third stage of the Cohen et al. (2005) study involved an exploratory analysis on a cross-validation sample in which they looked for other variables, aside from the extended time accommodation, that could explain test performance differences observed during the first stage of their study. They found that the differences were due to test content, not administration condition. In discussing these results, Cohen et al. concluded that

> [D]ifferential difficulty with types of mathematic content rather than the accommodation itself leads to group differences in item-level performance. Such a finding suggests that a hyperfocus on pointing the accusatory finger at accommodations is possibly inappropriate and redirects the needed attention of professionals on the failure of many students to attain curriculum goals. Accommodations are more appropriately viewed as leveling the playing field; they do not supply the knowledge necessary to pass the tests. (p. 231)

Oral Accommodation

As noted earlier, read-aloud accommodations on reading tests have not been supported in the literature for two reasons. First, an oral accommodation on a reading test is thought to change the construct measured.

Second, empirical studies investigating the "differential boost" between students with and without disabilities did not indicate gains for students with disabilities who received an oral accommodation relative to their nondisabled peers. Fletcher et al. (2006) addressed these issues by investigating the effect of a targeted oral accommodation. Rather than reading the entire test aloud, the oral accommodation involved reading aloud the proper nouns, the item stems following reading passages, and the answer choices. The item stems and answer choices were read aloud only after the students independently read the passages. Narrowing the accommodation in this manner was considered to retain construct measurement because the accommodation targeted word recognition difficulties.

Fletcher et al. (2006) randomly assigned students diagnosed with dyslexia (n = 91) and average readers from the same classrooms (n = 91) to standard or accommodated administrations of a practice version of the Grade 3 Texas Assessment of Knowledge and Skills reading test. In addition to the oral accommodation described earlier, students in the accommodation condition took the test over two separate testing sessions. Students in both groups had unlimited time to complete the test. They found a statistically significant interaction between student group and accommodation condition. Specifically, the effect size associated with the mean difference for students with dyslexia was almost one standard deviation (Cohen's delta = .91), while the effect size for the nondisabled students was negligible (Cohen's delta = .15). Based on the results, Fletcher et al. concluded the students with dyslexia had a seven times greater probability of passing the exam under the accommodation condition, than under a standard administration.

Huynh and Barton (2006) also studied the effects of an oral accommodation on a reading test. They analyzed archival data from the reading section of the South Carolina High School Exit Examination. There were three groups in their analysis. The first group comprised students with disabilities who took the test with an oral accommodation, the second group comprised students with disabilities who took the test under standard conditions, and the third group comprised students without disabilities who took the test under standard conditions.

Using confirmatory factor analysis, Huynh and Barton (2006) concluded the factor structure of the test was consistent across the three groups of students. This consistency of the internal structure of the test held up over separate-group and multi-group confirmatory analyses. They concluded that the oral accommodation did "not change the test's internal structure substantially and therefore the major construct underlying the test remained intact" (p. 35). Cook, Eignor, Sawaki, Steinberg, and Cline (2006) also used factor analysis to evaluate the consistency of test structure across accommodated and nonaccommodated versions of an English Language Arts test. Although the accommodations were not limited to oral accommodations, the results also suggested consistency of structure across standard and accommodated test administrations.). In addition, Huynh and Barton used analysis of covariance (with Grade 8 reading scores used as a covariate) to compare the covariate-adjusted mean test scores across the three groups. They found the means for the two groups of students with disabilities (one with the oral accommodation, one without) to be essentially equal, which they took as evidence of appropriateness of the accommodation. They concluded that "all these results contradict the stereotypical idea that reading the reading test changes what is measured" (pp. 35–36).

In an earlier study, Crawford and Tindal (2004) examined the effects of a read-aloud accommodation on a standardized reading test for fourth- and fifth-grade students with and without learning disabilities. The sample size was large ($N = 338$) but most of the students (78%) did not have a disability (76 students received special education services). The read-aloud accommodation was in the form of a video administration and so students could not hear the passage or test questions repeated. A repeated-measures design was used, with all students taking a form of the test under both standard and video (read-aloud) conditions. The order of the conditions was counterbalanced. There was no statistically significant difference between order of accommodation condition (standard first or read aloud fist) or grade level (4th or 5th). However, they found a statistically significant disability-by-accommodation interaction, reflecting a differential performance boost from the video presentation accommodation. Students with disabilities performed much better under the video condition (Cohen's delta = .71, or almost three fourths of a standard deviation), relative to their general education peers (delta = .28).

Computer-Based Oral Accommodation

Dolan, Hall, Bannerjee, Chun, and Strangman (2005) investigated the effect of computer-based oral accommodation on the test performance of 10 high school students with learning disabilities. (Earlier studies involving computerized oral accommodations include Brown and Augustine (2001) and Calhoon, Fuchs, and Hamlett (2000).) The results across these studies were mixed (see Sireci et al., 2005). The test studied consisted of two parallel forms of a United States history and civics test based on released items from the National Assessment of Educational Progress. The 10 students took the test under two conditions in counterbalanced order. One condition was a traditional paper-and-pencil format with no oral accommodation. The other condition was a computerized administration where text-to-

speech software was available so that the students could listen to the reading passages, test questions, and answer choices. The software also allowed for synchronized highlighting of words.

The results from Dolan et al. (2005) indicated that, on average, students scored about 1 point better on the 15 multiple-choice questions in the computerized read-aloud condition than in the paper-and-pencil condition. However, the result was not statistically significant. Given the small sample size for this study, and the fact that the oral accommodation was confounded with the computerized administration, it is difficult to conclude the read-aloud software leads to improved performance for students with learning disabilities. Nevertheless, it is interesting to note that the students had little difficulty navigating the computerized test delivery system, and so this accommodation should be studied further.

Dictation Software

MacArthur and Cavalier (2004) investigated the effects of using dictation software as an accommodation for students with disabilities on a writing test. According to the authors, 48 states consider dictation to be an allowable accommodation. The study involved 31 students, 21 of whom had a diagnosed disability, and 10 students who did not have a diagnosed disability. The students wrote an essay under three different conditions: handwritten, dictation to a scribe, and dictation to a computer using speech recognition software. The order of the test conditions was counterbalanced. The interaction effect between response condition and students' disability status was not statistically significant, but the authors attributed that result to a lack of statistical power. In looking at the effect sizes across the two student groups, in comparison to hand-written essays, they found a large effect size for the students with disabilities group when they dictated their essay to a scribe, and a moderate effect size when they dictated their essays using dictation software. The effect sizes for the students without disabilities were negligible for both dictation conditions. They concluded "Overall, the results of the study support the validity of dictation to a scribe and speech recognition as accommodations on tests that involve writing" (p. 55). However, they cautioned that dictation accommodations should consider the purpose of the test and whether dictation may alter the construct measured. As they described:

> When writing is used to assess knowledge in content areas such as social studies or science, the use of dictation would not change the constructs. However, when the test is intended to measure writing achievement itself, a conceptual question must be resolved about whether the construct of writing includes the mechanics of producing text or whether the tests are intended to assess composing independent of mechanics. If the construct focuses on composing, then speech recognition software would be a legitimate accommodation that compensates for a disability in text production. (pp. 55–56)

Individualized Accommodations

Kettler et al. (2005) evaluated the effects of accommodations on fourth-grade and eighth-grade students' performance on commercial math and reading tests. The study involved students with and without disabilities and the accommodations were based on the individualized education programs (IEPs) of the students with disabilities. Students without disabilities were randomly matched to students in the disability group and received the same accommodation as their yoked partner. In fourth grade, there were 118 participants, 49 of whom had IEPs. In eighth grade, there were 78 participants, 39 of whom had IEPs. Each student was tested twice, in standard and accommoda-

tion conditions, in counterbalanced order. Two parallel versions of each test were used, also in counterbalanced order. Each student within a yoked pair took the test in the same order. Hence, the study had strong internal validity.

On the fourth-grade reading test, Kettler et al. (2005) found a statistically significant interaction, where the students with disabilities had significantly higher scores under the accommodation condition (effect size = .42) and the students without disabilities had a negligible increase in their scores under the accommodation condition (effect size = .13). In addition, 43% of the students with disabilities increased at least one proficiency level under the accommodation condition (compared to 6% who decreased one level). For the students without disabilities, 22% increased at least one proficiency level, but 10% decreased one level. For the fourth-grade math test, both groups achieved higher mean scores under the accommodation condition, but the group-by-accommodation interaction was not statistically significant. Nevertheless, the effect size for the accommodation gain was noticeably larger for the students with disabilities (.46) than for the other students (.27). The differential with respect to improvements in the proficiency level was similar to that observed for reading.

The eighth-grade results in Kettler et al. (2005) were more modest. The interaction between student group and accommodation was not statistically significant for reading or math. In addition, the effect size for the gain under the accommodation condition was slightly larger for students without disabilities (.29) than for students with disabilities (.25) on the reading test. The effect sizes for the accommodation gain on the math test were negligible for both groups (.17 and .13 for the disability and non-disabled students, respectively). Based on these results the authors concluded "These findings seem to support previous research indicating the generally positive, yet highly individualized, impact of testing accommodations on test scores" (p. 47).

DISCUSSION

In general, the studies reviewed in this chapter support the findings from previous reviews regarding assessment accommodations. Test accommodations appear to have a positive effect on the test performance of many students with disabilities, and in some instances, they also lead to increased scores for students without disabilities. Our discussion of the validity issues surrounding test accommodations illustrates that it is difficult to determine whether a particular accommodation will facilitate valid interpretation of a particular student's test performance. Such decisions can be carefully made on an individual basis, but are hard to make on a statewide or other aggregate basis. States should consider allowing the popular accommodations found in the literature, if it can be assumed or demonstrated that the accommodation does not change the construct measured. Allowing such accommodations enables IEP teams to have more tools available for increasing the access of students with disabilities to educational assessments.

Testing agencies should develop clear definitions of the constructs measured on a test, as well as potential sources of construct-irrelevant variance. These definitions will help test users better evaluate the utility of the test and will help facilitate understandings of how accommodations may alter the construct measured. With respect to the determination of whether a particular test accommodation changes the construct, both qualitative and quantitative approaches are recommended. Qualitative approaches include convening groups of subject matter experts to determine the effects of the accommodation on the construct. Quantitative methods could include dimensionality analyses, studies of differential item functioning, and studies of differential predictive

validity, although the latter will be particularly difficult to conduct since valid external criteria are needed. Experimental designs to compare the gains for students with disabilities and other students under accommodation and nonaccommodation conditions have proven to be helpful for evaluating the equivalence of accommodated and standard test administrations, and so states and other entities are encouraged to conduct such studies. Fletcher et al. (2006) provides an excellent example of a comprehensive study organized at the state level with participation by the state department of education.

The literature also demonstrates that many accommodations are helpful to many students—some with disabilities and some without. Thus, building tests with more flexible time limits and flexibility in presentation and response formats is likely to increase the validity of test score interpretation for all students. Future test development designs should consider technology and the principles of universal test design (Thompson, Johnstone, & Thurlow, 2002) to promote valid score interpretations and to make testing conditions so flexible that accommodations are needed for far fewer students. The moral of the story we discovered through our review of the literature, and through our review of validity issues, is that more work needs to be done in providing accommodations to students, in evaluating these accommodations, and in developing more flexible assessments that are less likely to need accommodation for different types of students.

We realize it is difficult for schools, districts, and states to make broad policy decisions regarding test accommodations. Can the results from studies appearing in the literature help inform these policy makers? We think so. The results clearly illustrate the variability in students' test performance under both standard and accommodated conditions. Obviously then, a one-size-fits-all approach to accommodations is not likely to be successful. Instead, accommodation decisions need to be made on a case-by-case basis, but the list of allowable accommodations should be as numerous as possible while staying true to the construct measured.

With respect to extended time, our review suggests that this should be an allowable accommodation on any timed tests, unless speed of response is explicitly included in the definition of the construct measured. With respect to oral accommodation, the literature suggests that this should be an allowable accommodation on tests that do not assess reading. As for allowing oral accommodations on reading tests, three studies provided results to support this accommodation (Crawford & Tindal, 2004; Fletcher et al., 2006; Huynh & Barton, 2006); however, a concern still remains that this accommodation may change the construct measured in some cases. Thus, more research in this specific area is needed. At the present time, research associated with the National Accessible Reading Assessment Project is addressing this issue and so interested readers should consult the Web site (http://www.narap.info/) as the results from these studies become available.

In closing, we invite educators to participate more fully in the research on test accommodations. States, districts, and schools can use the results from published research on accommodations to help make accommodations decisions, but they can also add to this body of knowledge by providing data relevant to their specific situations. Given all the statewide testing that is underway in compliance with the No Child Left Behind legislation, there is a great opportunity to compile more evidence about the types of accommodations that benefit specific types of students. We encourage states, schools, and districts to evaluate the ways in which their test accommodations appear to be working and to share these lessons with others outside their jurisdiction.

REFERENCES

American Educational Research Association, American Psychological Association, & National Council on Measurement in Education. (1999). *Standards for educational and psychological tests.* Washington, DC: American Psychological Association.

Bolt, S. E., & Thurlow, M. L. (2004). Five of the most commonly allowed accommodations in state policy: Synthesis of research. *Remedial and Special Education, 25,* 141–152.

Brown, P. J., & Augustine, A. (2001, April). *Screen reading software as an assessment accommodation: Implications for instruction and student performance.* Paper presented at the annual meeting of the American Educational Research Association, Seattle, WA.

Calhoon, M. B., Fuchs, L. S., & Hamlett, C. L. (2000, Fall). Effects of computer-based test accommodations on mathematics performance assessments for secondary students with learning disabilities. *Learning Disability Quarterly, 23,* 271–82.

Chiu, C. W. T., & Pearson, P. D. (1999, June). *Synthesizing the effects of test accommodations for special education and limited English proficient students.* Paper presented at the National Conference on Large-Scale Assessment, Snowbird, UT.

Cohen, A. S., Gregg, N., & Deng, M. (2005). The role of extended time and item content on a high-stakes mathematics test. *Learning Disabilities Research & Practice, 20,* 225–233.

Cook, L., Eignor, D., Sawaki, Y., Steinberg, J., & Cline, F. (2006, April). *Using factor analysis to investigate the impact of accommodations on the scores of students with disabilities on English-language arts assessments.* Paper presented at the annual meeting of the National Council on Measurement in Education, San Francisco, CA.

Crawford, L., & Tindal, G. (2004). Effects of a read-aloud modification on a standardized reading test. *Exceptionality, 12*(2), 89–106.

Dolan, R. P., Hall, T. E., Bannerjee, M., Chun, E., & Strangman, N. (2005). Applying principles of universal design to test design: The effect of computer-based read-aloud on test performance of high school students with learning disabilities. *Journal of Technology, Learning, and Assessment, 3*(7). Retrieved August 5, 2006, from http://escholarship.bc.edu/jtla/vol3/7/

Fletcher, J. M., Francis, D. J., Boudousquie, A., Copeland, K., Young, V., Kalinowski, S., & Vaughn, S. (2006). Effects of accommodations on high-stakes testing for students with reading disabilities. *Exceptional Children, 72,* 136–150.

Hollenbeck, K. (2002). Determining when test alterations are valid accommodations or modifications for large-scale assessment. In G. Tindal & T. Haladyna (Eds.), *Large-scale assessment programs for all students* (pp. 395–425). Mahwah, NJ: Erlbaum.

Huynh, H., & Barton, K. E. (2006). Performance of students with disabilities under regular and oral administrations of a high-stakes reading examination. *Applied Measurement in Education, 19,* 21–39.

Kettler, R. J., Niebling, B. C., Mroch, A. A., Feldman, E. S., Newell, M. L., Elliott, S. N., et al. (2005). Effects of testing accommodations on math and reading scores: An experimental analysis of the performance of students with and without disabilities. *Assessment for Effective Intervention, 31,* 37–48.

Kosciolek, S., & Ysseldyke, J. E. (2000). Effects of a reading accommodation on the validity of a reading test (Technical Report 28). Minneapolis, MN: University of Minnesota, National Center on Educational Outcomes. Retrieved January 5, 2003, from http://education.umn.edu/NCEO/OnlinePubs/Technical28.htm

MacArthur, C. A., & Cavalier, A. R. (2004). Dictation and speech recognition technology as test accommodations. *Exceptional Children, 71,* 43–58.

McKevitt, B. C., & Elliott, S. N. (2003). Effects and perceived consequences of using read-aloud and teacher-recommended accommodations on a reading achievement test. *School Psychology Review, 32,* 583–600.

Meloy, L., Deville, C., & Frisbie, D. (2002). The effect of a read-aloud accommodation on test scores of students with and without a learn-ing disability in reading. *Remedial and Special Education, 23,* 248–255.

Messick, S. (1989). Validity. In R. Linn (Ed.), *Educational measurement* (3rd ed., pp. 13–103). Washington, DC: American Council on Education.

Pitoniak, M. J., & Royer, J. M. (2001). Testing accommodations for examinees with disabilities: A review of psychometric, legal, and social policy issues. *Review of Educational Research, 71,* 53–104.

Sax, G. (1997). *Principles of educational and psychological measurement and evaluation.* Belmont, CA: Wadsworth.

Sireci, S., Li, S., & Scarpati, S. (2003). *The effects of test accommodations on test performance: A review of the literature* (Center for Educational Assessment Research Report No. 485). Amherst: University of Massachusetts, School of Education.

Sireci, S., Scarpati, S., & Li, S. (2005). Test accommodations for students with disabilities: An analysis of the interaction hypothesis. *Review of Educational Research, 75,* 457–490.

Sireci, S. G. (2004, January). *Validity issues in accommodating NAEP reading tests.* Paper commissioned by the National Assessment Governing Board. Retrieved January 5, 2006, from http://www.nagb.org/pubs/conferences/sireci.doc.

Sireci, S. G. (2005). Unlabeling the disabled: A psychometric perspective on flagging scores from accommodated test administrations. *Educational Researcher, 34*(1), 3–12.

Thompson, S., Blount, A., & Thurlow, M. (2002). *A summary of research on the effects of test accommodations: 1999 through 2001* (Technical Report 34). Minneapolis: University of Minnesota, National Center on Educational Outcomes. Retrieved January 5, 2006, from http://education.umn.edu/nceo/OnlinePubs/TechReport34.pdf

Thompson, S. J., Johnstone, C. J., & Thurlow, M. L. (2002). *Universal design applied to large scale assessments* (Synthesis Report 44). Minneapolis, MN: University of Minnesota, National Center on Educational Outcomes. Retrieved September 29, 2006, from http://

education.umn.edu/NCEO/OnlinePubs/
Synthesis44.html

Tindal, G., & Fuchs, L. (2000). *A summary of research on test changes: An empirical basis for defining accommodations.* Lexington, KY: Mid-South Regional Resource Center.

Author Note: This article is from the *Center for Educational Assessment Research Report No. 609.* Amherst, MA: Center for Educational Assessment, University of Massachusetts. The authors thank April Zenisky for her help in locating some important articles for this review and Cara Cahalan Laitusis and Daniel Eignor for their careful editing of an earlier version of this chapter.

CHAPTER 5

Research Designs and Analysis for Studying Accommodations on Assessments

CARA CAHALAN LAITUSIS
Educational Testing Service

This chapter provides policy makers, researchers, and test developers with research-based approaches to determining the validity and reliability of test scores obtained under accommodated conditions. Although other areas of research (e.g., the development of universally designed assessments) are important, this chapter will primarily focus on determining if the outcome of accommodation use on a particular assessment yields valid test results. In addition to providing access to the test, testing accommodations are sometimes provided to remove construct-irrelevant variance and improve the validity of the test score. In some cases the use of a testing accommodation is controversial because the accommodation is believed to interfere with the construct being assessed or to alter the comparability of accommodated and nonaccommodated test scores. When this is the case, evidence needs to be collected to show that the test score resulting from the accommodated condition is valid.

Phillips (1994) argued that measurement specialists should consider the impact of test accommodations on the constructs measured and the validity of the scores obtained on the test. She expands this argument by saying that any change to testing conditions should be avoided if the change would (a) alter the skill being measured, (b) preclude the comparison of scores between examinees that received accommodations and those that did not, or (c) allow examinees without disabilities to benefit (if they were granted the same accommodation). This last criterion is debatable, and several researchers have argued that accommodations should only be provided if they offer a *differential boost* to students with disabilities (Elliot & McKevitt, 2000; Fuchs & Fuchs, 1999, Pitoniak and Royer, 2001). Differential boost indicates that students with disabilities receive significantly larger gains in overall test score (accommodated test score-nonaccommodated test score) from an accommodation than students without disabilities gain from the same accommodation. It is important to note that both groups can receive improved test scores from the accommodation, but the gains for the students with disabilities are differentially larger.

More recently Sireci, Li, and Scarpati (2005) have referred to the differential boost model as an interaction model, but the principle of differential performance between students with and without disabilities remains the same. The interaction model uses a repeated measures analysis of variance to look for a significant interaction between disability classification (disabled or not disabled) and accommodation (accommodated or standard) when all students have completed the test under both accommodated and nonaccommodated testing conditions.

Although there have been several articles examining what theoretical factors impact the validity of test scores, the specific procedures for identifying threats to validity are rarely discussed. This is partially due to the differences among testing programs, but it also stems from the fact that it is difficult for a single study to prove that a testing accommodation does not impact the validity of test scores. Rather a testing program should compile a body of evidence that provides indicators of whether a particular accommodation yields valid test results.

Over the last decade, the gold standard for examining the validity of test scores taken with accommodations has been an experimental research design that examines *differential performance boost* (Fuchs & Fuchs, 1999). These studies examine the performance of students with and without disabilities on tests taken with and without the accommodation of interest (by both groups). The primary purpose of a differential boost study has been to answer a simple question: *Would students without disabilities benefit as much from the accommodation as students with disabilities?* The primary purpose of asking this question is an assumption that students would benefit more from the accommodation if their disability resulted in an impairment related to the accommodation. For example there is an assumption that students with learning disabilities who receive extra time accommodations have disability related deficits in either

reading rate or processing speed and that extra time allows these students to demonstrate their true ability on the construct the test is designed to measure. The previous question focuses on an issue of test fairness because it implies that students who receive extra time may be given an advantage over students who do not receive extra time. However, this question does not focus on two more pressing validity questions:

- Does the accommodated test score more accurately measure the construct being assessed for students with disabilities than students without disabilities?

- Are the accommodated test scores for students with disabilities psychometrically comparable to the standard test scores for students without disabilities?

This chapter will review several different approaches to answering these critical validity questions as well as research focused on improving test development and delivery for students with disabilities. The next section will review the advantages and limitations of collecting data via special accommodations compared to the advantages and disadvantages of using data from operational testing programs. The subsequent section will describe special research studies for examining the validity of test scores and improving accommodation policy and practice. Next we will review the use of operational test data to examine the comparability of test scores under accommodated and standard conditions. The final section will focus on the implications of this research for practitioners, policy makers, and test developers.

SAMPLE SELECTION: SPECIAL DATA COLLECTION OR OPERATIONAL TEST DATA

Over the years researchers have used both operational test data and special data collections to examine the validity and comparability of test scores. The primary advantage of collecting data for a research study is the ability to collect specific data rather than being limited by existing or convenient operational test data. For example, data regarding the impact of the student's disability (and accommodation needs) can be isolated and examined separately. Other advantages of collecting data are the ability to control for other effects that might interfere with the interpretation of the results of the study, such as order effects from test form or accommodation use. Order effects refer to the degree that the order of administration (of test forms or accommodation conditions) can impacts results. In addition the sample of "students with disabilities" can be more specific (e.g., reading-based learning disability and no other disability rather than learning disability with or without ADHD). This more precise data can be examined to provide reasons why students perform differently with testing accommodations as well as to inform accommodation decision makers about what factors to consider when making a decision about testing accommodations for a particular student or test.

Although there are many advantages of collecting data via special data collection activities, there are several limitations that dissuade some testing programs from collecting such data. These limitations include (a) significant financial costs which are increased substantially when studying data with low incidence disabilities, (b) lack of motivation in test takers participating in research studies rather than taking operational tests, (c) significant time to collect data compared to using existing operational data, and (d) significant effort to obtain adequate sample sizes because students and schools often feel overtested (due to increased level of participation in state and national assessments) and are reluctant to participate in additional testing.

When these limitations cannot be overcome, testing programs may choose to use operational test data or supplemental data collections done under operational testing conditions. The use of operational test data to examine the validity of test scores is advantageous because it is cost effective (in terms of time and money), easy to replicate, and can include large samples of motivated test takers. However there are several limitations to using operational data. The first and most obvious limitation is that disability and accommodation use are confounded and no control group exists because students without disabilities do not use accommodations and students with disabilities who do use accommodations may vary in the type of disability they have or the severity of the disability. Other limitations include that data may not be precise enough (e.g., disability and accommodation categories may be too broad), and information on accommodations may not be accurate (e.g., approved accommodations may not be used). Although there are some limitations, the use of operational test data for psychometric research purposes is extremely valuable and should not be overlooked. This data is particularly valuable in examining the psychometric comparability of accommodated and standard test scores.

The next two sections will review different approaches to designing research studies (using both special data collections and operational test data) to answer the two critical validity questions mentioned earlier: (1) Which test score (accommodated or standard) is a better measure of the construct? and (2) Are the two test scores (accommodated and standard) psychometrically comparable?

RESEARCH DESIGNS FOR SPECIAL RESEARCH STUDIES

This section will primarily review the design of research studies that can be used to examine the validity of accommodated and standard test scores for students with and without disabilities. In addition we include other research studies that can be conducted to improve test design and accommodation policies for students with disabilities. The specific areas covered will include the differential boost design, special field testing, surveys, and small sample designs.

Differential Boost Design With Alternate Measure of Performance

This design can be employed to answer questions about differential boost (Would students without disabilities benefit as much from the accommodation as students with disabilities?) as well as a more pressing validity question identified earlier (Does the accommodated test score more accurately measure the construct being assessed for students with disabilities than students without disabilities?). In many cases the answer to both of these questions is obvious because the standard condition can not assess the construct with any degree of accuracy for the students with the disability (e.g., student who is blind taking print test). Some cases, however, do not offer obvious answers and require experimental research to answer these questions. The most controversial testing accommodations that have generated the most research are extra time, the use of a calculator, and having the test read aloud. Research studies have employed the premise of differential boost, but many are lacking in rigorous experimental design, adequate sample sizes, random assignment of students to accommodation conditions and test forms, an adequate measure of performance, or a combination of these factors. In addition none of these studies has examined the validity of test scores for students with and without disabilities under both accommodated and standard conditions.

The ideal differential boost study should examine students with and without the disability of interest across both testing conditions (with and without the accommoda-

tions). In addition an alternate measure of performance in the construct of interest should be collected for all students in the sample so researchers can examine if the accommodated or standard score is a better predictor of the intended construct. For example, if reading proficiency is your construct of interest, you may wish to collect data from another assessment of reading proficiency or collect teachers' ratings of reading proficiency.

In addition to examining the predictive validity of both accommodated and standard scores for both populations, this research design will allow researchers to determine if students with disabilities receive a differential boost in total test score from the accommodated condition than students without disabilities. Table 5-1 displays an example of an ideal differential boost design which includes randomly assigning students with and without disabilities separately to one of four groups which counter balance the order of testing condition and the order of test form. This random assignment of students is only possible when students with disabilities can provide some meaningful information without the accommodation. (For example, it may be possible to obtain some meaningful information on test takers with learning disabilities who participate in a standard administration, but it might not be possible to obtain meaningful information on students with significant visual impairments who are given a standard print test. See *Cautions for Standard Condition* section of this chapter for additional information on testing students with disabilities without a specific accommodation.) Assuming the effect size of interest is .20, the sample included in Table 5-1 is large enough to detect an effect size of .20 with a power of .80 at a significance level of .05.

Cautions for Standard Condition. Although the differential boost design provides information on test takers under both conditions, the standard testing conditions

TABLE 5-1

Example of Differential Boost Design Comparing Standard Administration to Accommodated Administration

Group	Category	Sample Size	Session 1 Test Form	Session 1 Condition	Session 2 Test Form	Session 2 Condition
1	No Disability	175	A	Standard	B	Accommodated
2	No Disability	175	A	Accommodated	B	Standard
3	No Disability	175	B	Accommodated	A	Standard
4	No Disability	175	B	Standard	A	Accommodated
5	Specific Disability	175	A	Standard	B	Accommodated
6	Specific Disability	175	A	Accommodated	B	Standard
7	Specific Disability	175	B	Accommodated	A	Standard
8	Specific Disability	175	B	Standard	A	Accommodated
Total	All Test Takers	1400				

may prove to be excessively frustrating for students with disabilities. When this is the case cautions should be issued and steps taken to ensure that the standard testing condition is as accessible as possible. These cautions and steps may include explaining to students the purpose of the study and then offering additional testing accommodations (not the accommodation of interest) under both the standard and accommodated conditions. For example, if the read-aloud accommodation is the accommodation of interest, it may be possible to provide extra time under both the standard and read-aloud condition. One then needs to separate out the direct impact of read aloud from the impact of both extra time and read aloud, but a more supportive testing environment for students with disabilities will have been provided.

Selection of Test Forms. One critical aspect of this study is selection of the necessary two test forms that will be used with the standard and accommodated conditions. In an ideal situation the two test forms would be equated. Some prior research studies have attempted to use nonequated test forms (e.g., randomly assigning items from one large test to create two shorter tests, creating two com-

parable forms using item statistics, content specifications, and expert judgment) but these approaches are not advisable since there is no guarantee that the process will result in comparable scores across the two forms. Such comparability will be assured only through the process of equating.

Reducing Financial Costs. Because the differential boost study requires a large sample size and thus is costly, it is reasonable to consider possible ways to reduce costs. Reduction of cost usually involves the use of reduced sample sizes, but this will decrease the chance of finding a significant difference. How much the sample size is reduced should be informed by prior research on the accommodation of interest as well as the expected differential performance boost. If prior research indicates that the performance boost is as large as a full standard deviation then the sample size can be reduced more than if prior research indicates smaller performance boosts from the accommodation. Other cost reducers may include randomly assigning students with and without disabilities to take either the accommodated or standard form, and then examining average group scores rather than individual boost. A

TABLE 5-2

Types and Examples of Additional Data to Collect

Additional Data	Examples
Alternate measure of construct	Additional test scores
	Grades
	Grade point average
	Teacher's rating of student's ability or performance
Survey	Information on how the accommodation was used
	Teacher's predictions of boost from accommodation
	Accommodation history
	Student observations and preferences
	Type of disability
Observational data	Amount of time spent on each test item
	Frustration level of student with test or using accommodation
	Number of times student read (or listened to) each item

final cost reducer may include using operational test data for one of the two test sessions; however, this approach would require randomly assigning students to take the research portion either before or after the operational test to reduce the impact of order effects.

Other Types of Special Research Studies

In addition to the differential boost study described, researchers are employing smaller research studies that focus on improving accommodation policy and practice. These studies include field testing new item types and test forms on a sample of students with disabilities, cognitive labs or think aloud studies, and the scaffolding of accommodations to examine the impact of testing accommodations at the item level. A description of these studies follows.

Field Testing. Another type of research study that can provide information on the validity of test scores and inform test development is an examination of the accessibility of test items in a field test or pilot test

prior to an operational administration. Often students with disabilities are excluded from field testing and pilot testing of new test questions. Although a large field test is often cost prohibitive, a small field test can be very cost effective and can identify major problems with new item types prior to operational administration.

Table 5-2 provides several types of data that can be collected during a field test and examples of each. One piece of data mentioned earlier is an alternate measure of performance on the construct of interest. Other pieces of evidence include survey data (from teachers, parents, and students) as well as observational data which can inform policy and training on test administration procedures. These types of data can be used to inform individuals who make decisions about testing accommodations at both the individual level and the policy level. For example information on the amount of time spent on each test item can inform policy on the amount of testing time required for both students who test under standard and accommodated conditions. Table 5-3 includes several survey questions that can be included in

TABLE 5-3

Types of Survey Questions and Observational Data to Include in Disability Field Test

Areas	Examples
Teacher or student perceptions	How well does the item appear to measure the intended construct (rather than the student's disability)?
	Did the students feel they had enough time to complete the items?
	Were the directions clear?
	How could the test item be improved?
Accessibility	How were the accommodations used?
	What specific accommodations would improve the item or item type?
	How many times did the student read (or listen to) each item?
	Which format did the student prefer?
	What obstacles and behaviors did the test administrator observe?
	Which presentation approach (A or B) did the test taker prefer? (This question can be used when a new item type is field tested under two or more presentation modes.)
Student data	What was the student's specific disability classification?
	Which constructs are impacted by the student's disability (e.g., reading or math)?

a field test as well as observational data that the test proctor can collect. These pieces of information can help to inform test development, to create alternate test formats, and to determine policy on the implementation of testing accommodations.

In addition to the observational and survey data, performance data can be collected to compare the percentages of students with and without disabilities who answer the item correctly. Test developers should pay particular attention to these data if the gap in performance (between students with and without disabilities) is larger here than what is typically observed. When this proves to be the case, the proposed items may need to be reexamined to determine if they are increasing construct-irrelevant variance for students with disabilities.

Cognitive Labs or Think Aloud Studies. One study design that is gaining in popularity is the use of think aloud protocols (also referred to as cognitive labs; see Johnstone, Bottsford-Miller, & Thompson, 2006, for a review of the use of think aloud methodology to examine issues of test design for students with disabilities and English language learners). One advantage of think aloud studies is that they can be completed with a small number of students (10–20). In addition the methodology provides a useful means for investigating how different test takers approach a particular item type. However, researchers need to be careful to first determine if the students have communication skills that are sufficient enough to clearly articulate their thought processes during test taking.

Scaffolded Accommodations. Another research design that has been employed is the use of scaffolded accommodations (Ketterlin-Geller, Yovanoff, & Tindal, 2007) to determine how a student performs with and without accommodations on the same item (rather than equated test forms as in the differential boost design). The scaffolded accommodation obtains information on the student's performance under standard conditions and then asks the student to attempt the item again with an accommodation that the student, teacher, or computer selects. Other slightly different research designs allow the students to select an accommodation after making a judgment of whether they can complete the item without the accommodation. This type of design provides additional information on a student's metacognitive skills in determining if they can complete the item without accommodations. Although the scaffolded accommodation designs provide some useful information, students who are able to accurately complete the item under both conditions (with and without accommodations) and students who are unable to complete the item under both conditions should not be included in the sample. In addition, the use of the same item under both conditions can result in the provision of practice on that item which is intertwined with the accommodation effects.

RESEARCH DESIGNS FOR PSYCHOMETRIC COMPARABILITY

Although the differential boost study that includes an alternate measure of performance can be used to examine one critical aspect of validity (predictive validity of test scores), other aspects of score validity (under accommodated and standard conditions) can be examined using operational test data. This section will review several psychometric indicators that can be examined to provide testing programs with additional evidence to include in a portfolio of research on the impact of testing accommodations. In 1982 the National Academy of Sciences (NAS; Sherman & Robinson, 1982) recommended five psychometric indicators for examining the impact of testing accommodations. These included

1. Test reliability
2. Test factor structure
3. Item functioning
4. Predictive validity
5. The impact of accommodations on admission decisions

The last item (admission decisions) focused on the interpretation of test scores that were flagged for nonstandard administrations of admissions tests (e.g., college entrance examinations) due to the use of extended time. It is not as relevant today given the decision made by many testing companies to discontinue the use of flagging of test scores.

In 2006 the U.S. Department of Education's Office of Special Education Programs (OSEP) released a paper that focused on large scale assessment for students with disabilities. This paper examined the validity of test scores and provided a framework for examining this validity which included seven different types of empirical validity evidence. This evidence included the first four NAS recommendations listed previously as well as evidence from test design and development, scoring, and scale comparability studies. Most of the psychometric evidence from the NAS and the Department of Education's recommendations can be collected using operational test data, which is relatively cost effective. This section includes a review of the procedures for examining reliability, factor structure, and item functioning with operational test data.

Reliability

All test scores contain some degree of error. This fact is true for tests in the physical sciences as well as tests used for educational and psychological purposes. It is very important when developing assessments to ensure that the degree of error in an assessment is appropriate for the purpose of the test. Tests that are used for accountability purposes, such as state standards-based assessments, need to have very little error. Another way of thinking about test reliability is that it is a measure of how consistently examinees' scores are rank ordered across administrations of a test. The measure of this consistency is provided by a correlation coefficient that theoretically can range between −1 and +1. Typically, reliability coefficients for psychological or educational assessments range from .5 to .9.

There are a number of different methods that can be used to measure the reliability of test scores. The most common methods are split-half reliability, measures of internal consistency, and alternate forms reliability. (See Anastasi, 1988 for a complete description of these reliability coefficients and how they are calculated.) Split-half reliability is a coefficient that is computed by dividing a test into halves, correlating the scores on each half, and then correcting for test length. The primary weakness of this coefficient is that it is inappropriate for speeded tests. Internal consistency measures focus on the degree to which the test items are correlated with each other. Many testing programs report internal consistency measures with test scores. Alternate form reliability is a method that is available to testing programs that administer alternate forms of the same test. The correlation of scores for one group of examinees taking alternate forms of the same test is used to estimate the reliability of the test. Regardless of how a reliability coefficient is computed, it is very important to compute this coefficient for all relevant subgroups of the test-taking population. In some cases, because of sample size issues, this may require combining low-incidence disabilities into a single category (e.g., blind and low vision could be combined to form a single visually impaired subgroup).

Factor Structure

The American Educational Research Association, American Psychological Association, and National Council on Measurement

in Education's *Standards for Educational and Psychological Testing* (AERA, APA, & NCME, 1999) suggest a study of a test's internal structure as part of the test score validation process (p. 13). For valid test score interpretation, scores on accommodated test forms given to students with disabilities should measure the same underlying construct or constructs as scores for students without disabilities who have taken the test under standard conditions. Knowledge about the underlying constructs of assessments that are taken by both examinees with disabilities and those without disabilities, and by examinees that take the test with and without accommodations, is critical in order to interpret scores on these tests and to compare or aggregate test scores for these populations.

Some of the questions that a factor analytical study can answer, provided the appropriate conditions are built into the study, are

1. Does the assessment measure the same underlying construct (s) for examinees with a disability who take the test *without* an accommodation as it does for the nondisabled population?

2. Does the assessment measure the same underlying construct(s) for examinees with a disability who take the test *with* an accommodation as it does for the nondisabled population?

3. Does the assessment measure the same underlying construct(s) for examinees with a disability who take the test *with* an accommodation as it does for the examinees with a disability who take the test *without* an accommodation?

Typically, a series of exploratory and confirmatory factor analyses are carried out using either item level data or parcel data. (See Cook, Dorans, & Eignor, 1988, for a discussion of issues involved with factor analyzing item level data.) Several researchers have recently used factor analysis to investigate the structure of an assessment for students with disabilities (Cook, Eignor,

Sawaki, Steinberg, & Cline, 2006; Huynh, & Barton, 2006; Huynh, Meyer, & Gallant, 2004). These studies are important because they provide an important starting point for gathering evidence that a test does or does not measure the specified construct for a particular group of examinees.

Item Functioning

Differential item functioning (DIF) analyses are another approach to examining what the test is measuring for different populations. There are several procedures for conducting DIF analyses (see Holland & Wainer, 1993, for a discussion of DIF analysis procedures) with advantage and disadvantages for each, but all examine the difference in item performance between two comparable groups of test takers (usually formed by matching students from the two groups on total test score). DIF exists if two groups of test takers who have the same underlying ability level are not equally likely to get an item correct. These groups are usually different demographic groups (e.g., male vs. female, or White vs. African American) but recently several research studies have used this methodology with disability subgroups (see Barton & Finch, 2004; Bielinski, Thurlow, Ysseldyke, Freidebach & Freidebach, 2001; Bolt & Ysseldyke, 2006; Cahalan-Laitusis, Cook, & Aicher, 2004; Cahalan-Laitusis, Morgan, Bridgeman, Zanna, & Stone, 2007), and English language learners (see Abedi, 2004; Laitusis, Camara, & Wang, 2004). These research studies have used DIF to examine if a fatigue effect exists from extended time accommodations and if specific item characteristics are more or less difficult for students who receive read aloud accommodations. Although DIF research can provide insight on the impact of testing accommodations on item characteristics, it is important to initially define disability subgroups as tightly as possible (e.g., students with learning disabilities who received extra

time) so that results can more easily be interpreted. That said, the sample size should not be less than 100 in each group for research studies or 300 in each group for operational tests. A final consideration before conducting DIF analyses is to ensure that the matching criteria (usually total test score) is unidimensional and equally reliable for both populations.

IMPLICATIONS

This chapter has provided an overview of the different types of research studies that can be conducted to examine the impact of testing accommodations on the validity of test scores. Because research is needed to provide information at many different levels, the concluding section will focus on the implications of the material in this chapter for three groups: school-based decision makers, policy makers, and test developers.

For School-Based Decision Makers

Since school-based decision makers have limited resources for conducting research on the validity of testing accommodations, this chapter has greater implications for policy makers and test developers. However, it is important for school-based decision makers to understand the results from research studies to determine which accommodations result in the most valid test results. Prior research (see chapters on individualized education program [IEP] decision making) have indicated that in many cases IEP teams are not making accurate decisions about what accommodations would benefit a particular student. One way to rectify this might be to implement some of the research designs described earlier at the individual student level (e.g., consider the impact of an accommodation on construct being measured and consider the student's performance with and without a specific accommodation).

For Policy Makers

Policy makers should rely on empirical evidence when setting policies on which testing accommodations should be allowed on specific tests and how test scores will be treated if a specific accommodation is used. These policy decisions should be made based on empirical research findings, as well as an argument-based approach to validation (see National Research Council, 2004, for more details on articulating the validation argument for testing accommodations). When empirical evidence is not available, the other methods for collecting evidence outlined in this chapter can provide policy makers with critical information to inform their decision. In addition, data analysis of existing operational data is also an excellent source of information for determining the impact of potential policy changes.

Another important area where policy makers can influence research is by implementing practices to encourage research on data from their testing programs. One potential area for increasing research would be to make operational test data available to researchers. Another important contribution would involve collecting information on which testing accommodations are approved, which testing accommodations were actually used, and information on the student's disability (e.g., learning disability, ADHD). In addition, policy makers can encourage research on low incidence disabilities by requiring the use of the same test forms for low incidence disabilities (e.g., Braille forms) for multiple years which then allows for the pooling of data across years for study purposes.

For Further Research/Test Development

This chapter is most important for research and test development activities because it provides information on how to design research activities to inform test development as well as policy decisions. Carrying out research studies for students with disabilities is challenging for a number of reasons, some of which have already been mentioned earlier in this chapter. In addition, many of the techniques typically used to analyze data for the studies are large-sample techniques; factor analysis is an example of this type of technique. It is also not advisable to perform DIF analyses on samples of less than 100 (Cahalan-Laitusis et al., 2004). However, it is often the case that it is impossible to obtain sample sizes of over 25 for some low-incidence disabilities. Students with visual impairments using a Braille accommodation are an example of this situation. The heterogeneity of the samples is another problem. Students are not simply deaf or blind. There are wide gradients of a disability and often the classification of students into disability categories covers a very broad definition of that disability. In addition, most accommodations are provided in a bundle (e.g., read aloud with extra time and individual administration) which make disentangling the impact of each accommodation more difficult. Also, many students will require a special setting as a result of the particular accommodation they are receiving. Consequently, it is very difficult to isolate the impact of a particular accommodation on the validity of test scores from the effect of the special setting. As pointed out earlier, this can be done through the manipulation of variables in an experimentally designed study. However, one must then ask how realistic are the results of a study that focuses on only a single accommodation, if that accommodation is administered in the study in a manner that is not typically used in the classroom or on standardized tests. In spite of all of these issues, progress in carrying out high quality research has been made (Sireci et al., 2003, and Chapter 4 by Sireci and Pitoniak in this book). It is important to continue this type of research in spite of the difficulties because it is only by finding answers to the most pressing questions, and using these answers to inform practice, that the validity and accessibility of assessments for students with disabilities can be achieved.

REFERENCES

Abedi, J. (2004, April). *Differential item functioning (DIF) analyses based on language background variables*. Paper presented at the annual meeting of the National Council on Measurement in Education, San Diego, CA.

American Educational Research Association, American Psychological Association, & National Council on Measurement in Education. (1999). *Standards for educational and psychological tests*. Washington, DC: American Psychological Association.

Anastasi, A. (1988). *Psychological Testing*. New York: MacMillan.

Barton, K. E., & Finch, H. (2004, April). *Using DIF analyses to examine bias and assumptions of unidimensionality across students with and without disabilities and students with accommodations*. Paper presented at the annual meeting of the National Council on Measurement in Education, San Diego, CA.

Bielinski, J., Thurlow, M., Ysseldyke, J., Freidebach, J., & Freidebach, M. (2001). *Read-aloud accommodations: Effects on multiple-choice reading and math items*. (Technical Report 31). Minneapolis, MN: National Center on Educational Outcomes. Retrieved February 18, 2004, from http://education.umn.edu/nceo/OnlinePubs/Technical31.htm

Bolt, S. E., & Ysseldyke, J. E. (2006) Comparing DIF across math and reading/language arts tests for students receiving a read-aloud accommodation. *Applied Measurement in Education*, 19(4), 329–355.

Cahalan-Laitusis, C., Cook, L. L., & Aicher, C. (2004, April). *Examining test items for students with disabilities by testing accommodation*. Paper presented at the annual meeting of the National Council on Measurement in Education, San Diego, CA.

Cahalan-Laitusis, C., Morgan, D., Bridgeman, B., Zanna, J., & Stone, E. (2007). *Examination of fatigue effects from extended time accommoda-*

tions on the SAT Reasoning Test. New York: College Board.

Cook, L. L., Dorans, N. J., & Eignor, D. R. (1988). An assessment of the dimensionality of three SAT-Verbal test editions. *Journal of Educational Statistics, 13*, 19–43.

Cook, L., Eignor, D., Sawaki, Y., Steinberg, J., & Cline, F. (2006, April). *Using factor analysis to investigate the impact of accommodations on the scores of students with disabilities on English-language arts assessments*. Paper presented at the annual meeting of the National Council on Measurement in Education, San Francisco, CA.

Elliott, S. N., & McKevitt, B. (2000, April). *Testing accommodations decisions: Legal and technical issues challenging educators*. Paper presented at the annual conference of the American Educational Research Association, New Orleans, LA.

Fuchs, L. S., & Fuchs, D. (1999). Fair and unfair testing accommodations. *School Administrator, 56*(10), 24–29.

Holland, P. W., & Wainer, H. (1993). *Differential Item Functioning*. Hillsdale, NJ: Lawrence Erlbaum.

Huynh, H., & Barton, K. (2006). Performance of students with disabilities under regular and oral administrations of a high-stakes reading examination. *Applied Measurement in Education, 19*(1), 21–39.

Huynh, H., Meyer, J. P., & Gallant, D. J. (2004). Comparability of student performance between regular and oral administrations for a high-stakes mathematics test. *Applied Measurement in education, 17*, 38–57.

Johnstone, C. J., Bottsford-Miller, N. A., & Thompson, S. J. (2006). *Using the think aloud method (cognitive labs) to evaluate test design for students with disabilities and English language learners* (Technical Report 44). Minneapolis, MN: University of Minnesota, National Center on Educational Outcomes. Retrieved December 11, 2006, from http://education.umn.edu/NCEO/OnlinePubs/Tech44/

Ketterlin-Geller, L., Yovanoff, P., & Tindal, G. (2007). Developing a new paradigm for conducting research on accommodations in mathematics testing. *Exceptional Children 73*, pp. 331–347.

Laitusis, V. , Camara, W. J., & Wang, X. B. (2004, April). *An examination of differential item functioning (DIF) between language groups on an assessment of math reasoning*. Paper presented at the annual meeting of the National Council on Measurement in Education, San Diego, CA.

National Research Council. (2004). *Keeping score for all: The effects of inclusion and accommodation policies on large-scale educational assessments*. (Judith A. Koenig & Lyle F. Bachman, Eds.). Washington, DC: The National Academies Press.

Phillips, S. E. (1994). High-stakes testing accommodations: Validity versus disabled rights. *Applied Measurement in Education, 7*(2), 93–120.

Pitoniak, M. J., & Royer, J. M. (2001). Testing accommodations for examinees with disabilities: A review of psychometric, legal, and social policy issues. *Review of Educational Research. 71*(1), 53–104.

Sherman, S. & Robinson, N. (Eds.). (1982). *Ability testing of handicapped people: Dilemma for government, science, and the public*. Washington, DC: National Academy Press.

Sireci, S. G., Li, S., & Scarpati, S. (2003). *The effects of test accommodations on test performance: A review of the literature*. (Center for Educational Assessment Research, Rep. No. 485). Amherst, MA: School of Education, University of Massachusetts Amherst.

Sireci, S. G., Scarpati, S. E., & Li, S. (2005). Test accommodations for students with disabilities: An analysis of the interaction hypothesis. *Review of Educational Research, 75*(4), 457–490.

U.S. Department of Education. (2006). *Validating assessments for students with disabilities*. In *Models for large-scale assessment for students with disabilities*. Retrieved October 31, 2006 from http://www.osepideasthatwork.org/toolkit/pdf/Validating_Assessments

CHAPTER 6

Validity and Accommodations: The Journey Toward Accessible Assessments

KAREN E. BARTON
CTB/McGraw-Hill

Evidence about the validity of accommodations on large-scale assessments is required by the *Standards and Assessment Peer Review Guidance* (U.S. Department of Education, ED, 2004). Critical Element 4.6.b requests not only that accommodations be made available, but that the "State (has) determined that scores for students with disabilities that are based on accommodated administration conditions will allow for valid inferences about these students' knowledge and skills and can be combined meaningfully with scores from non-accommodated administration conditions" (p. 40). In addition, the *Standards for Educational and Psychological Testing* (American Educational Research Association, AERA, American Psychological Association, APA, and National Council on Measurement in Education, NCME, 1999) state in Standard 10.4 that whenever accommodations are made for students during testing, "the [accommodations] as well as the rationale for the [accommodations] should be described in detail . . . and evidence of valid-

ity should be provided whenever available" (p. 106). The *Standards* go on to note that when comparability of test scores is desirable, test score validity should also be provided.

That these two widely accepted documents require validity evidence about accommodations cannot be ignored. There are challenges not only in collecting such evidence, but assuring the evidence collected provides trustworthy and useful information. Confounding variables in even the best experimental designs (see Sireci and Pitoniak, Chapter 4, for review of research) are extremely rare in accommodations validity research on large-scale assessments, and may often be outside the researchers' control and at the very heart of the assessment itself.

This chapter discusses ways to collect validity evidence at foundational levels across valid assessment systems, and where constructs, accessibility, and the minimization of error are key components in assuring valid accommodations and score comparability.

VALIDITY

Validity is the ongoing trust in the accuracy of the test, the administration, and interpretations and use of results. According to Messick (1995), "validity is not a property of the test . . . as such, but rather of the meaning of the test scores . . . [that] are a function not only of the items or stimulus conditions, but also of the persons responding" (p. 741).

Validation must encompass the full testing environment: standards, test constructs, items, persons, characteristics, administration, and interactions of each. This goes beyond scoring the validity of accommodating and to the heart of assessment validity. Within the constraints of various confounding variables, the validation process should include an evaluation of accessibility at the student and item level, and precision in light of targeted constructs and systematic error. From there, innovation in testing and research can help build valid assessment systems.

To build the case for a valid assessment system, various evidences about various types of validity must be gathered. According to Messick (1989, 1995) validity is an amalgamated concept that includes various types of evidences. Procedural validity evidence can be collected across the types of validity Messick describes (1989, p. 16; 1995, pp. 744–746). For example:

Type: Content—subject domains covered
Evidence: Standards Development Process, Item Specifications and Blueprints, Test to Standards Alignment Study

Type: Substantive—tasks within domains and regularity with which various individuals respond to them
Evidence: Internal Reliability

Type: Structural and Convergent—relationships among responses to tasks, items, or parts of a test (or the internal structure of test responses)

Evidence: Error Analyses, Score Comparability, Factor Analyses, Correlational Analyses

Type: Generalizability—Score meanings over time, across groups and settings
Evidence: Generalizability studies

Type: External and Divergent—Relationships of test scores with other measures and background variable
Evidence: Correlational analyses of different constructs

Type: Consequential—Social consequences, intended outcomes and unintended side effects
Evidence: Instructional surveys, predictive validity, social consequences, student work and item mapping studies, assessment literacy, classroom assessments

The *Standards* (AERA, APA, & NCME, 1999) address similar sources of inclusive validity evidence: evidence based on test content, response processes, internal structure(s), relations to other variables, and consequences of testing. Each of these sources of validity evidence can be researched and collected in a variety of ways. For instance, an expert review of an assessment's test specifications (or blueprints) and associating items provide evidence of test content, or content validity. The items within an assessment should not go beyond the test specifications, which are normally developed to represent the content to be covered within instruction, such that there is item to test alignment. Items unspecified by the blueprint, yet found on the assessment, might represent content areas unexposed to all students (introducing the issue of *opportunity to learn*).

Other approaches to gathering validity evidence include data about the reliability of the assessment. Reliability is a precursor to validity; however, reliability does not necessarily guarantee validity. Reliability is merely consistency and only in light of additional analyses can one determine if the consistency is further a reflection of accuracy. (One can be reliably wrong!) Further, correlational analyses of student responses and inferences made on one assessment and those responses and inferences on another assessment of the same construct (convergent) or of a different construct (divergent) can indicate the degree of "external" validity evidence (Messick, 1989, 1995). Error analyses, score comparability investigations, and factor analyses to examine the consistency of internal structures (Crocker & Algina, 1986) can also be used to gather validity evidence. The use of factor analyses to investigate constructs and convergent validity evidence has been conducted by various researchers (Enright, Rock, & Bennett, 1998; Rock, Bennett, & Jirele, 1988; Rock, Bennett, & Kaplan, 1987). Evidence of the predictive validity (the ability of a performance on one test to be predicted on future assessments) and social consequences, intended or otherwise, can be provided by documenting future student performances in other assessments and social situations, like college grade-point averages, rates of graduation, or frequency of obtaining jobs.

Both Messick (1989, 1995) and the *Standards*—and more recently, the collection of evidence for peer review (ED, 2004)—provide a clear direction on how to collect information about the entire system of assessment and is typically referred to as *procedural validity*. The collection of validity evidences in a variety of ways and along the life cycle of an assessment is a very solid, scientific approach to cross-validating through a variety of sources the overall validity of the assessment system.

VALID ASSESSMENT SYSTEMS

In the current state of educational testing, diverse examinees approach the assessment platforms with various accommodations; those accommodations may or may not be standardized in how they are chosen or how they are provided. What, then, can be done to improve the validity of the assessments and of the accommodations provided? The first step is to take a hard look at the assessment itself with a back-to-basics approach where assessments are built as part of valid assessment systems (VAS). The system includes various pieces that are driven by the purpose and end use of the assessment, including but not limited to

- Content standards.
- Test development (test blueprints, item specifications, accessibility issues).
- Test administration (accommodations decisions and provisions, eligibility and exclusion criteria, test dates, materials handling).
- Scoring (rubrics, range finding, anchor paper, training, interrater reliability).
- Data collection (test data—biographical, item specific, total test, interviews, think alouds, questionnaires).
- Data analyses (special studies, item and test level analyses, interpretation and use, instructional impact).
- Documentation via technical reports.

One way to summarize most validity evidence that can be collected for each of the VAS pieces is via a technical report. Past documentation on accommodation data and even alternate assessments has often not been included in traditional technical reports. Given the scores for the accommodated and alternate assessment, students deserve as much validation as do the scores for the general population; data for those students and assessments also need to be included in technical documentation. Research using solid documentation and actual test data must be conducted on the various pieces of the VAS to determine where the precision is threatened and to include threats due to accommodations.

However, actual test data are often inconsistent in regard to accommodations. For example, not all states collect the vital information needed to begin analyses: Who are the participating students and how are they being assessed (with or without accommodations)? One step to improve data collection, particularly in light of peer review process and the ED guidelines (2004), is to include subgroup data (disabilities, home languages) and the specific accommodations provided.

The technical report should begin with a description of the targeted student population and the eligibility criteria and guidelines needed for students to participate and receive accommodations. Content validity evidence can be achieved through consistent adherence to test blueprints and standards and through rubric and scoring specifications that truly represent what all students will know and will be able to do. The report should detail the standards, how they were developed and approved, and by whom. The standards are typically reviewed by content experts to decide which standards will be assessed. That leads then to the development of a test map or blueprint that guides all item and test development. The blueprint is critical to the evidence of the alignment between the test and the standards.

Often, there is an alignment study to further evaluate, cross-validate, and ensure test-to-standards alignment. Once the testing is complete, there are usually very clear and consistent rules on scoring and for open-ended type items, training scorers consistently and repeatedly on the rubrics, scoring philosophies, selecting and using anchor papers, and so forth, all the while collecting rater reliability data as evidence. All of the documentation on rubrics, anchor paper selection, training, and so forth further serves as the procedural evidence of validity. Finally, various data analyses, special studies, and student performance results should be provided.

Specific to the validation of accommodations, the first step is to establish exactly what the test is purposed to measure. One can not accommodate a student validly without knowing clearly the purpose; otherwise the accommodation and provision thereof could directly invalidate the test. According to Haladyna and Downing (2004), "the most fundamental step in validation is defining the construct" (p. 25). What is the test intended to measure as a whole and by the individual items? This is defined by the construct(s). According to Crocker and Algina (1986), a construct is "a product of informed scientific imagination, an idea developed to permit categorization and description of some directly observable behavior [while the] constructs are not directly observable. [The constructs] must first be operationally defined" (p. 230).

Although the construct is the *idea*, it can be defined in tangible ways. The *targeting of the construct* is the process of operationally defining the construct through targeting the specific, observable tasks or skills that define and provide evidence for the construct. This starts with a universe of possibilities, focusing in on the construct domain, observable behaviors, and finally the sample(s) of evidence (see Figure 6-1).

The operational definition of the construct and selection of evidence is merely the start. The operational definition includes the specification of observable tasks that, together, represent the (unobservable) construct, via empirical evidence and analyses to support what has been "imagined." Once the constructs are defined theoretically, the evidence such as item and test level performance must be analyzed empirically and validated. Only then can assurances be made that any interpretations of the evidence about the construct are valid and that there is comparability across the evidence collected about the construct.

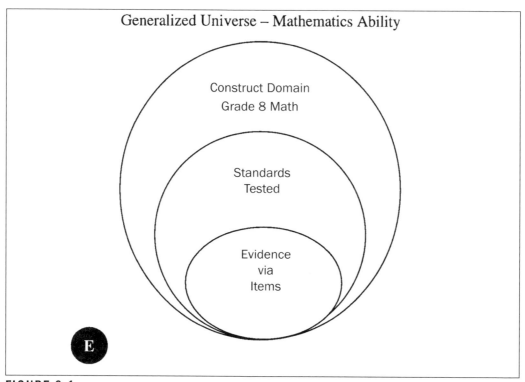

FIGURE 6-1

An Illustration of the Sampling Flow From Construct to Items as Evidence

ACCESSIBILITY AND "ACCESS ABILITY"

Targeting constructs is vitally important to any assessment because it can provide direct evidence on student performance that is specific to the construct and student progress validation on the construct. Such specificity not only helps to minimize error; it can be especially useful for instruction and important to the level of accountability associated with current educational assessment. In addition, it is equally important to assure that the response conditions of an assessment are also well known, defined, and targeted. When the response conditions of a test are not well specified, both random and systematic errors may be introduced. Based on Messick's (1995) statement, validity includes the interaction of items, stimulus conditions, and examinees. Therefore, response conditions encompass the interaction of (a) the student and the items and (b) the items and the student. (See Figure 6-2.)

The first interaction is much like the customary view of accessibility. Accessibility discussions are typically limited in definition to student access to test items or tasks and how such items or tasks can be edited to be more accessible by the student or examinee. The report by Thompson, Johnstone, and Thurlow (2002) on universal design of assessment (UDA) speaks quite clearly. All of the elements of Universal Design in that report describe ways in which the test can be designed such that students have increased access to the information about the items and that characteristics within the test items that present barriers to students are decreased. Accessibility should be further extended to the curriculum and content assessed. Prior to testing, students must be provided opportunities to learn what is being

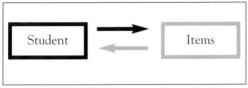

FIGURE 6-2

The Interactions Affected by Response Conditions

assessed. "Students who have not had an opportunity to learn the material tested will be disadvantaged during testing no matter how universal the design of the assessment" (Thompson & Thurlow, 2002, p. 2).

What is missing from accessibility discussions thus far is the second interaction of the items with the students, that is, how well test items access a student's ability or a test's "access ability." This goes well beyond the look and feel, readability, comprehensibility, and other such UDA characteristics. This gets to the power of each item to truly tap into and access ability.

Accessibility is therefore a two-pronged requirement of validity evidence: examinees' access to the test and test access to the examinee. To begin targeting evidence about each interaction one should ask the following:

- Can the examinee respond to the item(s) and provide evidence of their ability without systematic hindrance? (student access)

- Do the items provide the clearest, error-minimized (as none are error-free) path to eliciting a response that reflects the true ability of each examinee? (test access)

Accommodations are the access tools specific to the first interaction or student access. It is the accessibility of the student to the items that reduces the barriers and confounding variation (or construct irrelevant variance) about the items, which in turn increases the reliability and validity or trust in the accuracy of the test score as an indica-

tor of the students' performance. Accommodations should also maximize the access ability of the assessments such that disability or limited language skills do not misrepresent true performance (the second interaction). In order to improve test or item access to the examinee's ability, and thus to improve precision, reliability and validity of the test scores, the test must be built such that constructs are clearly defined and clearly communicated, minimizing construct irrelevant variance and errors (systematic and random).

ERROR

Error in measurement can easily threaten and compromise the accessibility and therefore the precision, reliability (to include accuracy), and validity of an assessment. There are two types of errors customarily defined in measurement: random and systematic. Both random and systematic errors can compromise interpretations of scores and hence the validity of the assessment.

In measurement, the belief is that random error can be minimized by standardizing test administrations so that differences in scores reflect differences among examinees and not test administrations (Geisinger, 1994). Random errors are just that—random. They are varied, inconsistent, and are usually inherent to the assessment or administration thereof. For example, there might be random errors due to variability in scoring by raters; distractions during the administration (a parade goes by during testing, the student is having an "off" day); or how well the content was sampled (the entire universe of possible tasks can not be measured on a single test); or because the test is a one-time, summative measure of student ability. There can even be random errors in defining the construct. These specifically affect the usefulness of results, and the reliability, validity, comparability, and generalizability of the assessment.

Systematic error arises, however, if the test and test administration in and of itself presents an inaccessible situation of students-to-items and items-to-student ability. These errors have typically been described as being inherent to the examinee and are consistent and persistent regardless of how the test is administered (except in cases where administration procedures systematically present situations in which student performance is directly impacted). An example of systematic error is when students with disabilities are administered a test without the accommodation(s) they require (giving a blind student a regular, non-Braille, non-large print form), or when items are inaccessible by students due to characteristics of the student.

Although many systematic errors are inherent to the examinee, there are arguably types of systematic errors that are inherent to the assessment. For example, if a constructed response writing sample is selected that is not representative of the full range of papers, the scores will narrowly represent the full range of papers and will limit the generalizability and accuracy of the scores. Other examples include test administrators that are trained improperly, test materials that are mishandled, or scanners that malfunction. Systematic errors reduce the accuracy of the test results, and threaten the reliability, validity, comparability, and generalizability of the assessment, just as do random errors, particularly with respect to test accessibility.

When error of either type is minimized, scores are more trustworthy. There are various ways to minimize error. Although systematic error can be minimized by improving the accessibility of the assessments, random error is typically thought to be minimized through standardization in testing administrations. However, providing either standard or nonstandard administration requires sacrifices. There is an increased potential for random errors in a nonstandard environment and for systematic errors when a test is standard and inflexible to students' access to test information. At what point are the sacrifices impeding measurement precision and the validity thereof?

Accommodations can either maximize or minimize either type of error. The variability in accommodation decision-making policies and in the provision of accommodations is directly related to random error. Improving the standardization of both would potentially reduce the (immeasurable) amount of random error. If the assessment systematically limits access to students or by students, say when students are not given needed accommodations or are given accommodations they do not need, then that is in fact systematic error. Therefore, decisions about accommodations and the provisions of the accommodations need to be taken very seriously.

COMPARABILITY

The minimization of error also improves the comparability of scores. With respect to Standards 10.4 (AERA, APA, & NCME, 1999), the scores for students with and without disabilities are often aggregated for accountability reporting, and scores on an accommodated test administration should have the same meaning as scores on a nonaccommodated test administration (Phillips, 1994; Willingham et al., 1988). There should be comparability of the tasks required, and item or performance tasks required should be similarly difficult or easy (Tindal, 1998; Willingham et al.). The constructs measured by items, tasks, and the test as a whole should not be different or measured differently for diverse examinees, making the tests standard for participating students and permitting valid comparability and interpretations of scores (Phillips; Thurlow, Ysseldyke, & Silverstein, 1995; Tindal; Willingham et al.).

Willingham et al. (1988) reminds researchers to investigate score and task comparability as well as other types of evidence for investigating validity:

- For score comparability—reliability, factor structure, differential item functioning (DIF), predicted performance, and college admission decisions.
- For task comparability—appropriate test content, accommodations, and timing.

Tindal (1998) offers three ways testing programs can study task comparability of test items, in order of increasing level of evidence for comparability: descriptive, comparative, or experimental procedures. With descriptive research, policies are reviewed for evidence, such as the number and kinds of accommodations offered and used by students (this evidence can be provided by surveys). Comparative research on post-hoc evidence, such as teacher reflections of the appropriateness of accommodations used and their possible influence on student performance, also exist. The highest level of research for finding comparability evidence when using accommodations is experimental. Such approaches attempt to provide evidence of cause and effect with sound experimental designs and methodology.

CHALLENGES

Past research on accommodations has focused on ways to validate accommodations through collections of evidence by conducting factor analyses, cluster analyses, qualitative reviews, DIF analyses, and the like. Most research studies on accommodations have led to results which are difficult to generalize. More recently, studies have focused on the *boost/no boost* or *interaction hypothesis* (Shepard, Taylor, & Betebenner, 1998). The hypothesis is that students who actually need an accommodation and receive it should see a boost or improvement in their scores, where students who receive an accommodation and do not need it show no boost or improvement in scores. There is controversy

over the validity and use of this approach (Koenig & Bachman, 2004; see Koenig & Bachman, 2004; Koretz & Barton, 2004; Sireci, Li, & Scarpati, 2003; Tindal & Fuchs, 1999; see also Sireci and Pitoniak, Chapter 4, and Cahalan Laitusis, Chapter 5, within this book for additional references on accommodation studies.)

In Chapter 5 of this book, Cahalan Laitusis provides a detailed description of both ideal and practical methodology for collecting validity evidence. Although these designs offer researchers a foundation, there are difficulties in conducting research about accommodations that include challenges with experimental designs which are rarely utilized in accommodation research. Obtaining a sample large enough to detect effects in the research is also difficult, particularly given the diversity of disabilities and the possibilities of accommodation combinations. Securing a sample that is not a convenient sample and providing a counter-balanced design, (e.g., where accommodations are provided to students who do not need them and not provided to students who do for sake of the experiment in the "over-tested" environment) is also challenging to say the least. Additionally, confounding variables are present due to (a) the variability in classifying students by disability, the assignment of and provision of accommodations, and student exposure to curriculum; (b) the inability to tease out single administration accommodations (as most students receive more than one accommodation) to improve generalizability of the results; and (c) the lack of available and consistent data on either accommodations and/or students with disabilities.

Even with the best experimental designs for gathering validity evidence, there are confounding variables that limit the interpretations of research results, specifically when the research is about the validity of testing accommodations. Confounding variables exist with persons and items or tests, as well as with accommodations. Person- and item-related confounding variables are prone to the variability across the nation, within states, and even within school districts. Table 6-1 describes a few potential confounding variables.

Accommodations can also represent confounding variables that occur when research attempts to investigate the validity of a single accommodation. Typically, students are given multiple accommodations concurrently, or when given a single accommodation, the single accommodation automatically requires an additional accommodation. For example, if the student requires a read-aloud accommodation, it may result in a separate testing environment, such as a small group or one-on-one administration, and often extended time. Teasing out the effect of any one accommodation is further confounded by the unknown effects of the others. In addition, accommodations are often provided in nonstandard fashion and so the actual effect of the accommodation may not be known (e.g., variation in policy decisions and administration procedures—no scripts for oral accommodations, limited training for scribes).

With confounding variables of both persons and items, accommodations cannot be validated apart from an in-depth look at the assessment and what it is trying to measure (constructs), in concert with how the accommodations and test items interact (see complete lists of accommodations research by Sireci et al., 2003 and Tindal & Fuchs, 1999). It must be clear how the accommodations affect the skills or abilities measured by the test. Therefore, future research should focus deeply on validity of the assessment in light of how the wide range of students approach assessments, with all their diversities (accommodations, disabilities, languages, giftedness) and, therefore, confounding variables. Regarding single administration of accommodations, it may simply not be appropriate to attempt to tease many accommodations apart when the reality of the situation is that accommodations are very often not used singly but as a group.

In order to provide data for sound research, even nonexperimentally designed research, better efforts must be made to support students and to improve decisions on accommodations and to standardize the provision of accommodations. There exists immense variability in the identification and classification criteria for students with disabilities and for English language learners (ELLs), as well as variability in accommodation decision-making procedures and the way in which accommodations are provided and utilized across test administrations. Given the variability, even available accommodation data currently are quite "dirty" and in dire need of improvement. Data improvements may or may not be possible in the near future and research on the validity of accommodations and testing in general for students with disabilities and ELLs will continue to be a challenge.

Tests are typically administered in as standard a fashion as appropriate and possible with considerable administrator training, materials, and guidance to maximize standardization. The same attention should be paid to accommodated testing. Accommodation policies or guidelines should be readily available, easy to understand, and communicated to those who decide which accommodation(s) a student needs as well as how to effectively and validly provide the accommodation during test administration. It is very important to provide training to those responsible for making the decision about student accommodations and specific training and direction for those actually providing the accommodation during testing.

Most importantly, when the typical educational assessment is designed, the target population for the assessment is generally all test takers in a particular grade, or all test takers who have had a particular type of educational experience. The test is usually designed to provide maximum discrimination

TABLE 6-1

Sources of Confounding Variables and Examples

Possible Confounding Variable	Description
Identification of disability	It is well known that disabilities are identified in various methods with nonstandard instruments. (Koenig & Bachman, 2004)
Accommodation policies, selection, and provision	There is some overlap in state-to-state policies about allowable accommodations, but there is also a great deal of variation. In addition, the way in which accommodations are selected and assigned to students and then provided and administered severely lacks the level of standardization needed to provide trustworthy results from which to interpret and make valid recommendations about accommodations and the validity thereof. For example, students within the same school may be allowed to be accommodated by an oral accommodation. However, Tindal's Accommodation Station early results (see Chapter 9 in this book) suggests teachers are not consistent in deciding which accommodation a student actually needs and receives in the classroom or on assessments. Adding further variability, unless the state requires a utilization of a standard format audio version for oral accommodation, students with different test administrators are likely to hear a range of inflections, emphases, and the like in the accommodation. Accommodation training can help standardize such administrations, short of providing standard audio versions.
Access to and instruction in varied standards and depth/breadth of coverage	Students with disabilities who receive accommodations vary in their exposure and level of depth in the instruction received on standards, particularly the general curriculum standards.
Access to test information and opportunity to accurately respond	Students often have limited test accessibility which limits their understanding of what the test is requiring of them so they can respond accurately. In addition, students have their own barriers to responding because most tests require standard response methods (answer documents vs. oral responses that are not scripted by an adult, or the opportunity to draw rather than write responses). In other words, there is little if any flexibility or optional response modes for students taking most state-level assessments.
Test selection	Very little research is available on the accuracy in which students are selected for alternate assessments, modified assessments, or standard assessments. Research on testing accommodation selection, however, indicates that IEP teams do not accurately predict which accommodations will improve students test scores (Fuchs, Fuchs, Eaton, Hamlet, Brinkley, & Crouch, 2000) so it is likely that test selection may also be a source of variance.
Acceptance and use of accommodations	Some evidence suggests that students are less likely to accept testing accommodations at higher grade levels and that the use of accommodations may vary based on school factors (e.g., available testing rooms or staff) rather than the needs of the student (see Ewing, Chapter 13, for more details).

among candidates in the center of the distribution of scores (where most test takers' scores will reside). Consequently, most of the measurement power of the test focuses on students whose scores are in the center of the distribution and scores in the extremes of the distribution are measured with less precision. Most students with disabilities have scores that fall into the lower end of the distribution of scores on these tests. Consequently, scores for these students may be less precise and may provide less reliable data for research purposes.

CONCLUSIONS

Future research on the validity of accommodations might provide more conclusive results if there is a focus on a re-evaluation of and clarity in defining test constructs, research on all students that is not limited to disability classifications, research on what students do not know via distracter or error analyses (Barton & Huynh, 2003), data collection on the actual instructional interpretation and impact of results, and think aloud studies focused on access and student response conditions. To improve the flexibility of assessments and make standard the minimization of systematic error introduced by inaccessibility and ability that is not precisely or accurately assessed, test developers should consider and research new item types and acceptable variations in student response conditions. The approach to flexible item types and research thereof could be treated as parallel item forms and formats the new item types and those are likely to be beneficial for more than just the "accommodated" sample. Finally, the magnification of the view on the lower (and upper) tails of the score distribution is certainly worth consideration and should be the starting point. From there, the construct should be well defined, targeted, and broadly communicated. If we cannot define what we want to

know, how then do we know that what we know is what we want to know?

Assessment development must better attend to the constructs of items, the administration conditions, and responsive conditions: the way in which examinees—*all* examinees—respond to and interact with the items. There are specific parts of the assessment that a student must be able to access and to which developers must pay close attention. Students must have access to the test information and be able to easily navigate through the full form. This means that information such as the directions, pagination, and item stimulus need to be very clear. In addition, the item specific requirements about how the student is expected to respond must be clear. The developer must have a clear understanding of the expectation and requirement of the item—in other words, the construct being measured, what an appropriate response would be, and typical errors. These must be known for both multiple-choice items where distracters must also be accessible, as well as for constructed response items where not only the visible item but also the expectations and intended constructs at each score level are clear within the rubric.

Response conditions or the way in which students respond need to be considered so that when various response capabilities are used (such as oral responding or the use of assistive technologies) they do not preclude a student from being able to respond and respond accurately. Attending to each of these not only increases the student accessibility to the test and items, but it also provides a solid foundation of construct understanding and test administration by the developer. There is an additional benefit when a test needs to be translated into another language or made into special versions such as audio, Braille, or large print and the developer has a firm understanding of how to maintain constructs across versions while developing an assessment whose construct(s) is not threatened by such versions or by administrative and response diversity (nonstandard and accommodated).

Policy and procedures should continue improved attention to disability classifications, accommodation decisions and provisions, and data collection. Policy may also consider a re-conceptualization of "standardization." A more valid conceptualization may be what is standard for each examinee (what is customary for the student during instruction and classroom testing) and how best to support standardizing the accommodation decisions and provisions.

The goal should be that all examinees are assessed reliably and validly regardless of how they access the assessment. The assessment should be built such that it is dynamically consistent at assessing ability across examinees for the full distribution of scores on the assessment.

REFERENCES

American Educational Research Association, American Psychological Association, & National Council on Measurement in Education. (1999). *Standards for educational and psychological testing.* Washington, DC: American Educational Research Association.

Barton, K., & Huynh, H. (2003). Patterns of errors made by students with disabilities on a reading test with oral reading administration. *Educational and Psychological Measurement, 63*(4), 602–614.

Crocker, L., & Algina, J. (1986). *Introduction to classical and modern test theory.* Fort Worth, TX: Harcourt Brace Jovanovich College Publishers.

Enright, M. K., Rock, D. A., & Bennett, R. E. (1998). Improving measurement for graduate admissions. *Journal of Educational Measurement, 35*(3), 250–267.

Fuchs, L. S., Fuchs, D., Eaton, S. B., Hamlett, C., Binkley, E., & Crouch, R. (2000). Using objective data sources to enhance teacher judgments about test accommodations. *Exceptional Children, 67*(2), 67–81.

Geisinger, K. F. (1994). Psychometric issues in testing students with disabilities. *Applied Measurement in Education, 7*(2), 121–140.

Haladyna, T. M., & Downing, S. M. (2004). Construct-irrelevant variance in high-stakes testing. *Educational Measurement: Issues and Practice, 23*(1), 17–27.

Koenig, J. A., & Bachman, L. F. (Eds.). (2004). *Keeping score for all: The effects of inclusion and accommodation policies on large-scale educational assessments.* Washington, DC: National Research Council, National Academies Press.

Koretz, D., & Barton, K. (2004). Assessing students with disabilities: Issues and evidence. *Educational Assessment, 9*(1&2), 29–60; (CSE Tech. Rep. No. 587). Los Angeles, CA: National Center for Research on Evaluation, Standards, and Student Testing.

Messick, S. (1989). Validity. In R. L. Linn (Ed.), *Educational Measurement* (pp. 13–103). New York: American Council on Education/Macmillan.

Messick, S. (1995). Validity of psychological assessment: Validation of inferences from persons' responses and performances as scientific inquiry into score meaning. *American Psychologist, 50*, 741–749.

Phillips, S. E. (1994). High-stakes testing accommodations: Validity versus disabled rights. *Applied Measurement in Education, 7*(2), 93–120.

Rock, D. A., Bennett, R. E., & Jirele, T. (1988). Factor structure of the graduate record examinations general test in handicapped and nonhandicapped groups. *Journal of Applied Psychology, 73*(3), 383–392.

Rock, D. A., Bennett, R. E., & Kaplan, B. A. (1987). Internal construct validity of a college admissions test across handicapped and non-handicapped groups. *Educational and Psychological Measurement, 47*, 193–205.

Shepard, L., Taylor, G., & Betebenner, D. (1998). *Inclusion of limited-English-proficient students in Rhode Island's grade 4 mathematics performance assessment.* Los Angeles: University of California, Center for the Study of

Evaluation/National Center for Research on Evaluation, Standards, and Student Testing.

Sireci, S. G., Li, S., & Scarpati, S. (2003). *The effects of test accommodation on test performance: A review of literature* (Research Rep. No. 485). Amherst, MA: Center for Educational Assessment Research, University of Massachusetts.

Thompson, S., Johnstone, C., & Thurlow, M. (2002). *Universal design applied to large scale assessments* (Synthesis Rep.No. 44). Minneapolis, MN: University of Minnesota, National Center on Educational Outcomes.

Thompson, S., & Thurlow, M. (2002). *Universally designed assessments: Better tests for everyone!* (Policy Directions No. 14). Minneapolis, MN: University of Minnesota, National Center on Educational Outcomes. Retrieved November 6, 2006, from http://education.umn.edu/NCEO/OnlinePubs/Policy14.htm

Thurlow, M. L., Ysseldyke, J. E., & Silverstein, B. (1995). Testing accommodations for students with disabilities. *Remedial and Special Education, 16*(5), 260–270.

Tindal, G. (1998, March). *Models for understanding task comparability in accommodated testing.* Paper prepared for Council of Chief State School Officers State Collaborative on Assessment and Student Standards Assessing Special Education Students (ASES) - Study Group III. Retrieved from http://education. umn.edu/nceo/OnlinePubs/Accomm/Task Comparability. htm

Tindal, G., & Fuchs, L. (1999). *A summary of research on test changes: An empirical basis for defining.* Lexington, KY: University of Kentucky, Mid-South Regional Resource Center.

U.S. Department of Education, Office of Elementary and Secondary Education. (2004). *Standards and assessments peer review guidance: Information and examples for meeting requirements for the No Child Left Behind Act of 2001.* Washington, DC: Author.

Willingham, W. W., Ragosta, M., Bennett, R.E., Braun, H., Rock, D. A., & Powers, D. E. (1988). Testing *handicapped people.* Boston: Allyn & Bacon.

CHAPTER 7

Developing Accessible Tests With Universal Design and Digital Technologies: Ensuring We Standardize the Right Things

ROBERT P. DOLAN

TRACEY E. HALL

CAST, Inc.

With the advent of standards-based reform in the early 1990s and the passage of the No Child Left Behind Act of 2001 (NCLB), the role of large-scale assessment in public education has expanded significantly. Accurate large-scale assessment is necessary to the success of standards-based reform efforts insofar as those efforts aim to improve student outcomes, especially for students with disabilities (American Educational Research Association, American Psychological Association, & National Council on Measurement in Education, 1999; Elmore & Rothman, 1999). Federal initiatives such as NCLB and the Individual With Disabilities Education Act of 1997 (IDEA '97) have legislated that large-scale assessment must be accurate for students within both the general and special education curricula (Nolet & McLaughlin, 2000). Unfortunately, available research indicates that current methods of large-scale assessment may be inadequate for many students with disabilities (Elmore & Rothman; Hollenbeck, 2002; Olson & Goldstein, 1996; Sireci, Li, & Scarpati, 2003; Thurlow et al., 2000).

The challenge facing educators is how to standardize assessment of nonstandard individuals—that is, to ensure adequate individualization of test delivery without compromising comparability. To accurately reflect student learning, large-scale assessments must be designed such that they carefully isolate knowledge, skills, and abilities (KSAs) related to intended constructs. Unfortunately, many assessments measure not only the target KSAs, but also those associated with other unintended constructs, such as those related to accessing test material or generating a response (Abedi, Leon, & Mirocha, 2001; Helwig, Rozek-Tedesco, Tindal, Heath, & Almond, 1999; Parkes, Suen, Zimmaro, & Zappe, 1999).

For example, taking a paper-and-pencil math test requires physical capabilities such as holding a pencil and manipulating the test booklet, sensory capabilities such as sight and hearing (of directions), and cognitive capabilities such as organization and attention, all of which fall outside the targeted construct of math skill. These test requirements may not be a problem for many students, but they leave some students at a disadvantage, particularly students with disabilities. For students with learning disabilities, the problem of unintended constructs in assessment is pervasive. Difficulties with fundamental testing tasks, such as selectively attending to a test item and recording responses on a separate answer sheet, potentially undermine these students' performance. Because reading is a requisite skill across subject areas, students who lack strong literacy skills—such as phonemic awareness, phonics/word recognition, vocabulary, fluency, comprehension, and engagement—may also be unfairly disadvantaged during assessment (Ehri, 1994; Graham & Harris, 1996; Helwig et al., 1999; Liberman, Shankweiler, & Liberman, 1989; Stanovich, 1988; Swanson, 1999; Torgesen, 1993). These students' abilities to demonstrate proficiency with the subject or skill area being tested may be hampered by unintended constructs such as facility with the test medium or format. To state the problem differently, accurate assessment of student progress vis-à-vis learning standards is compromised by efforts to standardize the means for demonstrating learning.

Testing accommodations represent an attempt to reduce the influence of construct-irrelevant factors during assessment. However, as retrofitted solutions, they generally provide "too little, too late." First, accommodations such as the read aloud and scribe rob students of their ability to progress independently through a test, and do not fully address many students' needs. Second, these accommodations often interfere with the intended constructs, and thus jeopardize the validity of claims drawn from test results. As such, accommodations fall short of the goal.

How can we ensure that large-scale tests provide adequate individualization of test delivery without compromising comparability? In this chapter, we discuss how the principles of the educational framework Universal Design for Learning (UDL)—as

well universal design of assessment—may help improve the accuracy and efficacy of assessments, especially when applied in technology-based settings.

In Part I of this chapter, we review the UDL principles and their application to assessment. We also consider the affordances of new technologies. In Part II, we examine the research and practice of universally designed assessment, including technology applications. In Part III, we discuss the implications for schools, policy, and assessment research.

PART I. THE PROMISE OF UNIVERSAL DESIGN AND DIGITAL TECHNOLOGIES

Universal Design for Learning (Rose & Meyer, 2000, 2002) and universal design of assessment (Thompson, Johnstone, & Thurlow, 2002) represent two related and complementary approaches that could redefine how assessments are designed and delivered. Both draw inspiration from the universal design movement in architecture and product development founded by Ron Mace (1991) at North Carolina State University. Universal design's objective is to build innately accessible structures by addressing the mobility and communication needs of individuals with disabilities at the design stage, a practice that has spread to areas such as civic engineering and commercial product design. Designs that increase accessibility for individuals with disabilities make everyone's experience better. A good example from product development is television captioning. Captioning was first developed for people with hearing impairments, who had to retrofit their televisions by purchasing expensive decoder boxes to access the captions. But captioning later became a standard feature of every television. This universal design feature now benefits not only individuals with hearing impairments but also viewers without disabilities who use the technology to view television in noisy health clubs and restaurants, build English or Spanish language skills, and so forth (Rose & Meyer, 2002).

Universal design of assessment seeks to design tests that allow greater participation by students with disabilities by directly applying Mace's universal design principles (Thompson, Johnstone, et al., 2002). Preliminary research findings suggest that students with disabilities—indeed all students—may perform significantly better on tests that apply universal design principles than on traditionally designed tests (Johnstone, 2003).

The educational framework of UDL extends universal design from a physical space to a pedagogical space. It guides the design of more flexible curricula, including more flexible assessments that offer multiple opportunities for recognizing, using, and engaging with curriculum content. UDL serves as a guide for minimizing learning barriers and maximizing learning opportunities by flexibly accommodating individual differences, as follows:

- To support individual differences in learning to recognize the world, provide multiple, flexible methods of presentation.

- To support individual differences in learning strategies for action, provide multiple, flexible methods of expression and apprenticeship.

- To support individual differences in what is motivating and engaging, provide multiple, flexible options for engagement (Rose & Meyer, 2002).

By applying the principles of UDL to assessments, it should be possible to create more accurate assessments that incorporate widespread student needs into the original design. It should be possible to create tests that more accurately assess the KSAs of all

students, including those with dyslexia and other learning, cognitive, or physical disabilities. In the process, the need for many accommodations that are used today as retrofit solutions should be reduced (Dolan & Hall, 2001; Dolan & Rose, 2000). Although UDL curricula can be designed with traditional media and instructional approaches, technology is seen as a key enabler due to its inherent flexibility (Meyer & Rose, 2005). New media, such as digital texts and images, are potentially powerful educational tools because they are malleable and flexible, enabling content to be represented and accessed in multiple ways (Rose & Meyer, 2002; Dolan, Hall, Banerjee, Chun, & Strangman, 2005).

The display of digital content can be manipulated to meet the diverse needs of a variety of learners, including those with physical, sensory, and learning disabilities (Edyburn, 2003; Rose & Meyer, 2002). This, in turn, can enable teachers to differentiate their instructional methods and materials in multiple ways, thus reducing barriers to learning for many students.

These media can also be used to differentiate classroom-based assessment of student learning, supporting timely intervention at the point of instruction (Bennett, 2001; Chudowsky & Pellegrino, 2003). New media also offer the opportunity to assess skill learning in a deeper and more meaningful way (Bennett et al., 1999; Russell, 2002). For example, virtual/digital lab experiments may provide a clearer indication of science students' understanding of processes, methods, and outcomes than do written or verbal tests (Rose & Meyer, 2002). Moreover, by tracking what supports a student uses, the kinds of strategies that he or she follows, the kinds of strategies that seem to be missing, and the aspects of the task environment that bias the student toward successful or unsuccessful approaches, classroom-based assessment can provide information about students as learners. If these data are combined with student responses and scores and teachers are given support in using these data to inform subsequent instruction, it may be possible to develop assessment approaches that can truly transform education. Such techniques allow for the development of large-scale assessments that provide a broader set of constructs than traditional testing techniques allow.

PART II. CURRENT EFFORTS IN UNIVERSAL DESIGN AND ASSESSMENT

The 2004 reauthorization of IDEA explicitly called for application of universal design principles to assessment. Nevertheless, efforts to apply universal design to assessment have generally been limited to improving old practices—namely making print-based assessments more accessible. Although these applications provide important guidance for the generation of current, traditional tests, they do not realize the full potential of UDL and digital technologies. Advances in technology have made computer-administered testing a possibility. Whereas the overall focus on computer use for assessment has been on decreasing costs and increasing timeliness associated with large-scale testing, a few states, most notably Kentucky (HumRRO, 2003; Salyers, 2002; Trimble, Lewis, Dolan, & Kearns, 2006), have been exploring the role of technology in improving statewide test accessibility for students with disabilities. In addition, guidelines are emerging for making computerized tests more accessible (Allan, Bulla, & Goodman, 2003; Association of Test Publishers, 2002; Thompson, Thurlow, Quenemoen, & Lehr, 2002).

Clearly, more research and development is also needed in this area. Following are examples of research and practice that suggest future considerations and directions for the field.

Keyboarding Versus Handwriting

As the nature of classroom instruction changes, and in particular the technologies used in the classroom evolve, there is an increasing disconnect between the media with which students learn and the media with which they are assessed. Research by Russell and colleagues (Russell & Haney, 1997; Russell & Plati, 2000) demonstrates quite clearly the broad importance of developing assessment forms that match the needs of the student and reflect the technologies that they are using in the classroom.

Recognizing the increasing incongruity between computer use in the classroom and assessment technology, Russell & Haney (1997) conducted a study that investigated mode of administration effects on performance on standardized assessment. One hundred twenty-one students in Grades 6, 7, and 8 completed each of three assessments: (a) an open-ended assessment with writing, science, math, and reading questions; (b) a test composed of National Assessment of Educational Progress (NAEP) language arts, science, and math items—primarily multiple choice; and (c) a performance writing assessment requiring extended written response. Students randomized to the control group completed all assessments using pencil and paper. Students randomized to the experimental group completed the open-ended assessment on paper, but completed the NAEP and performance writing assessments using a computerized version whose layout was matched to the printed version as closely as possible.

Russell and Haney's (1997) findings plainly reveal the impact of test medium on student performance. Comparison of student responses clearly demonstrated a significant mode of administration effect: students completing the short-answer and extended written responses on the computer performed significantly better than students completing these assessments by hand. A secondary analysis of the NAEP multiple choice and open-ended items individually revealed a large and significant mode of administration effect for the science and language arts short-answer questions that favored the computerized administration. In addition, the average student score on the performance writing assessment was significantly higher on the computerized versus paper-and-pencil administration.

These findings were confirmed and extended in a later study with 525 typically achieving students in Grades 4, 8, and 10 who responded to the 1999 MCAS Language Arts Composition Prompt on paper or computer (Russell & Plati, 2000). In all three grades, the mean writing score was significantly higher for students composing on the computer versus with paper and pencil, with a mean difference in scores of 1.6, 1.9, and 1.5 points for Grades 4, 8, and 10, respectively.

Russell and Haney (1997) proposed that increased student familiarity with writing on the computer was likely responsible for the mode of administration effects; indeed, students in both studies had a high level of access to computers. However, the broader importance of these findings is quite clear given the increasing role computers play in students' lives both inside and outside of school.

These results have important implications for the future of large-scale assessment, demonstrating that student performance may be strongly sensitive to differences in the mode of administration. As noted by Russell and Haney (1997), assessment validity must take into account not only the content of instruction but also the medium. For assessment results to be valid and to avoid construct-irrelevant variance in test scores, the assessment environment must provide access and supports comparable to those available and familiar to students during instruction. From a UDL perspective this means providing students with multiple options for expression. In view of the increasingly digital classroom, it also means that test designers need to find a valid means to incorporate computers and computer-based supports into large-scale assessment.

Thus not only is mode of administration important to students with disabilities, as Russell and colleagues' work shows, but mode of administration can also greatly impact the scores of students without disabilities. Thus, although the needs of students with disabilities have provided a strong impetus for those interested in applying universal design to assessment, the issue of matching assessments to the needs of the student is in fact far more fundamental. Russell and colleagues' findings provide support for the UDL premise that designing for the needs of students with disabilities can have far-reaching benefits. Their findings also highlight an important shortcoming of accommodations, which are geared solely toward problems affecting students with disabilities and thereby divert attention from the value of reducing construct-irrelevant variance for all students. To avoid construct-irrelevant variance in test scores, it is essential to match the assessment technology to the student-whether the student has a disability or not.

It is important to acknowledge, however, that the task of matching assessments to students is not necessarily straightforward. A study by Helwig, Rozek-Tedesco, & Tindal (2002) underlines this fact, demonstrating special education teachers' poor accuracy in predicting which students would benefit from a read-aloud accommodation. Moreover, students themselves may not make wise choices, according to additional research by Russell & Plati (2000).

Kentucky Online System Technology Skills Checklist

This need to establish a good match between assessment technology and the student was the primary consideration of the Kentucky State Department of Education when they developed an accessible online format for their statewide assessment, the Commonwealth Accountability Testing System (CATS). Development of CATS Online was part of a comprehensive, statewide UDL initiative (Trimble et al., 2006). The process underlying this development speaks directly to the considerations that must be made when developing universally designed, technology-based tests.

IDEA '97 requires that students be provided with appropriate test accommodations, alterations in test materials, or procedures to minimize the impact of disability on assessment performance. CATS Online leverages technology to accommodate students with disabilities more elegantly and less intrusively than with traditional accommodations and paper-and-pencil tests. CATS Online is a version of the Kentucky Department of Education's statewide assessment which delivers the Kentucky Core Content Test via an interactive Web site. The test items and scoring rubrics are identical to those on the paper-and-pencil test, but the assessment includes built-in accessibility supports for students with disabilities

A key feature of CATS Online is the availability of read-aloud support. The read-aloud is the most common test accommodation addressing test presentation for students with learning disabilities (Sireci et al., 2003; Tindal, Heath, Hollenbeck, Almond, & Harniss, 1998). Research studies have repeatedly demonstrated its ability to improve the performance of test takers with learning disabilities and in some cases even those without (Brown & Augustine, 2000; Burk, 1999; Cahalan-Laitusis, Cook, Cline, King, & Sabatini, 2007; Calhoon, Fuchs, & Hamlett, 2000; Crawford & Tindal, 2004; Fletcher et al., 2006; Fuchs, Fuchs, Eaton, Hamlett, & Karns, 2000; Hollenbeck, Rozek-Tedesco, Tindal, & Glasgow, 2000; Meloy, Deville, & Frisbie, 2002; Thompson,

Blount, & Thurlow, 2002; Tindal & Fuchs, 1999). Most read-aloud accommodations involve a live reading by teacher or aide to a group of students taking individual tests. However, in CATS Online, students can use a mouse or keyboard to select text to be read aloud by the computer using text-reader or screen-reader software. This removes a number of potential problems with the traditional read-aloud from the testing equation, including potential differences among readers, which can lead to nonequivalent test conditions (Landau, Russell, Gourgey, Erin, & Cowan, J., 2003) and imposition of a linear navigation path and set pace, which can negatively affect test performance (Hollenbeck et al., 2000). Thus, the digital read-aloud capability of CATS Online provides greater accessibility by offering an alternative to the written text, and greater flexibility—particularly, independent, self-paced navigation. In this way, the read-aloud helps to reduce the effect of reading ability as a construct-irrelevant factor affecting students with disabilities. In addition to this read-aloud capability, students are permitted to use the computer-based writing supports they use in the classroom. Thus, students are flexibly supported via multiple means of recognition and expression, which are somewhat customizable to the student.

Development of CATS Online was a three-part process whereby the Kentucky Department of Education defined the population of students who would take the assessment, provided student supports for using the assessment technology, and engaged in ongoing state and local planning and organization to implement CATS Online. The digital nature of CATS Online and the prominent role of text-reader and text-to-speech (TTS) software raised important issues regarding the technology expertise of students and support staff. Thus, a key activity during the development of CATS Online was to address the following question: What prerequisite technology skills do students need in order to use accessible computer-based accountability assessments?

Kentucky's approach to this question was to identify, directly observe, and validate a set of technology skills needed by students to access CATS online, which culminated in a technology skills checklist (Fleming, Kearns, Dethloff, Lewis, & Dolan, 2006). The fundamental rationale for the CATS Online checklist is that understanding of students' construct-irrelevant KSAs is important to providing students with the right assessment—minimizing the occurrence of irrelevant constructs and maximizing assessment validity.

Initial development of the technology skills checklist involved a variety of activities, including student and teacher observations, focus groups, and interviews; review of national, state, and school district technology standards and skills; and analysis of the CATS Online Demonstration Area, a Web-based tool designed to offer students and teachers the opportunity to gain experience with the assessment interface. The first draft of the checklist was subsequently validated based on input from teachers. The resulting checklist includes 121 items distributed across five categories:

- Basic computer skills (i.e., move mouse pointer on screen).
- Keyboarding skills (i.e., use enter/return key).
- Word processing skills (i.e., open existing document from a specific location).
- Text-reader/screen-reader skills (i.e., change voice quality of text/screen reader).
- Skills needed for interaction with CATS Online, specifically (i.e., type in login password).

This checklist can be used to prepare students and school staff—in Kentucky and elsewhere—for use and administration of electronic accessible assessments. Although the skills identified are necessarily specific to CATS Online, they are likely to be relevant to other technology-based assessments.

The impact of CATS Online on students has been assessed in two survey-based studies. Preliminary evaluation indicates that the assessment had a highly positive impact on students. For example data show widespread student improvement in the ability to work independently and stay on-task. In addition, data show widespread improvement in students' self-concepts. Data from the second study show that the overwhelming majority of students preferred testing on the computer and suggested that greater control and independence were important contributing factors.

The Kentucky experience demonstrates the potential of an approach that integrates UDL with a technology-based assessment to anticipate student needs, including differences in technology experience, and improve the testing experience. The success of CATS Online also reflects important changes in the classroom and in policy. As part of their UDL initiative, Kentucky trained 27 teachers in UDL and text-reader or TTS software, and acquired a site license for text-reader software in 95% of schools. This not only provided an important foundation for UDL, but also increased students' opportunities to work with technology at the point of instruction. Policy changes were equally significant. Kentucky Senate Bill 243, KRS 156.027 (Procurement for Publishers, 2002) stipulated that publishers who provide an accessible digital copy of textbooks for state adoption would be given first preference, "Preferential Procurement," by local schools during the next textbook adoption cycle. In addition, a Kentucky Accessibility Materials Consortium, a state repository for the distribution of accessible digital curriculum materials for students with disabilities, was established. Publishers have provided over 1,300 individual digital textbooks to the consortium, encompassing social studies, arts and humanities, practical living and vocational studies, and language arts. These policy changes directly support the development of digital curricula, which can itself have a significant impact on the success of technology-based assessment.

Pilot Study of a Computerized Test System With Text-to-Speech Read-Aloud, and Universally Designed Supports

The Kentucky experience provides highly valuable practice and policy information regarding computer-based testing with built-in supports. However, for universally designed computer-based testing to gain acceptance within the testing community, research studies are vital. Most research studies have used a human read-aloud, which is now recognized to have several associated problems that pose threats to construct validity (Harker & Feldt, 1993; Hollenbeck et al., 2000; Landau et al., 2003; Lee & Tindal, 2000; Meloy et al., 2002).

Although these concerns might lead some to reject or severely restrict the use of the read-aloud, we argue that the issue is one of need for greater diversity and flexibility in the read-aloud accommodation. It has become increasingly clear that not all students with disabilities benefit from the read-aloud accommodation (Helwig et al., 1999; Helwig et al., 2002; Sireci et al., 2003), with responsiveness varying by student (Elliot, Kratochwill, & McKevitt, 2001; Tindal, Glasgow, Helwig, Hollenbeck, & Heath, 1998) as well as by grade, test form, and problem type (Fuchs et al., 2000; Helwig et al., 1999). Indeed, prominent assessment researchers have asserted the need for greater attention to individual effects of accommodations (Elliot et al.; Helwig et al., 1999; Tindal, Heath et al., 1998), a request that is consonant with UDL. Thus, there are compelling reasons to consider implementation of a more individualized read-aloud accommodation.

In this regard, computer-based read-aloud may hold potential, its digital nature providing much greater flexibility, particularly if coupled to principles of UDL. In a previous pilot study (Dolan et al., 2005) we addressed this possibility by investigating the effectiveness of computer-based testing with TTS and universally designed supports as a means to provide individualized support to students with learning disabilities during multiple-choice testing.

Ten Grade 11 and 12 students with specific learning disabilities were administered two equivalent forms of a U.S. history and civics test based on released NAEP items on separate days. One form of the test was administered using traditional paper-and-pencil methods, the other using computer-based testing with TTS. Students were randomly assigned to four groups, controlling for any effects of test order and form. Both test forms included two accommodations typically provided for students with learning disabilities: (a) one-at-a-time presentation of test item sets (i.e., a reading passage stimulus and associated question or questions), and (b) elimination of a separate answer sheet. The computer-based administration included an additional accommodation, a TTS-based read-aloud feature with which students could select words, sentences, or entire sections in the reading passages, test questions, or student responses to be read aloud on demand, with or without synchronous highlighting. The computerized test was designed to offer students navigation options similar to a paper-and-pencil test (Figure 7-1). For example, students could view the reading passage, questions, and responses, at the same time, mark questions for review, and proceed through the test in any order and direction using a navigation bar.

Evaluation of student test scores showed that overall performance was slightly but not significantly better (approximately 7 percent-

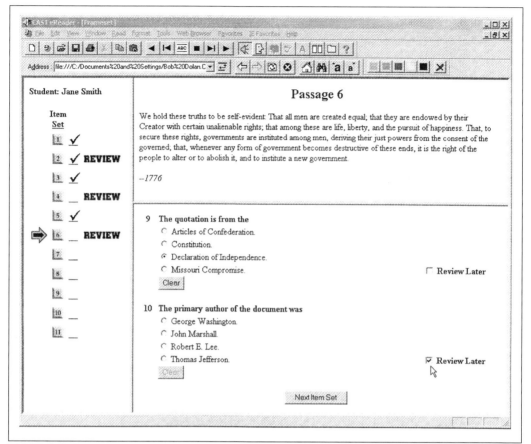

FIGURE 7-1

Screenshot of Prototype Computer-Based Testing System With TTS Support (CBT-TTS)

age points higher) on the computerized version of the tests than on the paper-and-pencil versions (Figure 7-2). However, analysis of the data after grouping items by question type (long or short reading passages) unmasked a marked difference in performance between the two test administrations. When responding to items associated with long reading passages (greater than 100 words in length), students scored approximately 22 percentage points higher on the computerized administration than on the paper-and-pencil administration, a statistically significant difference ($t = 2.26$; $p = 0.05$).

An important objective of this study was to look beyond group differences for potential individual differences in accommodation effects. Thus, we conducted further analyses to examine individual student performance across the two conditions. Test performance was re-examined at the individual level after categorizing students according to *low-average* (WIAT-II (Wechsler, 2002) reading composite scores below 80) or *average* (WIAT-II reading composite score above 80) reading ability. For the short-passage items, type of test administration did not impact the performance of low-average or average readers in any consistent way. However, for the long-passage items, all three low-average readers performed better when using the computerized versus paper-and-pencil test administration, scoring 17, 42, and 75 percentage points higher. In contrast, performance of the seven average readers was variable across the two test administrations. These results

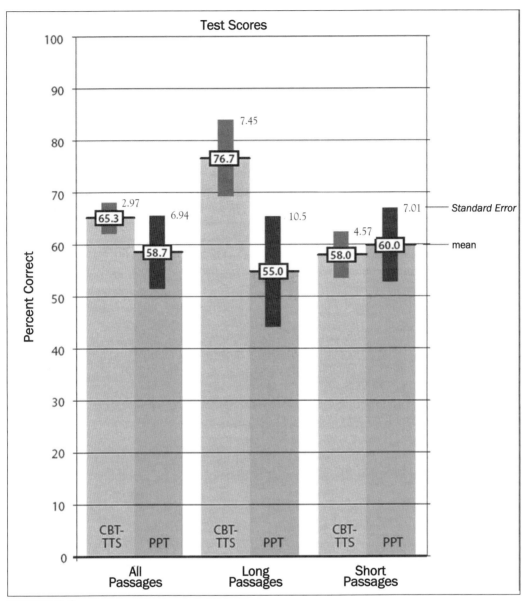

FIGURE 7-2

Mean Test Scores for Computerized and Paper-and-Pencil Administrations for All Test Questions, Test Questions With Long Passages, and Test Questions With Short Passages

suggest that within the overall population of students with learning disabilities, the computer-based accommodation may be more effective for students with low-average reading ability.

Students' overall impressions of the computerized test system were uniformly positive and suggested broad usability. Nearly all students responded with a "definite yes" when asked if they recommended the use of the computerized system to other students. An overwhelming majority of students (90%) reported having very few, if any, technical problems with the system. In fact, students said that the computerized system was "easier to use" and "easier to understand" than the paper-and-pencil system.

Our analyses suggested that the greater appeal of the computerized system was derived from its promotion of independence and flexibility, and from the TTS feature. Although 70% of students reported having no or limited experience with TTS, all of them used it to read passages during the study, and 70% said that TTS definitely helped their passage comprehension. In general, students preferred TTS to a human reader, a preference that seemed to be related to the tool's ease of use and opportunity for control, "TTS is easier to use. You can see and at the same time listen to it. I have more control when I use the computer." However, the inauthentic tone, prosody, and expression of the TTS were irritating to students. We found that the item display and item navigation features of the computer-based test were appreciated, but there was little indication that they made much difference to students relative to the TTS feature.

The results of this pilot study, while preliminary, underline the potential of technology and universal design for reducing construct-irrelevant variance during testing. Construct-irrelevant variance is a significant problem for students with disabilities, and a key factor in evaluating the effectiveness of any accommodation. The computerized read-aloud may be a potentially valuable tool for addressing the current problems inherent within the human-mediated read-aloud accommodation.

TTS read-aloud supports students' diverse ways of recognizing, strategically interacting, and engaging with an assessment by offering individualized, independent, and self-paced multimodal access to test content—on demand. Individual differences in each of these domains can be sources of construct-irrelevant variance. Unlike a human read-aloud, a TTS read-aloud provides students with consistent readings, free of poten-

tially directive or misleading intonation. In the Dolan et al. (2005) study, students appreciated the control available to them with the TTS tool, including the ability to select their own pace and review text on demand. This is consistent with the Kentucky Department of Education's feedback on CATS Online. Participants in the Dolan et al. (2005) study also appreciated the computer-based test's navigation features. Future investigations might directly address the relationship between the various features of the computerized test administration and changes in performance.

Students' usage patterns and responses suggest that they would use the computerized test system in real-world testing situations. Although a relatively small percentage of students in the study reported having experience with TTS, its availability during testing offers the potential for greater continuity between instruction and assessment, as listening is a core literacy activity in the classroom. Indeed, equivalence between the approaches and technologies used during instruction and assessment is essential to providing students with optimal assessment support (U.S. Department of Education, 2001). Ultimately, the link between instruction and assessment may be greatly strengthened through the use of embedded assessment approaches.

The results of this study provide yet further rationale for attention to individual differences when investigating the effects of accommodations. Meeting the challenge of diverse student needs is made easier by flexible, technology-based assessments. However, much more research is needed to establish effective means to realize this potential.

PART III. IMPLICATIONS OF UNIVERSAL DESIGN, TECHNOLOGY, AND ASSESSMENT

The research and practice described previously generally support the idea that universally designed assessment can improve student performance, but it is clear that we are only beginning to discover the full extent of variability in student needs and how to support them. It is our hope that future work in research and development, policy making, and school-based practices will address some of the critical questions that follow.

Universal design and technology have the potential to transform the development of assessments so that they are richer and more authentic measures of student learning. It is important to remember, however, that universally designed assessments must *from the outset* be built to serve the needs of diverse learners: Universal design is not a system for retrofitting poorly constructed assessment delivery systems. To reduce the effects of construct-irrelevant factors, the universal design approach must begin during test development (Dolan & Hall, 2001; Thompson, Johnstone et al., 2002).

A universal design approach to test development also considers the full range of challenges facing diverse learners. Providing access for those with physical or sensory disabilities is essential. However, assessment systems should also support and scaffold the assessment process for individuals with learning disabilities, those with executive function/organizational supports, as well as those with cognitive disabilities. Here the potential for new technologies is especially great (Bennett et al., 2001). However, developing novel computer-based assessment items according to universal design principles requires a grounded understanding of students' diverse abilities and the ways they interact with test items. A thorough consideration of the factors that impact construct validity, with an emphasis on identifying and eliminating sources of construct-irrelevant variance, is essential to this process. To help test developers understand and properly leverage the increased capabilities offered by digital technologies to offer new opportunities to deliver authentic, accessible assessments, the Universal Design for Computer-Based Testing (UD-CBT) framework has recently been proposed (Dolan, Burling, Harms, Way, & Rose, 2006; Harms, Burling, Way, Hanna, & Dolan, 2006; Burling et al., 2006). This framework is being used to direct the development of guidelines for designing novel computer-delivered assessments consistent with the goals of universal design.

To improve accuracy, attention must be paid to how best to engage students in the assessment process. Engagement is as important in assessment as it is in other areas of instruction, such as content presentation. Providing choice can be a powerful way of increasing the engagement of some (though not all) learners during instruction, especially if it develops their metacognitive awareness of how they learn best (Rose & Meyer, 2002). Test developers need to explore the effects of providing students greater choice during testing, keeping in mind the results of the aforementioned study by Russell and Plati (2000) in which students did poorly with even the most basic decisions about mode of response.

Test developers also need to be aware of the importance of matching instruction and assessment techniques and technologies. For example, assumptions are still often made about students' cultural experiences and reading comprehension abilities (on subject area tests); these assumptions cannot be "accommodated away" through retrofitting. Instead, they must be addressed during item development. Equally important is that the use of technologies such as TTS be matched to students' abilities and challenges as readers, and that such matching start in the classroom. The fact that in the third study summarized earlier only a few students had prior experience with TTS tools underscores the need for more appropriate use of such accommodations during the instructional process, not only during testing. Only then can we be assured that students are receiving the supports necessary to ensure their ability to learn, and their ability to be assessed fairly and accurately. A significant challenge lies in determining just how well matched the instructional and testing technologies must be. For example, in implementing CATS Online, the Kentucky Department of Education ensured that all students had access to exactly the same TTS software they used in the classrooms. However, for commercial test publishers developing solutions for use in multiple states, this requirement may prove problematic. It is therefore imperative that we better understand just how much difference in implementation is tolerable to students and is still consistent with the accommodations provided during instruction.

Finally, assessment needs to be woven into all levels of the instructional process so that it supports the most efficient and effective achievement of learning goals and standards. What do we want to achieve in the classroom? What do learners need to learn—and how? How can we leverage the power of universal design and new technologies to provide assessments that not only offer summative information about the learning process but, perhaps more importantly, provide the kinds of formative data that teachers need at the point of instruction to support successful learners to learn even more and to support struggling learners before events of failure turn into patterns of failure? With these questions in mind, test makers, policy makers, and school practitioners need to work together to develop and promote the use of universal design and new technologies to provide effective formative assessment in the classroom to support all learners as they engage in high-quality content.

CONCLUSION

To the extent that increased accountability can improve education, it must be based upon accurate and inclusive assessment practices, a goal that universally designed assess-

ments can help us reach. Only by creating fair and accurate tests that consider diverse students from the start and that allow them to demonstrate their learning progress regardless of how they learn, can we ensure that we are holding educational systems accountable for all students, including those with disabilities.

A small but growing body of evidence suggests that the UDL principles can inform the appropriate use of technology in assessment and that technology can help realize the flexibility necessary to accurately and fairly assess diverse students. Applying the principles of UDL makes it possible to create a new generation of assessments that leverage new media and technologies to more accurately assess the knowledge, skills, and abilities of all students by expanding the range of constructs that can be assessed. In the process we must distinguish measuring of individuals' progress toward standardized goals from standardizing the means by which we measure.

REFERENCES

Abedi, J., Leon, S., & Mirocha, J. (2001, April). *Validity of standardized achievement tests for English Language Learners.* Paper presented at the annual meeting of the American Educational Research Association, Seattle, WA.

Allan, J. M., Bulla, N., & Goodman, S. A. (2003). TEST ACCESS: *Guidelines for computer administered testing.* Louisville, KY: American Printing House for the Blind.

American Educational Research Association, American Psychological Association, & National Council on Measurement in Education. (1999). *Standards for educational and psychological testing.* Washington, DC: American Educational Research Association.

Association of Test Publishers. (2002). *Guidelines for computer-based testing.* Washington, DC: Author.

Bennett, R. E. (2001). How the Internet will help large-scale assessment reinvent itself. *Educa-*

tion *Policy Analysis Archives, 9*(5). Retrieved February 26, 2007, from http://epaa.asu.edu/epaa/v9n5.html

Bennett, R. E., Goodman, M., Hessinger, J., Kahn, H., Ligget, J., Marshall, G., et al. (1999). Using multimedia in large-scale computer-based testing programs. *Computers in Human Behavior, 15*(3–4), 283–294.

Brown, P. B., & Augustine, A. (2000). *Findings of the 1999–2000 screen reading field test.* Dover: Delaware Department of Education.

Burk, M. (1999). *Computerized test accommodations: A new approach for inclusion and success for students with disabilities.* Washington, DC: A.U. Software.

Burling, K. S., Beck, R., Jude, J., Murray, E. A., Dolan, R. P., & Harms, M. (2006, April 10). *Constructing innovative computer-administered tasks and items according to universal design: Illustrative examples with pilot data.* Paper presented at the National Council on Measurement in Education Annual Meeting, San Francisco, CA.

Cahalan-Laitusis, C., Cook, L. L., Cline, F., King, T., & Sabatini, J. (2007). *Examining the impact of audio presentation on tests of reading comprehension.* Princeton, NJ: Educational Testing Service.

Calhoon, M. B., Fuchs, L. S., & Hamlett, C. L. (2000). Effects of computer-based test accommodations on mathematics performance assessments for secondary students with learning disabilities. *Learning Disability Quarterly, 23*(4), 271–281.

Chudowsky, N., & Pellegrino, J. W. (2003). Large-scale assessments that support learning: What will it take? *Theory Into Practice, 42*(1), 75–83.

Crawford, L., & Tindal, G. (2004). Effects of a read-aloud modification on a standardized reading test. *Exceptionality, 12*(2), 89–106.

Dolan, R. P., Burling, K. E., Harms, M., Way, D. & Rose, D. H. (2006). *The universal design for computer-based testing framework: A structure for developing guidelines for constructing innovative computer-administered tests.* Unpublished manuscript.

Dolan, R. P., & Hall, T. E. (2001). Universal design for learning: Implications for large-scale assessment. *IDA Perspectives, 27*(4), 22–25.

Dolan, R. P., Hall, T. E., Banerjee, M., Chun, E., & Strangman, N. (2005). Applying principles of universal design to test delivery: The effect of computer-based read-aloud on test performance of high school students with learning disabilities. *Journal of Technology, Learning, and Assessment, 3*(7). Retrieved May 13, 2006, from http://escholarship.bc.edu/jtla/vol3/7/

Dolan, R. P., & Rose, D. H. (2000). Accurate assessment through universal design for learning. *Journal of Special Education Technology, 15*(4). Retrieved February 26, 2007, from http://jset.unlv.edu/15.4/asseds/rose.html

Edyburn, D. L. (2003). Measuring assistive technology outcomes: Key concepts. *Journal of Special Education Technology, 18*(2), 53–55.

Ehri, L. C. (1994). Development of the ability to read words: Update. In R. B. Ruddell & M. R. Ruddell (Eds.), *Theoretical models and processes of reading* (4th ed., pp. 323–358). Newark, DE: International Reading Association.

Elliot, S. N., Kratochwill, T. R., & McKevitt, B. (2001). Experimental analysis of the effects of testing accommodations on the scores of students with and without disabilities. *Journal of School Psychology, 39*, 3–24.

Elmore, R. F., & Rothman, R. (Eds.). (1999). *Testing, teaching, and learning: A guide for states and school districts.* Washington, DC: National Academies Press.

Fleming, J., Kearns, J., Dethloff, A., Lewis, P., & Dolan, R. (2006). Technology skills checklist for online assessment. *Special Education Technology Practice 8*(1), 19–32.

Fletcher, J. M., Francis, D. J., Boudousquie, A., Copeland, K., Young, V., Kalinowski, S., et al. (2006). Effects of accommodations on high-stakes testing for students with reading disabilities. *Exceptional Children, 72*, 136–150.

Fuchs, L. S., Fuchs, D., Eaton, S., Hamlett, C. L., & Karns, K. (2000). Supplementing teacher judgments of mathematics test accommodations with objective data sources. *School Psychology Review, 29*(1), 65–85.

Graham, S., & Harris, K. R. (1996). Addressing problems in attention, memory, and executive functioning: An example from self-regulated strategy development. In G. R. Lyon & N. A. Krasnegor (Eds.), *Attention, memory, and executive function* (pp. 349–365). Baltimore, MD: Paul H. Brookes.

Harker, J. K., & Feldt, L. S. (1993). A comparison of achievement test performance of nondisabled students under silent reading and reading plus listening modes of administration. *Applied Measurement in Education*, 6(4), 307–320.

Harms, M., Burling, K. S., Way, W., Hanna, E., & Dolan, R. P. (2006, April). *Constructing innovative computer-administered tasks and items according to universal design: Guidelines for test developers*. Paper presented at the National Council on Measurement in Education Annual Meeting, San Francisco, CA.

Helwig, R., Rozek-Tedesco, M. A., & Tindal, G. (2002). An oral versus a standard administration of a large-scale mathematics test. *The Journal of Special Education*, 36(1), 39–47.

Helwig, R., Rozek-Tedesco, M. A., Tindal, G., Heath, B., & Almond, P. (1999). Reading as an access to mathematics problem solving on multiple-choice tests for sixth-grade students. *Journal of Educational Research*, 93(2), 113–125.

Hollenbeck, K. (2002). Determining when test alterations are valid accommodations or modifications for large-scale assessment. In G. Tindal & T. M. Haladyna (Eds.), *Large-scale assessment programs for all students: Validity, technical adequacy, and implementation*. Mahwah, NJ: Lawrence Erlbaum.

Hollenbeck, K., Rozek-Tedesco, M. A., Tindal, G., & Glasgow, A. (2000). An exploratory study of student-paced versus teacher-paced accommodations for large-scale math tests. *Journal of Special Education Technology*, 15(2), 27–36.

HumRRO. (2003). *CATS Online: Logistic and construct evaluation of computer administered assessment* (No. FR-03-40). Alexandria, VA: Human Resources Research Organization.

Johnstone, C. J. (2003). *Improving validity of large-scale tests: Universal design and student performance* (Tech. Rep. No. 37). Minneapolis, MN: University of Minnesota, National Center on Education Outcomes.

Landau, S., Russell, M., Gourgey, K., Erin, J., & Cowan, J. (2003). Use of the talking tactile tablet in mathematics testing. *Journal of Visual Impairment and Blindness*, 97(2), 85–96.

Lee, D., & Tindal, G. (2000). *Differential Item Functioning (DIF) as a function of test accommodation*. Dover: Delaware Department of Education.

Liberman, I. Y., Shankweiler, D., & Liberman, A. M. (1989). The alphabetic principle and learning to read. In D. Shankweiler & I. Y. Liberman (Eds.), *Phonology and reading disability: Solving the reading puzzle* (Vol. viii, pp. 1–33). Ann Arbor: University of Michigan Press.

Mace, R. (1991). *Definitions: Accessible, adaptable, and universal design* (Fact Sheet). Raleigh, NC: North Carolina State University, Center for Accessible Housing.

Meloy, L. L., Deville, C., & Frisbie, D. A. (2002). The effect of a read-aloud accommodation on test scores of students with and without a learning disability in reading. *Remedial and Special Education*, 23(4), 248–255.

Meyer, A., & Rose, D. H. (2005). The future is in the margins: The role of technology and disability in educational reform (updated). In D. H. Rose, A. Meyer, & C. Hitchcock (Eds.), *The universally designed classroom: Accessible curriculum and digital technologies*. Cambridge, MA: Harvard Education Press.

Nolet, V., & McLaughlin, M. J. (2000). *Accessing the general curriculum: Including students with disabilities in standards-based reform*. Thousand Oaks, CA: Corwin Press.

Olson, J. F., & Goldstein, A. A. (1996). *Increasing the inclusion of students with disabilities and limited English proficient students in NAEP* (Focus on NAEP Vol. 2, No. 1). Washington, DC: National Center for Education Statistics.

Parkes, J. T., Suen, H. K., Zimmaro, D. M., & Zappe, S. M. (1999, April). *Structural knowledge as a pre-requisite to valid performance assessment scores*. Paper presented at the annual meeting of the National Council on Measurement in Education, Montreal, Quebec, Canada.

Preferential Procurement Status for Publishers, KRS 156.027 (2002).

Rose, D., & Meyer, A. (2000). *The future is in the margins: The role of technology and disability in educational reform* (U.S. Department of Education commissioned white paper). Peabody, MA: CAST.

Rose, D., & Meyer, A. (2002) *Teaching every student in the digital age: Universal Design for Learning*. Alexandria, VA: Association for Supervision and Curriculum Development.

Russell, M. (2002). How computer-based technology can disrupt the technology of testing and assessment. In Board on Testing and Assessment, National Research Council (Eds.). *Technology and assessment: Thinking ahead—Proceedings from a workshop* (pp. 63–78). Washington, DC: National Academy Press.

Russell, M., & Haney, W. (1997). Testing writing on computers: An experiment comparing student performance on tests conducted via computer and via paper-and-pencil. *Educational Policy Analysis Archives*, 5(1). Retrieved September 28, 2006, from http://epaa.asu.edu/epaa/v5n3. html

Russell, M., & Plati, T. (2000). *Mode of administration effects on MCAS composition performance for grades four, eight and ten*. (Rep. No.) Report prepared for the Massachusetts Department of Education. Chestnut Hill, MA: National Board on Educational Testing and Public Policy.

Salyers, F. (2002, August). Field study of Web-based core content tests goes statewide this fall. *Kentucky Teacher*.

Sireci, S. G., Li, S., & Scarpati, S. (2003). *The effects of test accommodation on test performance: A review of the literature* (pp. 1–100). (Center for Educational Assessment Research Rep. No. 485). Amherst, MA: University of Massachusetts Amherst, School of Education.

Stanovich, K. E. (1988). Speculations on the cause and consequences of individual differences in early reading acquisition. In P. Gough, L. Ehri, & R. Treiman (Eds.), *Reading acquisition* (pp. 307–342). Hillsdale, NJ: Erlbaum.

Swanson, L. (1999). Reading research for students with LD: A meta-analysis of intervention outcomes. *Journal of Learning Disabilities*, 32(6), 504–532.

Thompson, S. J., Blount, A., & Thurlow, M. (2002). *A summary of research on the effects of test accommodations: 1999 through 2001* (NCEO Tech. Rep. No. 34). Minneapolis, MN: University of Minnesota, National Center on Educational Outcomes.

Thompson, S. J., Johnstone, C. J., & Thurlow, M. L. (2002). *Universal design applied to large-scale assessments* (NCEO Synthesis Rep. No. 44). Minneapolis, MN: University of Minnesota, National Center on Education Outcomes.

Thompson, S. J., Thurlow, M. L., Quenemoen, R. F., & Lehr, C. A. (2002). *Access to computer-based testing for students with disabilities* (NCEO Synthesis Report No. 45). Minneapolis, MN: University of Minnesota, National Center on Education Outcomes.

Thurlow, M. L., McGrew, K. S., Tindal, G., Thompson, S. J., Ysseldyke, J. E., & Elliott, J. L. (2000). *Assessment accommodations research: Considerations for design and analysis* (Tech. Rep. No. 26). Minneapolis, MN: University of Minnesota, National Center on Educational Outcomes.

Tindal, G., & Fuchs, L. (1999). *A summary of research on test changes: An empirical basis for defining accommodations*. Lexington, KY: University of Kentucky, Mid-South Regional Resource Center.

Tindal, G., Glasgow, A., Helwig, R., Hollenbeck, K., & Heath, B. (1998). *Accommodations in large scale tests for students with disabilities: An investigation of reading math tests using video technology*. Paper prepared for Council of Chief State School Officers, Washington, DC.

Tindal, G., Heath, B., Hollenbeck, K., Almond, P., & Harniss, M. (1998). Accommodating students with disabilities on large-scale tests: An experimental study. *Exceptional Children*, 64, 439–450.

Torgesen, J. K. (1993). Variations on theory in learning disabilities. In G. R. Lyon, D. B. Gray, J. F. Kavanagh, & N. A. Krasnegor (Eds.), *Better understanding learning disabili-*

ties: New views from research and their implications for education and public policies (pp. 153–170). Baltimore, MD: Paul H. Brookes.

Trimble, S., Lewis, P., Dolan, R., & Kearns, J. (2006). *Universal design for learning: Assessment applications.* Manuscript submitted for publication.

U.S. Department of Education. (2001). *Clarification of the role of the IEP team in selecting individual accommodations, modifications in administration, and alternate assessments for state- and district-wide assessments of student achievement.* Washington, DC: Author.

Wechsler, D. (2002). Wechsler Individual Achievement Test – Second Edition (WIAT-II). (2002). San Antonio, TX: The Psychological Corporation.

Author Note: We dedicate this chapter to the memory of our dear colleague Sandy Thompson, who helped pioneer the application of universal design to educational assessment.

Practice

The previous chapters in this book have focused on *Policy* and *Research* and how these topics have influenced current practices in large-scale assessments for students with disabilities and English language learners (ELLs). Section III of this book, *Practice*, provides the reader with accounts of some "hands-on" experiences that both researchers and practitioners have had selecting and implementing appropriate accommodations for students with disabilities and ELLs in elementary, secondary, and postsecondary settings. The eight chapters included in this section cover a wide variety of topics that range from a description of how a progressive state department of education has responded to the challenges of inclusive testing brought about through IDEA and NCLB legislation (Wiener, Chapter 12) to discussions of Response to Intervention (RTI) models and the implications these models have for classification of students with learning disabilities (Lazarus and Ofiesh, Chapter 14); as well as the use of these models with culturally and linguistically diverse subgroups such as ELLs (Klingner & Solano-Flores, Chapter 15).

The primary focus of the chapters presented in this section of the book is on issues related to decision making for accommodations on assessments given to examinees with disabilities. However, these chapters are quite diverse in their perspective and address a broad range of issues that practitioners are faced with as they make decisions about assessment accommodations. Almond and Karvonen (Chapter 8) point to a recent survey by the National Center on Educational Outcomes that reminds us that there is limited agreement about, and little precedent for, determining which accommodations will best meet the needs of the individual child, while still preserving the meaning and comparability of the test scores. In their chapter, Almond and Karvonen describe one state's experience (Oregon) with a process for developing state policy about allowable accommodations for students with disabilities taking state assessments. These authors provide a detailed description of this process using a specific example of how a request for an accommodation (i.e., the use of a scribe on a math problem-solving assessment) was evaluated to make a judgment about the availability of the accommodation.

Crawford and Tindal (Chapter 9) focus on the teacher's role in the assessment accommodation decision process. In their chapter, they examine the teacher's role in the process as well as factors that may improve the teacher's ability to make appropriate decisions such as additional training. They describe four systems for understanding and supporting teacher decision making on accommodations for instruction and assessment. The four models differ primarily in the data sources that are used and, in some cases, in their technical adequacy.

Kopriva, Koran, and Hedgspeth (Chapter 10) also focus on the decision-making process for assessment accommodations at the large-scale K–12 assessment level. First, they discuss the pros and cons of a variety of approaches and systems for making large-scale assessment accommodations decisions for both students with disabilities and ELLs, arguing that research confirms that accommodations cannot be validly assigned to groups of students based on broad classifications or policies. They point out that most recommendations for accommodating ELLs are policy based, most often at the state level. Although there has been work towards developing systematic methods for improving the assignment process for students with

disabilities, understanding how to best accomplish this at the large-scale testing level is still being considered. Kopriva et al. then describe an informant-based computerized system for making assessment accommodation decisions on large-scale academic assessments administered to ELLs, the Selection Taxonomy for English Language Learner Accommodations. The authors point out that this system identifies critical variables and collects data about these variables from three sources. Afterwards, the data are combined with standard information regarding how accommodations perform, and, based on this information, the system produces a set of individualized accommodation decisions for students. Kopriva et al. discuss some of the implications for this and other types of decision-making accommodation systems for students with disabilities and ELLs, and suggest how the assignment work for both of these populations might proceed.

The chapter by Shriner and DeStefano (Chapter 11) includes discussion of two federally funded research and professional development projects that focused on individualized education program (IEP) team decision-making processes regarding participation and accommodation options for large-scale assessments. They highlight their technical assistance efforts with middle school personnel who wanted to improve the inclusion and performance of students with disabilities in both district and state assessments. The authors discuss the challenges of balancing the requirements for states' delineations of valid accommodations with the IEP team's authority to determine and assign accommodations for the individual student. They present four recommended plans given to the middle school decision makers to improve the quality of assessment and accommodation strategies for students with disabilities in both general education and special education environments.

The chapter by Wiener (Chapter 12) and the chapter by Ewing (Chapter 13) report on specific and contrasting experiences with two states in New England (Massachusetts and Rhode Island). Wiener explores the effects on students with disabilities in light of the dramatic changes that have occurred in state testing as a result of the passage of state and federal education reform laws beginning in the 1990s. He discusses how the mandate for schools to account for and improve the achievement of all students has had its most dramatic effects on student subgroups that have historically lagged behind the mainstream in academic performance. He also discusses the usefulness of alternate assessments and how high school graduation requirements have fundamentally changed the nature of instruction in high school for students with disabilities.

Ewing reports on a study of assessment accommodations that took place in Rhode Island with the goals of determining how IEP teams make assessment accommodation decisions for students, how assessment accommodations compared to instructional accommodations, and how assessment accommodations were implemented during statewide assessments. She found a general lack of awareness about how to tailor a set of assessment accommodations to match an individual student's testing needs. She also found that instructional accommodations were often not made available on assessments. Ewing provides some advice and guidelines for developing a clear process within schools to create a coherent and meaningful set of testing accommodations for individual students.

The chapter written by Lazarus and Ofiesh (Chapter 14) provides information about accommodating assessments for students with disabilities in a secondary and postsecondary school environment. The authors speak generally about major differences between accommodating examinees in a school age and in a postsecondary school environment. The major focus of the chapter is on accommodating tests such as the SAT, the Preliminary SAT (PSAT), and AP, administered by the College Board to examinees with disabilities. The authors discuss the process used to decide what accommodations an examinee with disabilities will receive when he/she takes these College Board tests. In addition, they discuss the use of RTI models to classify students with learning disabilities. They make the point that currently information on a student's response to interventions is additional qualitative information that the College Board considers as part of the student's entire documentation packet.

The last chapter in this section, by Klingner and Solano-Flores (Chapter 15), focuses on a very important change in the IDEA regulations: the introduction of RTI models to classify students with learning disabilities. The authors discuss how the models may be implemented and the implications for culturally diverse populations. They argue that since RTI is a form of assessment, it is very important to consider what accommodations may be required for these models when they are implemented with ELLs and with other culturally and linguistically diverse populations. Among other things, the authors discuss the skills and knowledge educators need to use RTI in their classrooms and the conditions schools need to meet if they are to properly implement these models.

CHAPTER 8

Accommodations for a K to 12 Standardized Assessment: Practical Implications for Policy

PATRICIA ALMOND
University of Oregon

MEAGAN KARVONEN
Western Carolina University

BACKGROUND

Large-scale assessments have been used by states (within the context of accountability systems), for multiple purposes at the individual and system levels. Test scores are used as indicators of such things as mastery of grade level content and competencies required for high school graduation. Some stakeholders, such as parents and employers, may interpret these scores as indicators of students' preparation for employment in a competitive global economy. At the system level, aggregated assessment scores may be used to document schoolwide performance, guide instructional improvement, and inform policy makers' decisions about how to allocate resources to address less effective elements of the educational system. When assessment results are used for multiple purposes, states are responsible for collecting evidence to support the technical adequacy for each purpose (American Educational Research Association, AERA, American Psychological Association, APA, & National Council on Measurement in Education, NCME, 1999, Standard 13.2).

Purpose of Accommodations

Accommodations refer to adaptations in presentation, equipment and materials, response accommodations, scheduling/timing, and setting that allow students greater access to the testing event and that do not alter the content or difficulty of what is tested. Testing accommodations allow students with disabilities, and in some states other students, to take the general education assessment with minor changes in test administration and have their scores "count." The adaptations are intended to ensure that all students, especially students with disabilities, are included in statewide assessment and accountability systems and in decisions about educational improvements that are made based on the assessment results.

There is disagreement from state to state about which adaptations are considered accommodations that do not change interpretations that can be made based on the test results. One example is the read-aloud accommodation in which a teacher or proctor reads the test to the student taking the test. It is accepted as an allowable accommodation in some states but not in others. In some cases reading aloud directions is acceptable but reading aloud questions and/or distractors is not acceptable. Clapper, Morse, Lazarus, Thompson, and Thurlow (2005) reported that 47 states permitted some or all tests to be read aloud; however, only 3 states permitted the use of this accommodation with no restrictions. They found 31 states that permitted questions to be read aloud on the math test but not the reading test. These policy differences from state to state point to the major challenges states face in setting accommodation policies.

Ideally, accommodations allow students with disabilities to obtain a score that represents their true knowledge and abilities, while avoiding either measuring construct-irrelevant variance (e.g., the effects of the disability) or giving an unfair advantage and yielding a score that overstates the student's proficiency. The basic purpose of accommodations is to level the playing field by providing students a fair chance to show what they know and can do.

States' Obligations: Determining Allowable Accommodations

States have the responsibility for designing, implementing, and ensuring appropriate district level use of accommodation policies. These responsibilities include determining which accommodations are appropriate for which students, taking which assessments, under which conditions. Under the No Child Left Behind Act of 2001 (NCLB) requirements for peer review of assessment systems, states must provide several types of evidence that their accommodations are appropriate and that accommodated assessments provide meaningful test scores (U.S. Department of Education, 2004). For example, one potential source of evidence is written documentation of the state's policies and procedures for the selection and use of

accommodations and alternate assessments, including evidence of training for educators who administer these assessments.

A House of Representatives Committee Report on the reauthorization of the Individuals With Disabilities Education Improvement Act (IDEA) 2004 provided a clear description of states' obligations:

> The bill also makes clear that States have an affirmative obligation to determine what types of accommodations can be made to assessments while maintaining their reliability and validity. The bill requires States to develop and implement guidelines on appropriate accommodations. The Committee intends that this provision will serve as a valuable tool for the IEP Team as they determine which assessments a child with a disability should take, and which accommodations are appropriate. (H. Report No. 108-77, 2003)

To "determine what types of accommodations" are appropriate, a state needs to identify alterations to standard test administration, or "changes that do not alter in any significant way what the test measures or the comparability of scores" (Thurlow & Wiener, 2000). When these standard or allowable accommodations are identified, states must develop and implement guidelines on appropriate accommodations. Many states provide lists of accommodations that can be used during testing that are acceptable for use in testing. These guidelines represent state policies and recommended procedures for test accommodations. Thus, accommodation policies must be sufficiently documented to support local individualized education program (IEP) team decisions about individual students. Without adequate guidance, the risk exists for IEP teams to choose inappropriate accommodations, accommodations for testing that do not match what was provided during instruction, or to provide more accommodations than necessary (Hollenbeck, Tindal, & Almond, 1998; Ysseldyke et al., 2001).

States are eager to increasingly include students with disabilities in statewide assessment and to fairly assess their academic achievement. In addition states are reluctant to incorrectly classify a student as below proficient, or for that matter to incorrectly classify a student as above proficient. States are focused on continually improving the technical quality of statewide assessments while at the same time ensuring that they are accessible to all students. Accommodations listed in a table of standard (allowable) accommodations are selected by IEP teams for individuals when they make decisions about which assessments students will take and which accommodations students will use. The decision to remove an accommodation from the *allowable* list has serious repercussions and will be very unpopular with IEP teams. Once states determine that an accommodation does not alter in any significant way what the test measures or the comparability of scores, that decision seems set in stone; therefore, the criteria for making the decision warrant careful attention.

Determining State Policy

Although there are numerous resources designed to help IEP teams make decisions about appropriate accommodations for individual students, fewer resources exist to guide states in determining appropriate policies for their own assessment systems. Some states rely on testing vendors to advise them about what constitutes a standard accommodation. Some turn to research that is at best confusing and at worst contradictory. For example, research on the use of dictation to a scribe reveals contradictory findings (Fuchs, Fuchs, Eaton, Hamlett, & Karns, 2000; Koretz, 1997; Koretz & Hamilton, 1999, 2000; Tindal & Fuchs, 1999). Much of the existing accommodations research is based on quasi-experimental designs, often with small homogeneous samples, or on archival data (Sireci, Scarpati, & Li, 2005). Although accommodation policies should ideally be supported by research, differential findings across subject areas, grade levels, or disability labels limit a state's ability to implement accommodation policies informed by conclusive evidence across studies. In light of research limitations, representatives from some states query colleagues in other states and search state Web sites for documentation and rationales to use as models in framing their own state policy around accommodations. Two potential resources include the National Center on Educational Outcomes (NCEO) online accommodations bibliography (NCEO, 2006, February), which is a searchable listing of research on various accommodations, and the *Standards for Educational and Psychological Testing* (AERA, APA, & NCME, 1999), which lists some best practices from a measurement perspective.

There is little agreement and limited precedent for how to determine what accommodations are allowable, and each state approaches the task differently. A recent NCEO survey indicated that states still needed several types of guidance related to their accommodation policies, including (a) determination of appropriate and allowable accommodations; (b) technical assistance on appropriateness of specific accommodations for both instruction and assessment; (c) professional development, especially for general education teachers; and (d) degree of specificity required in state guidance (Thompson, Thurlow, Johnstone, & Altman, 2005).

Although federal legislation such as NCLB and IDEA provide a set of requirements all states must meet in their assessment systems, states still have considerable latitude in designing, implementing, and evaluating accommodation policies. States determine what training to provide on the policies, and what standards of technical adequacy are appropriate for their assessments. Given the various (and sometimes competing) demands states face in designing and implementing accommodation policies, what processes might states choose to include and why?

This chapter describes one state's accommodation panel, including the process for nominating accommodations, criteria for considering the nomination, and procedures for reviewing and finalizing approval for allowable accommodations. This description, framed as a case study, illustrates one state's process for weighing empirical evidence and federal requirements along with litigation and social contingencies to create a process for considering and adopting allowable accommodations.

METHODOLOGY

An intrinsic case study is a methodology used to illustrate a particular, unique case that has value in and of itself; it is not necessarily intended to develop or test theory (Stake, 1995). The unit of study in this case is the Oregon Department of Education (ODE). In 2000, ODE had in place a unique system of assessment options and certificate requirements developed under state law. Pursuant to a lawsuit settlement, ODE was required to modify its process for reviewing and approving accommodations. The influence of litigation, along with other state and federal policy influences, created a unique set of circumstances that shaped the state's procedures for deciding what accommodations were allowable. As case study techniques are often used to bridge the gap between theory and practice (Berg, 2001), this approach was applied to ODE's experiences with accommodation decisions in order to explicate the decision-making process that evolved. Although the experiences in this state may not be immediately generalizable to other states' assessment systems, it is possible that ODE's review process includes features that may be adaptable for use in other states' systems.

Evidence for this case study came primarily from three sets of documents collected between 1999 and 2005: (1) ODE Web site and archived documents including descriptions of assessment practices, accommodation and modification tables; (2) documents from the accommodation review panel, including the manual, meeting minutes, and written communication about specific accommodation deliberations; and (3) other supporting documents such as the lawsuit settlement and ODE policy documents.

Analysis of data took two forms. First, trends across the 6-year period were examined to understand the broad impact of the contextual influences on the accommodations as a whole. Second, a detailed description of the review process was generated for a single accommodation to explicate the decision-making process. The first author, who was a member of the ODE staff during all the years of this case study, described the processes and trends using the archival data. The second author, who had no affiliation with ODE or the accommodations panel, reviewed written summaries from the first author and sought clarification from an outsider's perspective.

The case study emphasizes a description of the procedures for determining allowable accommodations, and provides an example of how the system worked in practice. First we provide an overview of the state's assessment options for students with disabilities.

OREGON'S ASSESSMENT SYSTEM

During the 1990s the Oregon Statewide Assessment Program shifted emphasis from principally a program evaluation purpose to a standards-based assessment. The change followed state legislation requiring alignment of the state assessments to the state's common curriculum goals or content standards and the requirement from Congress to use state tests for evaluating federally funded Title I programs. In 1996 Oregon performance standards, including cut scores for three perform-ance levels (i.e., meets, exceeds, and does not meet), were instituted for evaluating achievement in reading and mathematics. The state legislation, the Oregon Educa-tional Act for the 21st Century, established the Certificate of Initial Mastery (CIM) to be awarded at about Grade 10 to students who met the state's new world class stan-dards.

Along with the increasingly high stakes associated with statewide assessments, Oregon made a concerted effort to provide options for students to participate meaning-fully in their assessment system. Beginning in 1996, students that had been excluded from the assessment system were purposefully included, particularly English language learners and students with disabilities. By 2002, every student in Oregon's public school system was expected to fully partici-pate in the statewide assessment. Oregon's goal was to include all students in a single comprehensive assessment system and to avoid separate standards and assessments for subgroups of students. To achieve this goal, Oregon's system provided a number of options to students for participating in statewide assessments. With these options, more students were able to take tests and receive feedback on their performance than ever before. The multiple opportunities for participation that were available in 2002 are described below.

1. There were two versions of the general multiple-choice assessments available to schools: paper-and-pencil and computer-based testing. Both versions listed allow-able accommodations (i.e., adaptations that did not change the content or diffi-culty). *Accommodations* were available to students with or without an IEP who needed them in order to have access to the content being tested. Testing materi-als included tables describing allowable (standard) accommodations.

2. Manuals for the two versions of the gen-eral multiple-choice assessments also listed *modifications* (i.e., changes that an individual student may need in order to access the content or demonstrate what s/he knew but that had been demon-strated to change the content and/or dif-ficulty of what was being tested). Modifications were only available to stu-dents with IEPs and would result in *non-standard* scores.

3. In 2002, there were three variations that expanded the accessibility of the general assessment. The first was achievement-level testing that provided two addi-tional forms of the mathematics assessment: one with more easy items and one with more challenging items. A second variation was the addition of a plain language version of the general mathematics assessment, validated as assessing the same construct in mathe-matics and minimizing the language load. The third variation allowed stu-dents with disabilities to challenge a lower benchmark.

4. In 2002, there were two options for stu-dents taking an alternate assessment within Oregon's assessment system, one for students who could meet Oregon's challenging content standards on grade level but needed an alternative format, and one for students with significant cognitive disabilities who could not meet Oregon's achievement standards because they needed modifications and an assessment with reduced breadth and depth. These two options were called Juried Assessment and Extended Assess-ments, Oregon's alternate assessments for students with significant cognitive disabilities.

With the expanded alternatives for taking an assessment within the Oregon system, most students took the general assessment, that is, the standard administration with or without allowable accommodations.

It is important to note that, as it was introduced, the complexity of this system of options overwhelmed some administrators and practitioners/teachers in the field. It also baffled some psychometricians. Although the approach was grounded in a policy of inclusive instruction and assessment, it also confused some special education teachers and some parents of students with disabilities, less because the emphasis was on inclusion and more because the criteria for choosing an option were not yet clearly articulated. This approach did provide individualized alternatives for meeting the needs of individual students within the assessment system.

In the context of federal and state legislation supporting inclusive assessment practices, Advocates for Special Kids (ASK) brought legal action against Oregon in 1999. ASK alleged that the Oregon Statewide Assessment Program discriminated against children with learning disabilities in the Oregon public school system. In the lawsuit settlement arranged in 2001, the following language was used to describe how the state should handle accommodations on its assessments:

> Accommodations shall be considered allowable, valid, and scorable if they are used during instruction . . . and are listed on a student's IEP or Section 504 plan, unless [the department] can show that the accommodation invalidates the score interpretation. Rather than consider all accommodations first invalid until proven to be valid, [the department] shall consider all accommodations valid unless [it] can show that the accommodation would invalidate the score interpretation. . . . Any list of approved or not approved accommodations published by [the department] as a guide for school districts shall not be deemed exclusive. (*Advocates for Special*

Kids v. Oregon State Board of Education, 1999)

Thus, the burden of proof to show an accommodation would invalidate a score was placed on ODE.

It is important to note that in 2002 nearly all options except the extended assessments involved taking the general assessment in some format. As a consequence of the evolving regulations for NCLB, no state system has been static since its passage in 2001. The system that was in place in 2002 continued to evolve in response to regulation and presents an evolved constellation of options in 2006. Figure 8-1 provides an overview of the assessment system between 1997 and 2005.

THE ACCOMMODATIONS PANEL

ODE established an Accommodations Panel in 1997 to review proposals for allowable accommodations on specific assessments within the system. Guided by Panel members, the review process evolved over the course of about 18 months. The forms and processes described in this section came about during the interaction and deliberation of the Panel during their meetings. A process for consensus building evolved as Panel members worked through the process of advising ODE by recommending policy decisions.

Although the Panel had been meeting regularly for 2 years by the time the ASK lawsuit was filed, the lawsuit itself and the ultimate settlement agreement influenced the work of the Panel in at least two ways. First, the procedure for considering accommodations was clarified and became more transparent for the ODE, the Panel, and school districts. Second, the procedures for deliberation and documentation, and the stages in deliberating, building consensus, and finalizing recommendations for the associate superintendent, were structured, spelled out, and

				Time Period for Case Study			
Events	1997–1998	1999–2000	2000–01	2001–2002	2002–2003	2003–2004	2004–2005
Federal Legislation	IDEA			NCLB			IDEIA
Federal Requirements	• Gen Ed		• Alt Asmt • All tested	• AYP = All		• 1% Cap	
ASK vs. OR State Board		ASK vs OR	Settlement				Termination
OR Testing Options		• Standard[a] • Modified • Alt Asmt[b] • Exempt	• Standard • Challenge • Modified • Extended[c] • Exempt • Special • Juried	• Standard • Challenge • Modified • Extended • Exempt[d] • Special • Juried	• Standard • Challenge • Modified • Extended • Juried	• Standard • Challenge • Modified • Extended • Juried	• Standard • Targeted • Modified • Extended • Juried
KS[e] Accommodations & Footnotes Counts		29/2	29/4	35/7	43/10	43/10	44/13
KS Modifications & Footnotes Counts		15/1	13/2	14/3	18/5	19/5	19/6

FIGURE 8-1

History of Oregon's Assessment System

[a]Standard administration includes administration with and without standard accommodations.

[b]Alternate Assessment pilot testing.

[c]Alternate Assessment becomes Extended Assessment and field testing statewide.

[d]Final year in which exemptions were allowed.

[e]KS = Knowledge and Skills Assessments; Oregon's reading, mathematics, science, and social science assessments with selected responses items.

Date Submitted: *April 2*	
Adaptation: *assistance with spelling and grammar in his writing*	
For Which Assessments:	❑ Reading/Literature
❑ ✔ <u>Math Problem Solving</u>	❑ Mathematics
❑ Writing	❑ Science
Person Submitting: *Tiffanie* E-mail: *tiffanie@k12.district.or.gov*	School/District:

Description of Adaptation:
math problem solving test and assistance with spelling and grammar in writing

How students will use adaptation in assessment: describe for each assessment:
The student performs all math-related tasks individually on the test.

Please include sample of student work using adaptation.

Rationale for adding to the accommodations table:
Spelling and grammar are not part of the construct tested

Other factors that influence score validity when this adaptation is used (for example English proficiency):

FIGURE 8-2

Proposal Form to Add Adaptation to Accommodation Table

systematically followed. Eventually, the process stabilized and changed little from one meeting to another.

Accommodation Review Process

Under the review process, potential accommodations on specific assessments could be requested by teachers, parents, and other educators by using a form available on the ODE Web site (see Figure 8-2) and noted in the administration manual on the accommo-

dations and modifications tables. The person submitting the proposal was asked to specify a rationale under which the adaptation should be considered standard (allowable) for a particular assessment. Once the ODE staff received the proposal and reviewed the accommodation tables to be sure the requested accommodation was not already listed, ODE staff reviewed and analyzed relevant research and legal decisions about the effects of the proposed accommodation on the validity of test score interpretations.

Date of Review: _____
Adaptation Name:
For Which Assessments: ❏ Reading/Literature   ❏ Math Problem Solving ❏ Mathematics   ❏ Writing ❏ Science
Description of Adaptation:
How students will use adaptation in assessment—describe for each assessment:
Synopsis of Research and Legal Findings   1. Findings that show adaptation does *NOT* alter content and/or performance level: • —   • —   • —   2. Findings that show adaptation *DOES* alter content and/or performance level: • —   • —   • —
Copies of Abstracts or Annotated Bibliography of Most Relevant References:
References List:

FIGURE 8-3

Collection of Research and Legal Decisions

Findings from that review were summarized on another form (see Figure 8-3) and presented to the Panel. The Panel then considered these reports, examples of the adaptations, and relevant assessment materials, and deliberated about the appropriateness of the requested adaptation as a standard accommodation. The Panel eventually made a recommendation to include the adaptation either on the Accommodations Table or the Modifications Table, and submitted its recommendation to the ODE Associate Superintendent of Assessment and Evaluation (Figure 8-4). Once the Associate Superintendent determined whether to accept the Panel's recommendation, it was published in the test administration manual and appropriate table.

Adaptation Name:

Date Received:

Tracking Number:

Adaptation for Which Assessment(s). Please check one or more:

❑ Writing   ❑ Mathematics

❑ Reading/Literature   ❑ Math Problem Solving

❑ Science

---

1. Recommendation to include as accommodation/include as a modification. (Specify Below):

   • Accommodation

   • Modification

2. Rationale supporting adaptation being included on the specified table:

3. Conditions that must be met in order for this to be included on the accommodation table:

4. Wording for Table:

5. Footnote for Table:

6. Additional comments from the Accommodations Panel:

Date of Recommendation: _____

Approval (signatures and date): _____

FIGURE 8-4

Accommodation Panel Recommendation

The entire process for reviewing proposed accommodations is illustrated in Figure 8-5. From the time an initial proposal was submitted for consideration, the review process typically took between 1 and 3 months to complete. Because the settlement concluded that an adaptation was allowable until it was proven to undermine validity, the deliberation and determination needed to be made in a timely manner to meet analysis and reporting timelines for the statewide assessment system.

Panel Membership and Responsibilities

Members of the Accommodations Panel represented diverse perspectives and roles, including content area, special education, and measurement experts, as well as district stakeholders (e.g., district testing director and special education administrator, school principal, parent of a student with a disability). In total, 12 Panel members were appointed by the Superintendent of Public Instruction under advisement with the Offices of Assessment and Special Education. Five criteria were considered in nominating members to the Panel:

- Knowledge in their area (Master's degree or equivalent)
- Five years of experience in education
- Prior experience on assessment advisory or content panels
- Prior experience in statewide assessment
- Reputation as someone who could effectively work as a member of a group

Panel member responsibilities specified by the Assessment Office included

- Representation of own area of knowledge and expertise
- Familiarity with state assessments
- Attendance at all meetings

- Fair and ethical application of review criteria
- Collaborative work with other members of the committee

Once formed, the Accommodations Panel was responsible for reviewing all relevant materials, participating in deliberations, making judgments based on the review criteria, and providing the ODE with a recommendation regarding designating testing adaptations as either an accommodation or a modification. The Panel typically convened for 2 full days (9 a.m.–4 p.m.) and met three to four times per year. The frequency and duration of the meetings was dependent on how many adaptations had been submitted to the ODE following the most recent meting.

Twelve Panel members were present at each meeting. During reviews of research and discussion stages regarding the review criteria, the larger group divided into two small groups of approximately six members each. Attempts were made to balance representation so that each group had a general education teacher, a special education teacher, an administrator, a parent, someone knowledgeable about measurement, and some one familiar with interpreting research. The small groups conducted their own deliberations and nominated a note taker to capture the discussion. As they responded to the questions and criteria they worked toward consensus by crafting wording for the recommendation of the smaller group. Once each group had a recommendation that an adaptation should be classified as an accommodation or modification the groups reconvened as a Panel and negotiated a consensus by merging the two recommendations. When the recommendations were contradictory, Panel members articulated the perspective from each small group's deliberations and worked toward a revised agreement. This final Panel deliberation was characterized by persuasion by making a case

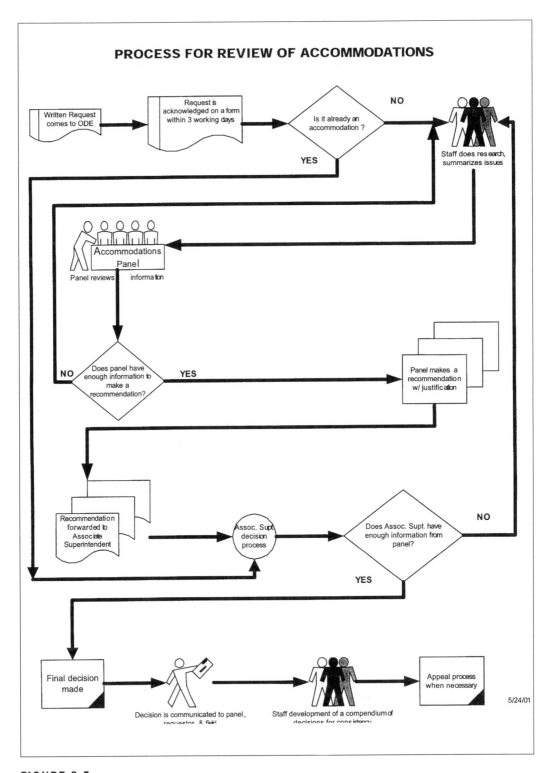

FIGURE 8-5

Flowchart Outlining Process for Review of Accommodations

and defending a position supported by an articulated rationale.

Two facilitators from the ODE, one a specialist from the Office of Special Education and one a specialist from the Office of Assessment (the first author), supported the work of the Panel by doing the legwork. In addition to the responsibilities described above, the ODE specialists acted as meeting organizers and conveners. They provided forms, materials, and research summaries, along with laptop computers and LCD projectors for note taking and group editing. The ODE staff assisted with note taking and provided clarification about the content being assessed, the procedures for test administration, and the reason provided for considering the adaptation. They did not participate in deliberations by giving opinions about the outcome of the deliberations. Staff pursued additional research or information as requested by panel members.

Review Criteria

This section describes the review criteria considered by the Panel in making its recommendations.

Criterion 1: Content and Performance Standards. The Panel was responsible for reviewing information about what was intended to be measured by the assessment. To assist the Panel in understanding the answer to this question, ODE staff presented information including a sample assessment, test specifications, the Oregon Standards, a sample individual score report, and in some cases the scoring rubric.

Criterion 2: The Requestor's Purpose. Panel members considered information on the proposal form (Figure 8-2) to determine the requestor's intent. For example, was the requestor hoping to enhance access to the test for an individual student who needed a particular accommodation, or proposing an accommodation that would allow a group of students to take the test with accommodations rather than modifications? Why was the request made to add the adaptation? Some adaptations were nominated for the accommodations table because a student used the adaptation during daily instruction and a teacher or IEP team believed that the adaptation did not change the construct or difficulty level. The desire was to have the adaptation added to the accommodations table so that the student's score would count. In other words, allowing the accommodation would provide the student with the opportunity to demonstrate proficiency in the standards.

Criterion 3: Function of the Adaptation. For this criterion, the Panel considered both how the adaptation functioned and what effect it had on student access to the content. The Panel also considered how the accommodation would be used and what structure needed to be in place to guide the use of the accommodation.

Criterion 4: Consequences of the Adaptation. In light of the intended inferences of scores on the assessment in question, the Panel next considered the impact of the proposed adaptation on those inferences. What possible misinterpretations could be made if the adaptation was approved as a standard accommodation? For instance, CIM proficiency indicates that the student meets the standard and is eligible for the certificate. Would proficiency under accommodated conditions erroneously indicate the student was ready for more challenging material? The panel was concerned about the possibility that listing an adaptation as an accommodation could start a trend that actually lowered teacher expectations or started a trend in the more frequent or casual use of a class of accommodations. For example, they were concerned that once reading the mathematics test aloud was permitted, teachers would start reading tests to students who didn't need them or try reading the same test to a group of students in a manner that *did* change what was measured. Besides potential consequences to students, the Panel also considered whether the proposed adaptation would somehow change or weaken the standards. For example, calculator use as an accommodation may lead to the relaxing of computation standards.

Criterion 5: Social Consequences of the Adaptation. The Panel considered the potential impact of the adaptation on students across settings and also on public perceptions of the validity of score interpretations from the assessment. For example, a potential consequence of allowing a word processor as an accommodation for writing might be to disadvantage students in schools without access to word processing, or inordinately advantage students from homes with more computer literacy and more resources.

Criterion 6: Potential System Change Resulting From Panel Decision. Finally, the Panel considered whether its decision might impact other parts of the assessment and educational system beyond its own scope. Would their decision change the assessment system itself or the established content and performance standards? For instance, in deliberating the addition of word processing with spell checking the Panel identified two possible system changes: (1) if spell checking was allowed, the state would potentially need another form of assessment to measure spelling; or (2) if spell checking was allowed and no new assessment component was added to test spelling, this combination might lead to a change in the state standards for spelling.

Application of the Criteria. The Panel considered the proposed adaptation by applying all six criteria. They wanted to know what the assessment was measuring and examined sample tests and test specifications. They discussed how an accommodation would be used; that is, what the test proctor did and what the student did. They also considered how the accommodation's use might affect other students. Through group discussion, Panel members docu-

mented their discussion of each criterion, taking notes that became part of the permanent record of their deliberations. The teachers on the Panel would usually describe the accommodation from personal experience in the classroom. Although Panel members began their discussion by walking through the criteria in sequence, discussion about one area often triggered a new understanding about a point that was mentioned previously. The group's understanding evolved as members came to a common understanding about the adaptation, its use, the effects it would have on the content and the student, and the confidence that could be placed in the resulting score.

Example Panel Deliberation: Use of Scribe for Math Problem Solving Assessment

The Mathematics Problem Solving assessment was an on-demand performance assessment in which a student received an open-ended mathematics problem and was asked to solve the problem showing his or her work and documenting the steps s/he went through to come to a solution. The student was also asked to verify the solution with evidence, in effect checking his or her answer. Students typically spent up to one class period to complete the assessment. A teacher nominated the accommodation in which a student would dictate his or her math problem-solving response to a scribe. Problems were scored by trained raters at a scoring site.

The Panel's handwritten notes indicated that the Panel considered the scribe adaptation as a way to capture a student response that would otherwise be unavailable and that the use of a scribe would minimize the interfering behaviors that prevented a student from writing. One type of disability that would necessitate a scribe was a significant motor impairment where the ability to respond or illegibility of the response might confound the interpretation of the student's solution. Panel members were concerned about a scribe providing assistance in a way that resulted in coaching the student instead of acting strictly as a recorder.

Panel members saw the problem-solving task as requiring the student to interpret the concepts in the problem and translate them into mathematics, choosing strategies and carrying them out to solve the problem. From their perspective, the second look at the solution allowed the student to defend the solution. Conveying the solution involved using pictures, symbols, and vocabulary. One concern expressed was that the scribe might alter or augment a student's response. The function of allowing the scribe would be to allow participation by more students but it might also result in more low scores. There were two concerns over fairness. On one hand the scribe's skill in being a scribe could influence the student's score. Would an inept scribe disadvantage the student? On the other hand, students would need skill and practice to effectively use a scribe. In addition, the Panel felt that over the long term, students should learn to respond independently without a scribe.

The Panel members discussed the pros and cons with the overarching question being whether they could prove that the use of a scribe in mathematics problem solving would invalidate the inferences that could be made based on the score. Their recommendation was that use of a scribe be added to the list of allowable or standard accommodations with several conditions. The first was that the scribe must be trained in being a scribe. The second was that the student's response must be transcribed verbatim and that the scribe's role was strictly as a recorder. Finally, they determined that translating, interpreting, and clarifying student's intention would not be permitted.

The Panel's recommendation was presented to the Associate Superintendent for Assessment, who conditionally approved the recommendation pending guidelines for the use of scribes and procedures for training scribes. The Panel provided the following clarifications: To ensure a literal transcription a scribe could ask a student to repeat a statement but could not ask the student to explain. A scribe could read back and make changes when the student requested this. Training should cover rate, conventions of scribing, as well as format or layout for a transcription. It was recommended that training be conducted through a video recording. The wording and the detailed footnote provided for the scribe accommodation appears in Figure 8-6.

IMPLICATIONS

The Accommodations Panel described in this chapter evolved over an 18-month period in a unique context created by state and federal reform legislation, a lawsuit settlement, and a complex array of assessment options. The requirement that all accommodations be allowable unless sufficient evidence existed to support their exclusion created the need for a Panel deliberation process that could meet a unique burden of proof, even when sufficient research to guide decision making did not exist. With the need to rely heavily on professional judgment in the absence of empirical evidence, ODE needed a system that was consistent with the testing standards and yielded accommodations that were fair and maintained the validity of test score interpretations and uses. Through the Panel review process, both the number of standard (allowable) accommodations and the level of detail describing those accommodations have increased considerably (see Figures 8-1 and 8-6).

Accommodation in 2000: Point to or dictate multiple-choice responses to a scribe (used only for multiple choice knowledge and skill assessments)

Footnote: Test administrators, proctors, scribes, page-turners, educational assistants, and others supporting a student's test taking must be neutral in responding to the student during test administration. Assistance in test administration must not give away the correct answer. The student's response must accurately represent the student's own choice.

Accommodation in 2001 (after Panel deliberation): Student requiring a scribe dictates mathematics problem solving.

Footnote: A scribe needs to provide a literal transcription of the student's response without inserting any information not presented directly by the student. The following three clarifications should be followed and assume that the student has the scoring guide or knowledge of it. The purpose of these clarifications is to ensure the response is that of the student not the scribe.

1. When the scribe does not understand (e.g., misses or tracks) what the student has said, s/he may ask a clarifying question such as "could you repeat that?" Scribes may not ask any other questions.
2. Scribes may not ask questions to clarify information when they know what the student has said but do not understand what it means or why it was said.
3. If asked by the student, the scribe is allowed to read what the student has said. They are then allowed to make changes, insertions, or deletions that are initiated by the student.

At the end of the session the scribe should ask as a final question "Did I accurately record what you have said?" Students should review (look at) what they have had scribed to edit the total response.

Both the student and the scribe need to sign off at the bottom of the test protocol to reflect agreement that all recorded information is correct. Scribes need to be familiar with the needs of the student (and have worked with students and scribing before) and not be scribing for the first time with a student during the test.

Training of scribes needs to address three important issues to ensure accurate recording: (a) speed or rate of recording, (b) conventions for (en)coding symbols, and (c) format and layout of the response. Practice sessions should be held with students and scribes in advance of actual use so the scribe understands students' articulation. During the administration of the test, school districts, students and/or parents have the option to request an audio or videotape of the session.

FIGURE 8-6

Example of Change in Footnote Detail Before and After Accommodation Panel Review: Use of a Scribe

General Implications

The broadest and most overarching implication of the Accommodations Panel process and experience revealed in Oregon's case example is the challenge to reframe the question about accommodations and validity from the perspective of the individual student. A statement that appears prominently on the NCEO accommodations Web page reads as follows:

> Accommodations are changes in testing materials or procedures that enable students to participate in assessments in a way that allows abilities to be assessed rather than disabilities. They are provided to "level the playing field." Without accommodations, the assessment may not accurately measure the [individual] student's knowledge and skills. (NCEO, 2006, December)

It is this emphasis regarding drawing the appropriate inferences for an individual student that are emphasized when challenged, as Oregon was, to operate its assessments in accordance with the first point in their settlement: "Accommodations shall be considered allowable, valid, and scorable if they are used during instruction or classroom assessment and are listed on a student's IEP or Section 504 plan, unless ODE can show that the accommodation invalidates the score interpretation" (*Advocates for Special Kids v. Oregon State Board of Education*, 1999). (As indicated in the Blue Ribbon Panel Report, not all instructional accommodations are considered appropriate for the Oregon statewide assessment system (OSAS); only those that "accurately reflect an individual students performance"; Tanzer, Elliott, Engelhard, Schrag, & Vogel, 2000, p. 15.) It is this shift in perspective toward the individual student, the inferences that are made, and the consequences of assessment, that may hold the greatest impact for large-scale assessment.

Implications for School-Based Decision Making

One of a state's roles in setting accommodations policies is to provide sufficient guidance to support school-level decision makers in identifying appropriate accommodations for individual students. ODE had tables listing accommodations and an accommodations panel in place before the legal action. However, the process became more structured and assertive about increasing the number of allowable accommodations and more carefully prescriptive about how to administer testing accommodations. In addition, ODE described accommodations with both "is" and "is not" examples—uses of an accommodation that will and will not invalidate the assessment results—to communicate appropriate and allowable uses of testing accommodations. The level of detail in the footnotes after Panel deliberation provides additional guidance to IEP teams that need to interpret the contents of the state testing manual when making assessment participation decisions for individual students. This additional guidance may help IEP teams, who are responsible for determining which tests students will take and under what conditions students will participate, select appropriate accommodations given individualized student needs.

The Accommodations Panel review process also had two other impacts on assessment decisions at the school level. First, when adaptations were classified as *modifications*, that outcome triggered a demand for an alternate route or appeals process when decisions about certifying individual students depends on the assessment results. Second, the process of allowing all members of the educational community to submit nominations to the Accommodations Panel empowered teachers to think creatively about adaptations and draw links between instructional accommodations and those that would be appropriate for large-scale assessments. Nominating accommodations can provide a form of training for teachers. The form itself requires them to provide a rationale for nominating adaptations—and asks them to be knowledgeable about the process and to be familiar with both the accommodations and modifications tables in order to know what to propose. Involving the teachers in the process of identifying accommodations could be a support in increasing teacher knowledge, given the NCEO survey findings in which states say they still aren't sure how to educate teachers about accommodations.

Implications for Policy Makers

As the test sponsor, a state carries the major weight for establishing policy and procedures around test accommodations and is dependent on research that informs judgments about appropriate and allowable accommodations. Just as panels convened for item review or standard setting require careful training, an accommodations panel needs guidance on the broad purposes and function of the panel, and familiarization with the review criteria and processes. State education officials must give careful thought to the structures and supports that need to be in place for the panel to function effectively, and must be prepared for the panel to evolve over time. For example, ODE's Accommodation Panel was structured so that no more than one third of its membership changed each year and the representation of various roles remained balanced, to preserve some continuity. Also, each meeting began with a review of processes and procedures to remind the Panel members about its goals for the meeting.

States have the primary responsibility for appropriately using available information to render solid judgments about allowable accommodations. As seen in the case of ODE, decisions about allowable accommodations must be made regardless of what information is available from the field.

When no legal or empirical foundation exists to justify a single, clear decision, an accommodations panel must rely primarily on expert judgment. Under these circumstances, documenting the decision-making process is important for determining the evidentiary basis for the panel's outcomes.

Implications for Research and Test Development

Ideally, decisions about allowable accommodations would be made based on a clear body of research with consistent findings that are applicable to a state's particular assessment system. Although the body of accommodations research has grown dramatically in the past few years, the job of sifting through evidence is still an onerous one. The NCEO online accommodations database continues to serve as a repository for individual studies that state department of education representatives may access. As the field continues to develop stronger research methodologies and complete more studies, research syntheses around particular accommodations or types of tests, such as the recent review by Sireci et al. (2005), should be periodically developed and widely disseminated. Once an accommodation is approved for use on a particular assessment, that state and other interested parties (test vendors, researchers) should conduct research to see whether the accommodations are functioning as the panel anticipated, or whether the panel decisions should be reviewed and revised.

Finally, as universal design principles are increasingly applied to test development, accommodations will be integrated at the test design phase and made available to a wide range of students. Creating a range of standardized presentation and response options will require accommodation panels to apply different criteria when considering the impact of accommodations on scores, and will require researchers to implement new designs that capture the continuum of assessment features and the population of students who take them.

REFERENCES

Advocates for Special Kids v. Oregon State Board of Education, No. CV99-263 (D. Or. Filed 02/22/1999).

American Educational Research Association, American Psychological Association, and National Council on Measurement in Education. (1999). *Standards for educational and psychological testing.* Washington, DC: American Educational Research Association.

Berg, B. L. (2001). *Qualitative research methods for the social sciences* (4th ed.). Boston: Allyn & Bacon.

Clapper, A. T., Morse, A. B., Lazarus, S. S., Thompson, S. J., & Thurlow, M. L. (2005). *2003 state policies on assessment participation and accommodations for students with disabilities* (Synthesis Rep. No. 56). Minneapolis, MN: University of Minnesota, National Center on Educational Outcomes. Retrieved July 29, 2006, from http://education.umn.edu/NCEO/OnlinePubs/Synthesis56.html

Fuchs, L. S., Fuchs, D., Eaton, S. B., Hamlett, C. L., & Karns, K. M. (2000). Supplementing teacher judgments of mathematics test accommodations with objective data sources. *School Psychology Review, 29,* 65–85.

Hollenbeck, K., Tindal, G., & Almond, P. (1998). Teachers' knowledge of accommodations as a validity issue in high-stakes testing. *Journal of Special Education, 32,* 175–183.

Improving Education Results for Children With Disabilities Act of 2003, H.R. Rep. No. 108-77. (2003).

Koretz, D. (1997). *The assessment of students with disabilities in Kentucky* (CSE Tech. Rep. No. 431). Los Angeles, CA: UCLA, Center for the Study of Evaluation, Center for Research on Evaluation, Standards, and Student Testing.

Koretz, D., & Hamilton, L. (1999). *Assessing students with disabilities in Kentucky: The effects of accommodations, format, and subject* (CSE Technical Report No. 498). Los Angeles, CA: UCLA, Center for the Study of Evalua-tion, Center for Research on Evaluation, Standards, and Student Testing.

Koretz, D., & Hamilton, L. (2000). Assessment of students with disabilities in Kentucky: Inclusion, student performance, and validity. *Educational Evaluation and Policy Analysis, 22,* 255–272.

National Center on Educational Outcomes. (2006, February 10). *Online accommodations bibliography.* Minneapolis, MN: University of Minnesota, National Center on Educational Outcomes. Retrieved July 15, 2006, from http://education.umn.edu/NCEO/AccomStudies.htm

National Center for Educational Outcomes (2006, December 21). *Special topic area: Accommodations for students with disabilities.* Minneapolis, MN: Author. Retrieved February 27, 2007, from http://www.education.umn.edu/NCEO/TopicAreas/Accommodations/Accomtopic.htm

Sireci, S. G., Scarpati, S. E., & Li, S. (2005). Test accommodations for students with disabili-ties: An analysis of the interaction hypothe-sis. *Review of Educational Research, 75,* 457–490.

Stake, R. E. (1995). *The art of case study research.* Thousand Oaks, CA: Sage.

Tanzer, J., Elliott, J., Engelhard, G., Schrag, J., & Vogel, S. A. (2000, December 4). *Report of the blue ribbon panel: Students with learning dis-abilities and the Oregon statewide assessment system.* Report submitted to the Advocates for Special Kids and the Oregon Department of Education.

Thompson, S. J., Thurlow, M. L., Johnstone, C. J., & Altman, J. R. (2005). *2005 State special education outcomes: Steps forward in a decade of change.* Minneapolis, MN: University of Minnesota, National Center on Educational Outcomes. Retrieved February 12, 2006, from http://education.umn.edu/NCEO/OnlinePubs/2005StateReport.htm/

Thurlow, M., & Wiener, D. (2000). *Non-approved accommodations: Recommendations for use and reporting* (Policy Directions No. 11). Minne-apolis, MN: University of Minnesota, National Center on Educational Outcomes. Retrieved July 15, 2006, from http://

education.umn.edu/NCEO/OnlinePubs/Policy11.htm

Tindal, G., & Fuchs, L. (1999). *A summary of research on test changes: An empirical basis for defining accommodations.* Lexington, KY: University of Kentucky, Mid-South Regional Resource Center.

U.S. Department of Education. (2004). *Standards and assessments peer review guidance: Information and examples for meeting the require-* *ments of NCLB.* Washington, DC: Author. Retrieved May 2, 2005, from http://www.ed.gov/policy/elsec/guid/saaprguidance.doc

Ysseldyke, J., Thurlow, M., Bielinski, J., House, A., Moody, M., & Haigh, J. (2001). The relationship between instructional and assessment accommodations in an inclusive state accountability system. *Journal of Learning Disabilities, 34,* 212–220.

CHAPTER 9

A Teacher's Role in the Implementation of Assessment Accommodations

LINDY CRAWFORD
University of Colorado at Colorado Springs

GERALD TINDAL
University of Oregon

TEST DESIGN AND USE

Universal design of large-scale tests includes multiple means of representation, multiple means of engagement, and multiple means of expression (Center for Applied Special Technology, 2006). A focus on accessibility of test items and overall test format ensures that all students are provided equal opportunities to demonstrate their knowledge and skills. Even with the creation of universally designed assessments, some students will require accommodations in order to fully access test questions and demonstrate their knowledge and skills of the constructs assessed. In this chapter, we briefly explore the impact of teacher training and decision making on use of accessible tests and use of test accommodations. In the end, it is teachers who will (or will not) implement tests as designed, or assign accommodations as allowed.

Teachers and Test Administration

To date, research into teachers' accurate implementation of universally designed assessments has not been published. Research on teachers' use of assistive technology has been published, however, and is indirectly related to implementation of universally designed assessments. Many advocate the use of assistive technology devices to aid in instruction (Edyburn, 2000; Marino, Marino, & Shaw, 2006) and assessment (Thompson, Johnstone, & Thurlow, 2002), but implementation is often impeded by a lack of adoption by school personnel (Cuban, 2001). School personnel, and in particular teachers, do not consistently provide students with the assistive technology they need to participate fully in academic settings (Abner & Lahm, 2002; Zascavage & Keefe, 2004). Some reasons for the inconsistent provision of assistive technology devices include the complexity of the equipment, time to learn how to use the equipment, and the need for more on-site assistance (McGregor & Pachuski, 1996). Lack of teacher willingness has not been identified as a barrier.

Teachers must be fluent in the use of technology and assistive technology if they are to help students make use of universally designed assessments. A related issue of importance is teachers' administration of test items in a manner that ensures students with disabilities are provided the opportunity to demonstrate their knowledge and skills. Skills identified as useful (and often required) for testing students with disabilities include use of three-dimensional models, scaffolding, and the targeting of responses for students with restricted movement. Training on how to validly administer tests to students with various disabilities has been found to improve teacher skills and positively impact student performance (Browder, Karvonen, Davis, Fallin, & Courade-Little, 2005). This positive relationship between teachers' facility with test administration and students' opportunity to fully demonstrate their knowledge and skills has also been reported by Crawford and McDonald (2005).

Accommodations and Large-Scale Testing

A need exists for accommodations in large-scale testing, though it is somewhat uncertain how and why they appear to be effective and with which students. Empirical support for accommodations is inconsistent within and across subject areas and even though they sometimes appear to be effective, they also appear to be either inert (not work for anyone) or overly effective (work for everyone). It is not yet possible, therefore, to simply move research to practice in embracing wide-scale adoption of specific accommodations that have passed the test of replicable empirical support. Yet, large-scale testing requires their application. To bridge this gap, the research on accommodations has begun to focus on how teachers make the decision to recommend specific changes in testing.

TEACHER DECISION MAKING ON ACCOMMODATIONS

Very little is known about the intricacies of teacher decision making. Early findings reported by Hollenbeck, Tindal, and Almond (1998) indicate that only 55% of general and special education teachers are correct in determining whether or not an accommodation is allowable for use with the particular assessment they are administering. Even more problematic, according to these authors, is the finding that special and general education teachers do not differ from each other in their knowledge of allowable accommodations.

Though not directly focused on accommodations, Crawford, Almond, Tindal, and Hollenbeck (2002) studied teachers' perceptions of the participation of students with disabilities in large-scale testing by organizing their comments into three categories: (a) teacher knowledge, (b) teacher attitude (in which the comments were not as abundant but were quite emotional), and (c) teacher decision-making (which contained the majority of comments). In this last category, they reported findings similar to those reported by Jayanthi, Epstein, Polloway, and Bursuck (1996): Many decisions about participation in large-scale tests are made by individual teachers, not by individualized education program (IEP) teams. Individual student characteristics (and basic skills) were the primary reference in making these decisions. As Jayanthi et al. conclude: "Teachers should be trained to use student performance data to validate these [inclusion] decisions . . . special service providers should develop a firm understanding of test accommodations available to students with disabilities" (p. 114). As two teachers so eloquently stated the problem in the Crawford et al. (2002) study: "I think we need to be trained and more information should be disbursed for us" and "We have some accommodations and some modifications but it looks like it's not clear how far we can push the envelope" (p. 107).

Using a similar focus group methodology, Ysseldyke and colleagues (2001) investigated the alignment of test accommodations with those used in instruction (specifically IEPs): "If a student had an IEP goal, it was very likely that the student received an accommodation for instruction in that area" (p. 216). Indeed, 82% of the students in their sample received some form of accommodation though no differences were found by disability prevalence or type. Importantly, 84% had instructional accommodations that matched their testing accommodations. (Though they distinguished between accommodations and modifications, it appeared that this distinction was based solely on the orientation to the content standards, as reading the reading test was viewed as an accommodation.)

Given that teachers may or may not be knowledgeable about allowable accommodations and with the pressure to ensure that accommodations in their classrooms are consistent with those used in the testing situation, it is important to support teachers' decision-making practices at the same time as basic research on accommodations is proceeding. This kind of support must come from supplemental information that is collected in addition to the purely descriptive information on state test results for two reasons. First, such outcome data usually represent post hoc results and teachers need information to make the initial decision. Second, descriptive information on state test results from accommodated and nonaccommodated conditions is confounded by student characteristics. (Nonaccommodated students are likely to be a different population of students than those who have been recommended to receive an accommodation.)

Four systems have emerged for understanding teacher decision making on accommodations, differing primarily on the source of data that they use. For Fuchs and Fuchs (2001) the focus has been on using curriculum-based measurement (CBM) as companion data for making decisions about accommodations and their effects. Teachers administer a basic skills measure in reading or mathematics to make a prediction about the need for an accommodation; in the Fuchs and Fuchs research designs, this prediction is compared to those made by teachers using informal information. For McKevitt and Elliott (2001), the source of information is a checklist on accommodations that help structure teachers' rationale for recommending accommodations. DeStephano, Shriner, and Lloyd (2001) focus on students' IEPs to ascertain the need for accommodations (and consistency with instructional use). Finally, Tindal and colleagues (Alonzo, Ketterlin-Geller, & Tindal, 2004; Ketterlin-Geller, Alonzo, Carrizales, & Tindal, 2005; Ketterlin-Geller, Yovanoff, & Tindal, 2007) use CBM as part of a diagnostic prediction that can be confirmed by documenting the effects of accommodations. Following are some specific findings from these four systems for recommending accommodations.

Fuchs and Fuchs

"One major obstacle to valid participation is the lack of standard methods for determining which testing accommodations preserve the meaningfulness of scores" (Fuchs & Fuchs, 2001, p. 174). Because the research base is thin, the population of students with disabilities is heterogeneous, and teachers have difficulty making recommendations when using informal judgments; Fuchs and Fuchs propose making data-based decisions. Their system— Dynamic Assessment of Test Accommodations (DATA)—is designed to assist teachers in making recommendations for test accommodations that include extended time, reading problems aloud (in math), use of calculators, a scribe writing nonmathematical responses, and large print. Accommodations are recommended by comparing a student's boost to that which can be expected (based on normative information from a population of students with learning disabilities).

In comparing accommodations recommended in this system with those recommended by teachers (or assigned at random), they reported significant differences: "Students to whom DATA had awarded accommodations earned larger boosts as a function of having those accommodations, compared to the subset to whom DATA had denied accommodations. The effect size was 0.34 standard deviations" (p. 179). Teachers both awarded and denied accommodations in a manner that reflected false positives and false negatives.

McKevitt and Elliott

McKevitt and Elliott (2001) studied teachers' selection of assessment accommodations and the impact of those accommodations on students' test performance using a modified version of the Assessment Accommodations Checklist (AAC; a checklist with 67 accommodations divided among eight categories and rated on use, potential helpfulness, and fairness). They reported multiple findings, but those findings most important to this discussion include:

1. Few differences existed in the selection of accommodations for students with and without disabilities.

2. Group analyses revealed that accommodation packages were equally ineffective for both these student populations.

3. Individual students benefited greatly from some accommodations (specifically, a read-aloud accommodation).

4. "[Teachers] believed that testing accommodations were 'somewhat helpful,' 'useful,' and 'fair' for helping students with disabilities show what they know" (p. 32).

5. Teachers selected only those accommodations they perceived as fair and valid.

DeStephano, Shriner, and Lloyd

DeStephano and colleagues (2001) developed a model for training teachers on decision making for participation in large-scale assessments that was based on present levels of performance in their IEPs. Working from the perspective that assessment accommodations should be parallel with those used in instruction (using the IEP as a proxy for instruction) and assuming that accommodations should be implemented to "mediate the effects of access deficits but not invalidate the assessment of target skills" (p. 9), they created six scenarios for participation and trained teachers how to make decisions about accommodations. In their training, they included information about IDEA requirements, IEP modifications, familiarity with content standards, and a flowchart illustrating how IEPs could be used for accommodation and participation decisions. Finally, they considered the participation of the student in the general curriculum, the use of accommodations, and the roles of both general and special education teachers. They reported significant changes in the participation rates and accommodation patterns as a result of their training and in relation to accessing the general curriculum with appropriate accommodations. "After training, teachers' decisions about assessment participation and accommodation did show a stronger link to students' access to the general curriculum and needed instructional accommodations than decisions prior to training." (p. 18)

Tindal and Colleagues

Ketterlin-Geller, Alonzo, Carrizales, & Tindal (2005) approached the process for recommending accommodations with a computer-based Accommodation Station

(AS) in which a series of basic skills assessments are administered and perceptions are documented with a report generated for IEP teams to use in making a recommendation. The AS has the following measures embedded in the computer programming.

1. A silent reading measure is used in which students are directed to move to the next screen where a passage is presented for them to read and, when done, 'click next'. When the screen is first presented, a clock begins timing the student and it is stopped when the student 'clicks next.' This measure is based on the work of Miller (1990) and Yule (1987) and allows the rate of silent reading to be calculated.

2. A series of sentences are presented for a fixed period of time, each of them replaced by a blank screen, which is then followed by a literal comprehension question addressing information from the sentence. Students with reading problems often click immediately to move off the passage (presumably because they cannot read the full passage); this task allows calculation of correct responses on easy-to-read text and easy-to-answer questions.

3. A cloze test measures student comprehension and is based on the technical work summarized by Shin, Deno, and Espin (2000). In this task, a passage is presented with the first sentence left intact and thereafter every nth (frequently every 7th) word is deleted and the student is directed to select one of four options to correctly complete the sentence. This measure includes 16 fill-in-the-blanks to document the student's understanding of syntax, grammar, and semantics.

4. Various mathematics problems are presented in both accommodated and standard fashion to determine whether or not the student's performance is differentially affected. These accommodations include simplification of language, reading the mathematics problem aloud, and presenting the problem in Spanish (see Ketterlin-Geller, Yovanoff, & Tindal, 2007).

5. A series of statements are presented that address student skills, interests, and benefits from various changes to the testing situation. Teachers and students respond on a scale of agreement, representativeness, or likelihood. These items reflect the field-testing work conducted by Alonzo, Ketterlin-Geller, and Tindal (2004).

SUMMARY OF TEACHER DECISION MAKING ON ACCOMMODATIONS

The four models for making accommodations recommendations vary primarily in the data sources that are used and may vary in their technical adequacy. At this point, the CBMs from Fuchs and Fuchs (2001) look very promising; the accommodations checklist from McKevitt and Elliott (2001) appears very popular; the focus on IEPs by DeStephano et al. (2001) highly relevant; and the AS (Ketterlin-Geller, Alonzo, Carrizales, & Tindal, 2005) potentially useful for IEP teams. Yet, further research is needed on all of them.

As Bolt and Thurlow (2004) recommend, the following practices should be followed by teachers:

1. Make the skills explicit prior to making accommodations decisions.

2. Use the least intrusive accommodations.

3. Align assessment with instruction.

4. Train test administrators in implementation of the accommodation.

5. Anticipate difficulties and be prepared to address challenges.

6. Monitor accommodations outcomes for individual students.

It is quite likely that the experimental research on accommodations needs to move to a field-based platform that both allows teachers to make decisions and systematically investigates the effects using randomized designs. In this process, more careful analysis of the achievement construct is needed at the item level and more rich descriptions are needed of the populations being tested.

REFERENCES

Abner, G. H., & Lahm, E. A. (2002). Implementation of assistive technology with students who are visually impaired: Teachers' readiness. *Journal of Visual Impairment and Blindness, 96*(2), 98–106.

Alonzo, J., Ketterlin-Geller, L., & Tindal, G. (2004). *Instrument development: Examining the appropriateness of student and teacher surveys for determining the need for testing accommodations.* (Tech. Rep. No. 31). Eugene, OR: University of Oregon, Behavioral Research and Teaching.

Bolt, S. E., & Thurlow, M. (2004). Five of the most frequently allowed testing accommodations in state policy. *Remedial and Special Education, 25*(3), 141–152.

Browder, D., Karvonen, M., Davis, S., Fallin, K., & Courade-Little, G. (2005). The impact of teacher training on state alternate assessment scores. *Exceptional Children, 71,* 267–282.

Center for Applied Special Technology. (2006). *What Is Universal Design for Learning?* Retrieved August 5, 2006, from http://www.cast.org/research/udl/index.html

Crawford, L., Almond, P., Tindal, G., & Hollenbeck, K. (2002). Teacher perspectives on inclusion of students with disabilities in high-stakes assessments. *Special Services in the Schools, 18*(1/2), 95–118.

Crawford, L., & McDonald, M. (2005). *2004 Colorado Student Assessment Program Alternate (CSAPA): Interrater reliability & administration fidelity.* Retrieved August 5, 2006, from http://www.cde.state.co.us/cdesped/download/pdf/CSAPA2004_Interrater.pdf

Cuban, L. (2001). Why are most teachers infrequent and restrained users of computers in their classroom? In J. Woodward & L. Cuban (Eds.), *Technology, curriculum and professional development: Adapting schools to meet the needs of students with disabilities* (pp. 121–137). Thousand Oaks, CA: Corwin Press. (ERIC Document Reproduction Service No. ED451621)

DeStefano, L., Shriner, J. G., & Lloyd, C. A. (2001). Teacher decision making in participation of students with disabilities in large-scale assessment. *Exceptional Children, 66,* 7–22.

Edyburn, D. L. (2000). Assistive technology and students with mild disabilities. *Focus on Exceptional Children, 32,* 1–23.

Fuchs, L. S., & Fuchs, D. (2001). Helping teachers formulate sound test accommodation decisions for students with learning disabilities. *Learning Disabilities Research & Practice, 16*(3), 174–181.

Hollenbeck, K., Tindal, G., & Almond, P. (1998). Teachers' knowledge of accommodations as a validity issue in high-stakes testing. *The Journal of Special Education, 32*(3), 175–183.

Jayanthi, M. E., Epstein, M. H., Polloway, E. A., & Bursuck, W. D. (1996). A national survey of general education teachers' perceptions of testing adaptations. *The Journal of Special Education, 30*(1), 99–115.

Ketterlin-Geller, L., Alonzo, J., Carrizales, D., & Tindal, G. (2005). *Reading between the lines: Testing methods of capturing silent reading fluency.* Eugene, OR: University of Oregon.

Ketterlin-Geller, L., Yovanoff, P., & Tindal, G. (2007). Developing a new paradigm for conducting research on accommodations in mathematics testing. *Exceptional Children, 73,* 331–347.

Marino, M. T., Marino, E. C., & Shaw, S. F. (2006). Making informed assistive technology decisions for students with high incidence disabilities. *TEACHING Exceptional Children, 38*(6), 18–25.

McGregor, G., & Pachuski, P. (1996). Assistive technology in schools: Are teachers ready, able, and supported? *Journal of Special Education Technology, 13,* 4–15.

McKevitt, B. C., & Elliott, S. N. (2001). *The effects and consequences of using testing accommodations on a standardized reading test.* Madison, WI: Wisconsin Center for Education Research.

Miller, S. D., & Smith, D. E. P. (1990). Relations among oral reading, silent reading and listening comprehension of students at differing competency levels. *Reading Research and Instruction, 29,* 73–84.

Shin, J., Deno, S. L., & Espin, C. (2000). Technical adequacy of the maze task for curriculum-based measurement of reading growth. *The Journal of Special Education, 34*(3), 164–172.

Thompson, S. J., Johnstone, C. J., & Thurlow, M. L. (2002). *Universal design applied to large scale assessments* (Synthesis Rep. No. 44). Minneapolis, MN: University of Minnesota, National Center on Educational Outcomes. Retrieved August 5, 2006, from http://education.umn.edu/NCEO/OnlinePubs/Synthesis44.html

Ysseldyke, J., Thurlow, M., Bielinski, J., House, A., Moody, M., & Haigh, J. (2001). The relationship between instructional and assessment accommodations in an inclusive state accountability system. *Journal of Learning Disabilities, 34,* 212–220.

Yule, V. (1987). Assessing children's silent reading. *Educational Researcher, 29,* 192–196.

Zascavage, V. T., & Keefe, C. H. (2004). Students with severe speech and physical impairments: Opportunity barriers to literacy. *Focus on Autism and Other Developmental Disabilities, 19,* 223–234.

CHAPTER 10

Addressing the Importance of Systematically Matching Student Needs and Test Accommodations

REBECCA KOPRIVA
University of Wisconsin

JENNIFER KORAN
University of Maryland

CAROL HEDGSPETH
Howard University

Several authors in the area of accommodations research point out that consistent and appropriate accommodations decision making is critical to the validity of standardized academic testing programs and the ability to properly use scores to compare student performance across states and districts (e.g., Fuchs, Fuchs, Eaton, Hamlett, Binkley, et al., 2000; Hollenbeck, Tindal, & Almond, 1998; Kopriva, 2000; Kopriva, Carr, & Koran, 2006). At the individual level when accommodations decisions are not appropriate to meet the needs of individual students, test results misrepresent their knowledge and skills (Hipolito-Delgado & Kopriva, 2006). At the aggregate level, when accommodations decisions are inconsistent from classroom to classroom or district to district, comparisons across classrooms and districts may be unfair and meaningless (Abedi, 2006; Fuchs, Fuchs, Eaton, Hamlett, Binkley, et. al., 2000; National Center for Education Statistics, 2001).

In the large-scale assessment literature, research on the most effective accommodations for both English language learners (ELLs) and students with disabilities is ongoing. Concurrently—due to the requirements of the No Child Left Behind Act of 2001—movement is also being made to appropriately integrate these students in standardized testing systems designed for the broad range of students being educated in U.S. schools. It is generally believed that accommodations should be selected to meet the needs of the individual student. Research confirms that one cannot validly assign accommodations to groups of students based on some broad classification or status (Sireci, Li, & Scarpati, 2003). Emerging work suggests that systematic methods of assignment may work better than relying on current policy approaches. Further, it presents evidence that using systematic methods to match the particular needs and strengths of individual students to specific accommodations which address these needs and strengths may increase validity and be superior to using educator directed decision making alone (Kopriva, Emick, & Hipolito-Delgado, 2006; Koran, Kopriva, Emick, Monroe & Garavaglia, 2006; Tindal, 2006).

This chapter will review traditional, current, and promising literature associated with how the field assigns accommodations for students who need them. Policy- and research-based approaches will be highlighted and an example of how one team is addressing this need for ELLs will be summarized.

DEFINING THE TASK

Studying test accommodations and understanding how they work can be quite complicated. Tindal and Ketterlin-Geller (2004) note that in accommodations research, "few accommodations can be viewed as single, isolated variables," and that "accommodations are best thought of as a package in which no one accommodation is ever studied very well in isolation" (p. 7). On one hand, test changes that we think of as a single accommodation, such as reading a test aloud to a student, may have multiple facets that remove or contribute construct-irrelevant variance for a particular student. For example, if a test is read aloud to a group of students, it is possible that students may benefit from the effect of having the test administrator pace them through the test, which is different from the benefit derived by having the reading demand of the test eliminated or reduced (Hollenbeck, Rozek-Tedesco, Tindal, & Glasgow, 2000; Weston, 2003).

Furthermore, groups of such accommodations may also be thought of as packages (Hollenbeck et al., 2000), as the multiple facets of various accommodations interact to produce a net increase or decrease in construct-irrelevant variance. Linguistic accommodations in particular (such as different forms of the test that incorporate linguistically oriented changes in the presentation of items or the availability of language aids, for instance a bilingual word list or increased visuals) function most optimally as packages. For example, side-by-side (dual language) administrations require extra time because working back and forth between the two language versions of each item takes more time than completing a comparable test in one language (Choi & McCall, 2002). For ELLs this seems to be particularly true because they may be especially affected by their previous schooling environments, past experiences, and current home environments which may be very different than those associated with mainstream U.S. students (Kopriva, in press).

One may think of multiple possible combinations of accommodations that function together to meet the student's need. One package of accommodations may be considered the preferred package for a particular student although other packages compensate for the student's need nearly as well. For example, an ELL may have a level of English proficiency such that a bilingual word list may not be needed if the student is to receive a form of the test where items are presented in plain or simplified English or in the student's native language. However, if that student were to receive a standard English version of the test form, he or she would need the bilingual word list to help him or her access the items. In selecting accommodations for students with disabilities and ELLs, most accommodation researchers are now recognizing that the package must be tailored to the needs of the individual student. Further, overaccommodating can be just as problematic for the student as not providing the needed accommodations at all (Kopriva, 2005a). Administering a test with all possible accommodations may be overwhelming, and administering a test with improper "bells and whistles" (particularly unnecessary additions to the test items or forms) that are not needed can be distracting (for instance, see Sharrocks-Taylor & Hargreaves, 1999).

The need to make individual accommodations decisions is common to both ELLs and students with disabilities. However, little research has been published regarding the processes used to make accommodations decisions for ELLs. In the next sections selected information on policy-based methods and research approaches for both populations are briefly summarized. Policy methods generally reflect current practice in selecting appropriate test accommodations for individual students in both groups, although the mechanisms associated with these assignments are somewhat different. Research-based methods are emerging which approach the task from the perspective of how theory and empirical literature might help structure the decision process and narrow down choices for students with particular needs.

POLICY-BASED APPROACHES

Current guidelines for selecting accommodations for students with disabilities primarily stems from authorizations of federal legislation (Individuals With Disabilities Education Act, IDEA, 2004). Regulations or instructions for assigning accommodations to individual ELLs, on the other hand, are generally policy-based, most often at the state level. The practice for assigning large-scale accommodations for students with disabilities typically focuses on the role of the individualized education program (IEP). In addition to developing and evaluating each student's learning goals and instructional plans, the IEP addresses the proper test accommodations appropriate for each student at both the classroom and standardized testing levels. Current practices typically used to assign large scale test accommodations to individual ELLs reflect that decisions are generally made by a single person (commonly the student's teacher or the school ELL specialist). A recent review of ELL test accommodations, policies, and practices both across the United States and within certain states and districts confirmed that ELL teachers still are the primary decision makers when it comes to ELL accommodations (Kopriva, Hedgspeth, Koran, & Carr,

2007). Some educational agencies are beginning to use teams of people which are similar to IEP teams for students with disabilities (for instance, parents, teachers, specialists, and administrators) to make the decisions (Kopriva, Carr, & Koran, 2006). However these teams differ in major ways from IEP teams, particularly in the scope of their charge. For English learners the scope is much more constrained and standardized test-focused than that defined under federal statute for students with disabilities.

Some disability researchers emphasize the importance of the IEP as a decision-making process as well as a document (Shriner & DeStefano, 2003). However, the protocol for IEP as a process is often not well defined or straightforward for a team of people to implement, and similar problems may be found in the guidelines for teams making accommodations decisions for ELLs. In both situations guidelines tend to offer broad parameters rather than specific guidance for those who must make accommodations decisions. Both individual teachers and teams making accommodations decisions attempt to work within the policies given to them by the federal, state or local educational agency, but these policies generally do not contain specific recommendations for selecting appropriate accommodations for individual students. Thurlow and colleagues (e.g., Thurlow, Moen, & Wiley 2004; Thurlow, Wiley, & Bielinski, 2002) routinely collect information documenting a great deal of variation and inconsistency in allowed accommodations across states for students with disabilities and ELLs. A more in-depth look at selected agencies found substantial variation in the explicitness and formality of policies for both populations among partner states and districts (Kopriva & Hedgspeth, 2005).

The educational agency using the ELL team decision-making approach assembled teams that were composed of a campus administrator, bilingual educator, transitional language educator, and a parent of an ELL student (not the child's parent). While this local education agency (LEA) is to be commended for bringing multiple perspectives together to make decisions, specific guidelines for choosing accommodations for ELLs with specific needs were sparse and spread out over multiple manuals. This makes the guidelines less straightforward for a team of people with varying backgrounds to work effectively together to make good accommodations decisions. Even when team members are well versed, Swierzbin, Anderson, Spicuzza, Walz, and Thurlow (1999) express concern that IEP teams with similar compositions (combinations of parents and school personnel) in similar circumstances (working with written guidelines presented in a text format and handed down by the state education agency) struggle to make consistent decisions across students and districts.

At present, both ELL individuals or teams and IEP teams tend to rely heavily on the implicit and ill-defined sense of knowledge about the student obtained from the child's primary teacher(s) and/or well-meaning adults. Research on accommodations decisions for students with disabilities shows that, with little additional guidance, they tend to be inconsistent decision makers when it comes to assigning appropriate accommodations for individual students. Ysseldyke, Thurlow, McGrew, and Shriner (1994) cite vague accommodations guidelines and altruistic motivations (such as assigning an accommodation to lessen emotional distress to the student rather than because the student needs the accommodation to receive a valid score) on the part of the local decision making team as contributing to the inconsistencies found in assigning accommodations for students with disabilities. Fuchs, Fuchs, Eaton, Hamlett, Binkley, et al. (2000) found that teacher judgments about whether to assign accommodations for students with disabilities were associated

with some demographic and performance variables where there were no such associations with the accommodations decisions made by an objective accommodations decision making system.

Douglas (2004) found that ELL teachers had difficulty articulating the specific decision-making process that they use in assigning accommodations. Koran and Kopriva (2006) found that teacher recommendations, unfortunately, were not statistically different from random assignment of accommodations to ELL students. This was true when teachers were asked to provide guidance without additional training from that provided by their states or districts. However, it was true even when the teachers took the leadership role themselves in a standard data collection process designed especially for this purpose. Similarly, Fuchs, Fuchs, Eaton, Hamlett, Binkley, et al. (2000) reported that teacher judgments did not correspond very well to students with learning disabilities demonstrated differential boost using each of three accommodations on different alternated forms of a reading assessment. In another study, teachers predicted with no more than a chance level which special education students benefited from read-aloud accommodation on a mathematics test (Helwig & Tindal, 2003). Further, Weston (2003) found that teachers did not do any better than chance at predicting which students with learning disabilities would gain the most from a read-aloud accommodation on a mathematics achievement test. Of interest, however, Koran and Kopriva found that teachers could easily and clearly specify the different needs of students. What they appeared to struggle with was the assignment of accommodations to students based on these particular needs. This was echoed in a recent Plake and Impara (2006) report where educator experts of students with disabilities could reliably differentiate needs of students across a broad spectrum of disability but had trouble linking these needs to appropriate accommodations. It seems that, while teachers may be proficient in identifying needs of individual students, at this time they have problems assigning differential testing accommodations based on these needs.

The focus group results reported by Douglas (2004) were revealing of the strategies ELL teachers use when given imprecise guidelines for making accommodations decisions for individual ELLs. In particular, teachers seem to work within the guidelines given to them, such as policies restricting the range of allowable accommodations, but, in general, they assumed that more accommodations were better. This is consistent with researchers' findings that teachers tend to over-assign accommodations for students with disabilities (Fuchs, Fuchs, Eaton, Hamlett, Binkley, et al., 2000; Fuchs, Fuchs, Eaton, Hamlett, & Karns, 2000) and that accommodations decisions tend to be an "all or nothing" phenomenon (DeStefano, Shriner, & Lloyd, 2001). The common attitudes seemed to be "When in doubt, give the accommodation" and "If you are going to accommodate, give them everything you can." In large-scale assessments, the focus groups suggested that teachers felt it was better to have a higher rate of false positives (giving accommodations to students who don't truly need them) so as to reduce the chance of false negatives (failing to assign an accommodation to a student who really needs it).

In general, present policies did not provide the level of explicit instruction necessary to allow teachers to make reliable decisions. Among the policies there appear to be few student-specific guidelines for assigning specific types of accommodations. As such, it does not appear that the policy-based guidance alone would provide appropriate guidance for making specific accommodations decisions for individual students who need them. It is hoped that, with more specific training and additional information to make good decisions, both

the rates of false positives and false negatives could be decreased. An early computer-based system, the Minnesota Online Decision-Making Tool, used a policy-based approach for making accommodations decisions with students with disabilities and ELLs (Anderson & Spicuzza, n.d.; Swierzbin et al., 1999). This model provided little support, however, for answering the questions of whether the student needed accommodations and which accommodations would meet that student's needs. It did attempt to systematize a process, though, that to date had been given only scant attention. Further, a pilot of this system found mixed initial acceptance among IEP team members who used the system in making accommodations decisions for students with disabilities (Swierzbin et al.). Recently, Elliott (2006) has developed a structured approach for focusing IEP teams on systematically addressing the diverse needs of the students with disabilities population. Rivera and Collum (2006) provided theory-driven guidance for teachers and districts about how they might better approach the assignment of accommodations based on linguistic student-specific variables, but no research on how this will work has been found to date.

Some authors attribute poor educator and possibly parent judgment with regard to assigning accommodations to inadequate training in the areas of measurement, standardized assessment, and accommodations (Hollenbeck et al. 1998). Indeed, DeStefano, Shriner, and Lloyd (2001) found that their intensive and comprehensive teacher training program improved the quality and extent of accommodations decisions for students with disabilities. However, their results were confounded with two substantial changes in the state's testing program that may have also contributed to dramatic changes in accommodations decisions (Shriner & DeStefano, 2003). Although it is important that teachers receive proper training in the areas of measurement, standardized assessment, and accommodations, teacher training alone may not entirely solve the problem. Fuchs, Fuchs, Eaton, Hamlett, Binkley, et al. (2000) found that even when teachers read background information about test accommodations, discussed and reviewed this information with a research assistant, and had the opportunity to ask questions about the material, they still did not do a good job at assigning accommodations. Their work suggests that increased teacher education with regard to accommodations in general, by itself may not be sufficient to improve accommodations decision making.

In other areas of standardized testing, such as grading constructed responses and setting cut scores, human judgment is commonly and successfully used within highly structured, defined, and systematic approaches that involve routine oversight and auditing mechanisms. That is, detailed guidelines are given, judges are trained, and checks are put in place to assure the quality and consistency of the decisions. To not take a systematic approach to the assignment of accommodations seems to represent a breakdown of the systematized chain of evidence that leads to valid inferences (Mislevy, 1994). Such an approach to accommodations decision making may help ensure not only the quality of the decision, but also the consistency of the decisions across students, both of which are needed in order to make meaningful comparisons across schools, districts, and states. There has been a call for more systematized accommodation decision support systems for students with disabilities (e.g., Solomon et al., 2001).

With ELLs, as with students with disabilities, there are many critical variables to consider in each student's background and many potential options for meeting the student's need. A structured systematic approach is probably necessary in providing support for the decision makers who must take so much information into account in making the decisions, and more attention needs to be paid to assure that the essential decision-making elements are being included and fairly utilized.

RESEARCH-BASED APPROACHES

There are a few possible research-based approaches for assigning accommodations to individual students based on their unique needs. Such systems are generally not intended to take the place of the persons who currently make accommodations decisions for ELLs and students with disabilities, but rather, they are intended to provide a solid recommendation of accommodations which can be used as a basis for the person or team making accommodations decisions. In describing and discussing these approaches, we distinguish between those which are inductive and deductive in nature. Both foundations hold the promise of guiding high quality, consistent accommodations decisions. Each approach discussed combines a data collection phase with an accommodations assignment phase. Kopriva (2005b) and others (Kopriva, Carr, and Koran (2006) have recently emphasized that there appear to be four steps to developing a proper method for assigning accommodations, not just two. Key variables need to be identified, data need to be systematically collected, data from multiple sources needs to be thoughtfully combined in order to inform the assignment process, and, finally, a logic method of assignment that fairly and sensitively recognizes and matches salient student and accommodation characteristics needs to be built and implemented.

In most approaches where information must be combined to make an accommodations recommendation, building the system on a computer-based platform has been found to be quite valuable. Computerized decision support technology has been used successfully for many years in other fields, such as business, medicine, and law enforcement. Unlike in many noneducational situations where computerized decision support systems have been found to be helpful for improving expert judgment, teachers and any other team members are not called upon to routinely make large-scale test accommodations decisions on a daily basis. This constitutes an even more powerful reason for developing systems to help agencies make good accommodations decisions. Yet there seems to be a reluctance or lack of resources to develop this technology in order to address some of the more problematic decision-making problems in education. It is only very recently that researchers in education have begun investigating ways in which computerized decision support systems may contribute to accommodations decision making for individual students.

Inductive Methods

In making accommodations decisions for ELLs and students with disabilities, it is possible to take an approach that is inductive, that is, to take specific incidences and make some sort of generalization. One reasonable inductive approach for assigning accommodations to individual students is the direct trial-and-error approach. In this approach different accommodations are tried with a student, one at a time or one package at a time, to see which ones help the student perform better in testing. This approach has been applied both informally and formally in making accommodations decisions for individual students. In the focus groups with ELL educators, many of them stated that they used an informal trial-and-error approach to calibrate the appropriate accommodations for a specific student by trying various accommodations in the classroom and tracking which accommodations worked best with that student (Douglas, 2004). Teachers felt they could use their observations to inform their accommodations decision making for large-scale testing even in the face of

a lack of clear, consistent guidelines for assigning specific accommodations to individual students.

One set of researchers has proposed and applied a formalized empirical version of this approach with students with disabilities (Fuchs, Fuchs, Eaton, Hamlett, Binkley, et al, 2000; Fuchs, Fuchs, Eaton, Hamlett, & Karns, 2000). In this method the student is administered a short mini-test without accommodations and other parallel forms of the mini-test with a different accommodation each time. The boost in performance on each accommodated mini-test over the performance on the unaccommodated mini-test is calculated and compared against normative data for general education students who did not need accommodations. If the student's boost exceeds a certain cutoff in the normative data, then the student is deemed to need the accommodation. The researchers found they could successfully predict for which students test scores on a large standardized test would improve substantially when administered with the specific accommodation or accommodations supported by the mini-test data. Recently, these researchers have published their operational approach which uses this methodology. It is known as DATA, the Dynamic Assessment of Test Accommodations (Fuchs, Fuchs, Eaton, & Hamlett, 2005).

The formalized trial and error approach seems to effectively identify students who stand to benefit from test accommodations in research situations. However, limited work has been done to identify how well this works for large-scale testing purposes on a routine basis. Further, in contrast to a formalized trial and error approach, it has not been documented that informal teacher trial and error is effective in the same way. Other limitations need to be considered as well. First, this method is clearly time-consuming. This needs to be taken into account for high school classes or other situations in which the teachers or specialists work with many students. Second, unfortunately, the mini-testing can confound itself with some accommodation needs, such as the need for more frequent breaks. Testing conditions for the accommodation assignments need to be as close to those for which the accommodations are being considered. This is particularly important for large-scale testing where several conditions, including test length and duration over days, are usually constrained.

Third, while Fuchs, Fuchs, Eaton, Hamlett, & Karns (2000) found that their systematic formal approach was effective, small *n*'s suggest caution. Fourth, as with any approach, students need enough time to practice any accommodation. This is true whether the students are preparing for a test or for the trial and error assignment process. Finally, the pure trial and error approach typically does not account for interaction effects when multiple accommodations are needed, unless packages are tried out as well as individual accommodations. Other researchers are investigating the use of a hybrid form which combines trial and error and other methods. These and others will be considered next.

Deductive Methods

Deductive approaches based on theory, or generalized notions which have been found to hold promise, also have been proposed. Theory-driven deductive approaches focus on identifying critical factors that are related to the individual needs of students and the active characteristics of test accommodations. Abedi (Chapter 2 in this book) emphasizes that only a small subset of accommodations is most appropriate for ELLs. In reviewing the ELL literature for key student indicators, the researchers who developed the system compiled a list of 139 different variables important for learning and evaluation in general. For the particular purpose of large-scale testing accommodations, however, their analysis found that only a small number of these seemed to be salient

for this type of situation. The extensive review was useful, however, because it helped to identify some nuances not generally considered in large-scale assessment to date, and provided information which could be used in the development of the logic systems. For example, August, Calderon, & Gottlieb (2004) reported that access to bilingual glossaries have been found to be effective for understanding test requirements in English when ELL students have at least some literacy in their home language. This is because they could transfer cognate cues across languages. The students did not need to be fully literate in their home language to begin using this skill; however, the more literate they were in their native language the more they could avail themselves of this benefit. Her work provided guidance to the developers of the system about how to assign this accommodation and to whom.

Theory-driven approaches have been classified as those that focus on a direct assessment of ancillary skills and those which use an informant approach. The hybrid system will be discussed in the next section.

Direct Assessment of Ancillary Skills. This approach attempts to directly assess selected ancillary skills of individual students that are unrelated to what the test is intending to measure but may block the student's access to the test if he or she does not have a sufficient command of this skill. Skills related to what the test is intended to measure may also be used provided they are predictive of what accommodations would help the student overcome access barriers in taking the test. Researchers interested in improving accommodations decisions for students with disabilities have attempted to use measures of ancillary skills, in particular reading, to predict whether those students would benefit from a specific accommodation (Helwig & Tindal, 2003). Tindal and others have also included measures of these skills in more comprehensive systems, such as their recent method, the Accommodation Station, which is identifying and evaluating the impact of selected student data related to accommodations and what that might mean for accommodations assignment (Ketterlin-Geller, 2003; Tindal, 2006). Directly measuring the level of access skills within the assignment system may be helpful in selecting individual accommodations for ELLs, particularly because some of the skills clearly impact student access to large-scale tests in other content areas as they are currently conceived.

Like the trial-and-error approach, the direct assessment of ancillary skills involves testing the student directly. Thus, the measurement of the particular ancillary skills must also be accurate to get valid results, and this in itself, is a large undertaking. For those who assess ancillary skills, specific domain and theory-driven variables need to be identified and measured, and logic about how to combine these to obtain proficiency levels would need to occur. Initial attempts at this approach that used an assignment system to making accommodations decisions for students with disabilities were largely unsuccessful (Ketterlin-Geller, 2003). A current project is attempting to build on this work by beginning to identify decision-making logic partially informed by the ancillary skills information that the latest version of the Accommodation Station provides (Siskind, 2004; Tindal, 2006).

Although Tindal's (2006) method utilizes a direct measure of some skills, he and others also recognize and have attempted to incorporate other "informant data" in their system. Helwig & Tindal (2003) used reading and math pretest scores to try to build student profiles that might better predict whether students with disabilities would benefit from having the read-aloud accommodation. However, the results were often in conflict and their system did not perform much better than teacher judgment. They suggested that their analysis failed to take into account a potentially critical variable,

namely the linguistic complexity of the items in their test of ancillary skills. This complexity is widely recognized in the ELL literature (see Kopriva, 2000; Abedi, Courtney, Mirocha, Leon, & Goldberg, 2001; Abedi, Lord, Hoffstetter, & Baker, 2000). Student performance with accommodations related to linguistics can be very complicated behavior to model and predict because of possible interactions with the characteristics of the test items. As such, data on the language complexity of the large-scale assessment the student will be using seems to be necessary in determining the effectiveness of some accommodations. Helwig and Tindal also speculated that their system was too simplistic and failed to benefit from the teachers' intimate knowledge of their own students. They proposed that math and reading screening test scores in tandem with teacher knowledge of individual students might produce better accommodations decisions. Lately, Tindal (2006) has attempted to address this limitation by including questionnaire data from teachers and the students. Finally, Tindal's current system uses some of the Fuchs and Fuchs (1999) trial-and-error methodology in that they test students with and without a read-aloud accommodation. To date, it is unclear how data from the direct assessment of ancillary skills, the informant data, and the trial and error data will be combined to provide guidance to IEP teams (Tindal). Structuring a system that incorporates different methods, however, is interesting, and it is anticipated future work will focus on these next steps.

Informant Approach. The informant approach relies directly on the insights of those who know the student personally and/or other extant skill information such as that which would be available in the student's record or about the large-scale academic test materials and conditions. In this sense, it has benefits over the other approaches discussed so far because it is not limited to skills or needs that can be tested or measured directly. In fact, it may not be necessary for the student to be directly involved in the process at all. Using this approach, information about the student may be collected from one source only (for instance, the teacher) or gathered from multiple sources, such as the student, the student's teacher, and the student's parent. As defined here, the informant approach is distinct from the policy-based teacher or team approaches in that specific information is gathered using standard instruments which focus on critical variables and is specifically designed for the purpose of assigning large-scale test accommodations. It does not rely solely on instinct or sources of information about students and accommodations that are vaguely and implicitly utilized and combined in a nonstandard way. On the other hand, depending on the informed source(s) and whether it is collecting data obtained from other test(s) or relying on the judgment of adult(s) who know the student well, the informant approach may rely on systematically collected information that is skewed (human judgment of parents or teachers) or outdated (for instance, information in the student record). The quality of the data relies on the quality of the information gained from the informant sources. Further, the quality of the decision is dependent on the quality of the informant's knowledge and the acumen of the system developer who interprets theory and research findings and builds the algorithms. Like any approach, the quality also is bound to be variable for different students.

No literature has been found which systematically links only student records information and accommodations assignments for large-scale assessments for students with disabilities or ELLs. Likewise, no research has been reported which combines uniformly collected information about student needs collected from only one "human" source (for instance teachers or parents) with this one human source making assign-

ments based on this information. As noted earlier, Koran and Kopriva (2006) reported results when ELL teachers, by themselves, were asked to assign accommodations based on a standard collection of data from multiple sources, including themselves. Even when standard instruments were used, teacher assignments proved to be no better than a random assignment of accommodations for individual students.

It may be argued that, when multiple sources are consulted, the informant approach may mark an improvement over the policy-based team approach not only by formalizing the contribution from each informant, but also by separating the role of student advocate from that of primary decision maker. Douglas (2004) concluded that ELL teachers felt, in the policy-based methods currently in use today, that they are asked to simultaneously take on competing roles as both expert decision maker and student advocate. This may present a dilemma for teachers who are asked to make decisions with minimal guidelines and support while maintaining the best interests of the child. Koran and Kopriva (2006) and Plake and Impara (2006) suggest that educators may be better at some roles than others in this accommodation assignment process.

The Selection Taxonomy for English Language Learner Accommodations (STELLA), the newly developed system for ELLs, discussed next, utilizes findings from the multiple sources and systematic student data collection procedures. It identifies critical variables, collects data, combines the data with standard information regarding how accommodations perform, and then uses a standard series of computerized algorithms based in theory and formative empirical input (Kopriva, Carr, & Cho, 2006; Kopriva, Hedgspeth et al., 2007). Two initial verification studies found that this system seems to be producing appropriate decisions for individual students.

STELLA

Although there has been more written about how to match students with disabilities with appropriate test accommodations, very little prior research had been conducted to look into the testing needs of individual ELLs and establish systems for matching them with appropriate test accommodations. STELLA has been developed over the last 3 years and is in a draft final form (Kopriva, 2002; Kopriva, 2005b; Kopriva & Carr, 2005; Kopriva, Carr, & Koran, 2006). STELLA was built by researchers at the Center for the Study of Assessment Validity and Evaluation, now at the University of Wisconsin, in partnership with several states and districts (South Carolina Department of Education, North Carolina Department of Public Instruction, Maryland Department of Education, Austin, Texas, Unified School District, and the District of Columbia Public Schools). STELLA is intended to be used with K–12 students to assign accommodations to the range of ELL students for use on large-scale academic assessments. It is a computerized system, research-based, and empirically developed and verified. It has been built, most recently, from research conducted as part of two large, multi-year projects. STELLA is continuing to be refined and it is anticipated that a beta version will be available to the public in 2007.

STELLA uses a multisource, informant data collection method where information is obtained from student records and relevant test scores, from teachers, and from parents or guardians. A complex series of algorithms take the data from each source, converts applicable information to common scales, consolidates data from more than one source or more than one related question, and finally, applies results to a decision-making system that systematically connects student needs to appropriate accommodation characteristics. The flexible computerized platform was designed to adjust to the needs and obligations of different users, and has been designed to be compatible with and flexible enough to accommodate information from a direct approach if future research suggests this is a viable addition to the system. The output for each individual student is designed to select appropriate accommodations from each agency's set of allowable accommodations. The output also illustrates accommodations STELLA would recommend that are not currently allowable. Including any additional STELLA recommended accommodations provides information for teachers and others who are not constrained by legislatively defined sets of accommodations. This output also provides users some guidance about how policies may be improved in the future for individual students. Finally, a student profile is produced that provides additional information to teachers and other interested parties about the particular needs and strengths of students. In its present form STELLA does not involve the student directly. Thus, it can be used with students who are quite young.

Relevant student factors that were addressed in STELLA can be found in Figures 10-1 to 10-4. They include salient information about English and home language proficiency in the four domains (reading, writing, speaking, and listening). Additionally, select cultural proximity data are collected. Cultural proximity is defined as the similarity between the student's native country schooling (if applicable) and selected home school-like experiences, relative to U.S. schooling and testing opportunities. Information obtained focuses on native country schooling experiences, including resources, time and pedagogical approaches, and purposes of testing. The time and consistency of their experience in U.S. schools is also obtained under this category as this is an ongoing issue with this population of students. Finally, information on teacher judgments of student needs and strengths, and U.S. ongoing classroom experiences with

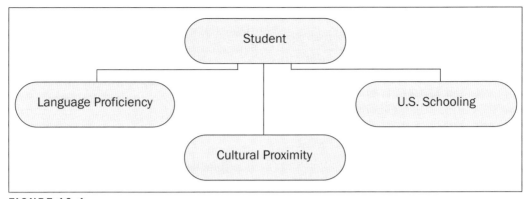

FIGURE 10-1

Overview of Relevant Student Factors

accommodations and other testing forms and formats are collected. In this system teachers are not asked to recommend large-scale accommodations.

At the present time, the data collection records form is based on information that is in the student's file at the school, such as English language and native language proficiency test scores and other information about the student's schooling in the United States. The teacher form is based on observations the teacher has made about the student's needs, language proficiencies on an ongoing basis in the classroom as well as compensatory preferences and classroom accommodation experiences. The parent/guardian form is based on an interview with the student's parent or guardian regarding the student's proficiency in the home language, prior schooling opportunities, and prior experiences with classroom and standardized testing.

Seventeen promising accommodations were selected and preloaded into the STELLA system. These accommodations were selected based on an analysis of their active characteristics and what affect each has in addressing the ELL students' needs or strengths (or both). The list of these can be found in Table 10-1. Also preloaded and recommended as appropriate are two types of pretest accommodations support approaches: a family assessment night and individually

tailored classroom support. The former type of support focuses on working with the family to understand the cultural experiences of the students as they relate to attitudes and experiences with testing and impact how students might be able to conceive of both classroom and standardized U.S. assessment experiences in the future. The latter focuses on a range of support that a teacher can provide to students which addresses considerations native language students take for granted (such as, practice with types of items that ask questions and items that ask for student's original thinking). Some indicators about a student's classroom needs are part of the output in the STELLA system and are designed to be utilized to support pretest opportunities in one or both ways. More information about the importance and types of pretest support useful for ELLs can be found in Emick, Kopriva, Monroe and Malagon-Sprehn (2006).

Another project offered important early insights into salient student and accommodation characteristics and how a matching model using an informant approach might work as an operational system. The Valid Assessment of ELLs (VAELL) project was funded in 2001 and was recently completed (Kopriva & Mislevy, 2001, 2005). In the project some relatively simple matching systems were developed, each designed exclusively for the specific accommodations study

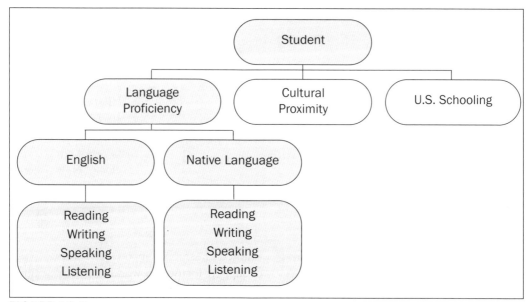

FIGURE 10-2

Relevant Language Proficiency Student Factors

at hand (Emick & Kopriva, 2007; Kopriva, Emick, Winter, & Chen, 2006). Because the focus of this first project was elsewhere, the second project built on this work and focused exclusively on developing a rigorous assignment system for ELLs (Kopriva, 2002). Once funding was retained, the forms were conceptualized, designed, and developed after extensive developmental work that (a) reviewed current large-scale and instructional accommodation literature, (b) conducted focus groups, (c) obtained recommendations from

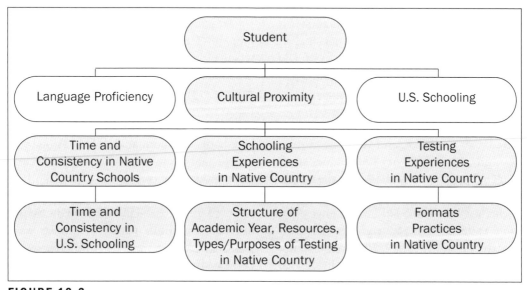

FIGURE 10-3

Relevant Cultural Proximity Student Factors

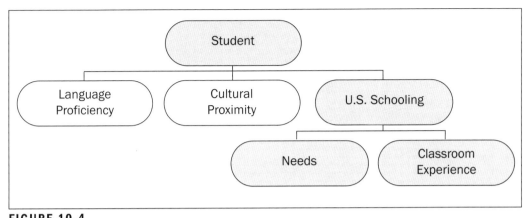

FIGURE 10-4

Relevant U.S. Schooling Student Factors

targeted practitioners, and (d) subsequently narrowed down the most salient student variables. Key variables were selected and interviews with teachers and parents combined with feedback from partner educational agency staff refined the questions on the forms. Concurrently, project staff, with guidance from educational agency participants, built on knowledge gleaned from the earlier project, identified the most promising accommodations, and completed an evaluation of the active characteristics of the final set of accommodations. Algorithms were developed by project staff and consultants and were reviewed and edited by partners and an expert panel (see Kopriva, et al., 2007 and Kopriva, Carr, and Koran, 2006 for an explanation of the formative studies and related development work).

Once the STELLA system was completed, two validation and verification studies were conducted in 2005. One study collected data on the feasibility of the system (Kopriva & Hedgspeth, 2005). It also researched how the STELLA findings compared to teacher recommended assignments (Koran & Kopriva, 2006). Nineteen teachers who spanned the range of K–12 participated from three states, each selecting six beginner to advanced ELL students for which to submit data. A total of 114 sets of data were completed with each set comprised of three completed forms per student. Feasibility results showed that teachers, who were the coordinators of the data collection on each student, could clearly identify needs of diverse students across schools and states. Findings also suggested that the system, in general, collected consistent data from like questions over forms, to be used for triangulation and confirmatory purposes, and that each form also appeared to contribute unique data about each student from the unique vantage point of each source.

In addition to completing the STELLA protocols for their students, the participating teachers were also asked to provide their own accommodation recommendations for each student at three points during the form completion process; before the forms were completed, directly after the data collection and based only on information STELLA had collected, and then later with any additional information they considered to be important about each student (but which was not represented on the STELLA forms). Subsequently, a blind panel of three ELL practitioners and an ELL researcher were convened and asked to independently rate how each of the teacher accommodation recommendations, the STELLA recommendations, and a randomly generated set of

TABLE 10-1

Preloaded Accommodations

Test Forms	Standard or some Universal Design forms
	Access-based form (These are forms for the emerging language learner. They include minimal language and central use of compensatory additions which, for the purposes of apprehension, support the use of avenues other than reading. The use of visuals would be one frequently used compensatory strategy that is often used in tests.)
	Native language or dual language forms as available
Tools	Bilingual word list, general or test specific
	Picture-word dictionary
	Problem-solving tools (An example of problem-solving tools are mathematics manipulatives.)
Administration	Oral English
	Oral home language
	Small group
	Individual administration
	Language liaison/small group (Language liaisons are trained L1 aides who have constrained responsibilities with new arrivals.)
	Extra time
	More frequent breaks
Response	Written in native language or code switching (Code switching is when students use both English and their native language. This often occurs within sentences or even phrases.)
	Oral English
	Oral in native language or code switching
	Demonstrated or modeled response (Most often feasible on computer-based tests, this is when students can drag and click or otherwise demonstrate their response without any language.)

accommodations compared to the data on the forms. These raters did not know the students; rather, they made their ratings after reviewing form data for each of the 114 students. Rater findings were subjected to goodness of fit analyses which determined how well the panel ratings fit the student data that occurred on the teacher, parent, and records forms. Results indicated that STELLA was found to consistently and significantly be the best fit, over students and over all recommendation alternatives. However, teacher recommendations disappointedly did not prove to be different from each other even as teachers potentially learned more about their students during data collection. Nor were any of these teacher recommendations significantly different from the random assignment. No significant recommendations were obtained from teachers about any additional kind of information needed to be added to the STELLA forms to properly assign students to accommodations.

The second study investigated if students who received selected STELLA-recommended accommodations performed better on the test relative to those who received improper accommodations or no accommodations whatsoever (Kopriva, Emick, & Hipolito-Delgado, 2006; Kopriva, Hedgspeth et al., 2007). It was designed to provide information about the validity and effectiveness of particular STELLA assignments utilized in the study. Initially, 276 third- and fourth-grade South Carolina ELL students who spanned the range of English language proficiency completed a computerized mathematics test under randomly assigned accommodations that were implemented electronically as the students took the test. Three accommodations were used (oral English, bilingual word translation, and picture-word "translation") and students randomly received one, two, or three of them. One group received no accommodations. Afterwards, additional data about the students was used to assign students to one of the three groups (proper accommodations, improper accommodations, or no accommodations), as per the STELLA framework. Findings showed that students who received proper accommodations performed significantly better on the test than either students receiving improper accommodations or no accommodations. It also showed that students who received inappropriate accommodations (as per the STELLA assignment) scored no better than those who received no accommodations. This study not only verifies the reasonableness of the affected STELLA assignments, but also suggests how important it is for students to receive proper accommodations versus improper ones.

It is anticipated that future work with STELLA will continue to investigate its usefulness and effectiveness. Developers are interested in studying if the system works well for ELL students of all backgrounds and at all proficiency and grade levels.

IMPLICATIONS

No matter how adroitly and carefully accommodations are selected and created, if they do not get to the students who need them, they are not useful. Emerging research suggests that use of improper accommodations may result in scores that are not substantially more valid for these students than if they received no accommodations. This is very troubling for many reasons but particularly two. First, individual performance on large-scale academic tests and scores may misrepresent the skills of students who do not receive proper accommodations. This can have profound consequences for future learning opportunities for these students, including improper placement or other student-level decisions, as well as inappropriately impacting educational agency level decisions and possibly resource allocations. Second, improper accommodations may help explain why the findings from accommodations research have, to date, been so mixed. It may be suggested that only when researchers employ rigorous means of matching students to accommodations they are empirically testing will their work provide clearer results about which options are useful and which are not. Currently, many of us are left with the vague notion of which accommodations are helpful but we're not sure how or when. The real question may well be "Useful for whom?" It is argued here that this is the question researchers should be investigating.

Many student factors are critical in understanding how to properly instruct ELLs and students with disabilities. This chapter suggests that a subset of these key indicators appear to be salient in determining which large-scale testing options a student should receive, especially as long as standard assessments of academic content remain similar to those which are currently in use today. Test purposes, environments, standardized conditions that assume few if any procedural or material adaptations and reliance on written language (most typically in English) mean that some student issues as compared to others take on more importance in the current testing climate. Likewise, certain accommodations or testing options should be clearly highlighted as being especially useful for students with certain needs or strengths. In tandem, the recognition of these characteristics appears to set the stage for developing matching systems which can be useful for both practitioners and researchers.

To date, the form that these systems should take is not entirely clear. Simple policy guidelines do not appear to be sufficient. It is possible more specific guidance may be helpful and effective, with some type of systematic training and rigorous oversight procedures in place. Certainly, teachers often know the students well, and IEP teams utilized with students with disabilities, suggest that other personnel, or even the students themselves provide important and unique insights. Relying exclusively on the knowledge and time associated with compiling materials, educating and utilizing overtaxed educators, parents and students, however, may not be practical or reasonable even though in less demanding circumstances they may be "up to the task." Also, research suggests teachers or other educational specialists are particularly well positioned to identify needs but, to date, appear to struggle with how to assign accommodations. This may or may not extend to parents, other school personnel, and students. Computerized systems that guide personnel through the policy process provide standardization and, in the future, may also provide selected educational opportunities as the needs arise within more complex programs.

Electronic systems that provide differential boost information or that directly test the levels of students' ancillary skills are interesting because they provide up-to-date needs information that offset records or other data which may be dated or educator judgments that may be skewed. However, to date, they appear to be time consuming for students. Informant approaches should help streamline the process; however, unless stringent evaluation is part of development and ongoing implementation, they may provide a too-simplistic set of recommendations which would not properly address the nuanced and ever-changing needs of these populations. All in all, it appears that theory-driven systems need to be computerized as long as the algorithms appropriately address the complex realities associated with accommodations assignment.

As system designs mature, they need to have the ability to handle relevant data in such a way that sensitive decisions can be made not only for each student, but consistently and even-handedly across students. It is also anticipated that most future systems will be hybrids in some form or another. Such systems will need to have the capacity to prompt, include and combine large numbers of discrete pieces of information in complicated ways with ease and be able to update frequently and store algorithms and output for use by different educational agencies. All in all, methodologies would probably represent variations of expert (or knowledge-based) systems used in other disciplines (see Wright & Bolger, 1992) where sources include humans as well as other knowledge-based data about students and characteristics of testing practices. Whereas more attention is being given to getting the right accommodations options matched with the right students based on individual student need, the next link in a valid inferential chain is making sure that the accommodations actually get administered to the student, and get administered properly. Limited research and practical experiences suggest that there may be issues with implementing test accommodations that have been recommended through current operational processes (e.g., Jayanthi, Epstein, Polloway, & Bursuck, 1996; Solomon, Jerry, & Lutkus, 2001).

Finally, some researchers envision accommodation assignment approaches that are integrated into computerized content area testing systems. Kopriva, Carr, and Cho (2006) and Kopriva (in press) discuss future testing systems that are sensitive to a number of nuances about the ELL students and alter accommodations by item. These systems would not only allow for matching algorithms to operate in them, such as that produced by STELLA, but they would include algorithms that address item characteristic data which are more finely tuned to student needs. For instance, Solano-Flores, Trumbull, and Nelson-Barber (2002) suggest that ELL students differentially use native language or English items when presented with dual language forms. While others (e.g., Duncan et al., 2005) suggest students use primarily one form or another, Solano-Flores suggests that his more fine-grain research points to small preferences depending on a number of linguistic factors. In a similar fashion, Ketterlin-Geller (2003) predicts that the students with disabilities' Accommodation Station may one day implement recommended accommodations directly within a computer-administered academic test system. That is, similar to the thinking of Kopriva and others, she suggests that the accommodations matching system could be embedded in a larger assessment system that also administers the accommodations.

REFERENCES

Abedi, J. (2006, April). *Accommodations for English language learners that may alter the construct being measured.* Presentation at the Annual American Educational Researchers Association, San Francisco, CA.

Abedi, J., Courtney, M., Mirocha, L., Leon, S., & Goldberg, J. (2001). *Language accommodation for large-scale assessment in science.* Los Angeles: UCLA, National Center for Research on Evaluation, Standards, and Student Testing.

Abedi, J., Lord, C., Hoffstetter, C., & Baker, E. (2000). Impact of accommodation strategies on English language learners' test performance. *Educational Measurement: Issues and Practice, 19*(3): 16–26.

Anderson, M., & Spicuzza, R. (n.d.) Minnesota Assessment Project decision making tool. Minnesota Assessment Project, Minnesota Department of Children, Families and Learning and National Center on Educational Outcomes (NCEO). Retrieved on May 9, 2005, from http://education.umn.edu/nceo/map/

August, D., Calderon, M., & Gottlieb, M. (2004, October). *Developing literacy in English language learners: Key issues and promising practices.* Paper presented at the third annual summit of the Office of English Language Acquisition, Washington, DC.

Choi, S. W., & McCall, M. (2002). Linking bilingual mathematics assessments: A monolingual IRT approach. In G. Tindal and T. M. Haladyna (Eds.), *Large-scale assessment programs for all students.* Hillsdale, NJ: Lawrence Erlbaum.

DeStefano, L., Shriner, J., & Lloyd, C. (2001). Teacher decision making in participation of students with disabilities in large-scale assessment. *Exceptional Children, 68,* 7–22.

Douglas, K. (2004). *Teacher ideas on teaching and testing English language learners: Summary of focus group discussions* (Tech. Rep. No. 246). University of Wisconsin, Center for the Study of Assessment Validity and Evaluation.

Duncan, T. G., Rio Parent, L., Chen, W. H., Ferrara, S., Johnson, E., Oppler, S., et al. (2005). Study of a dual-language test booklet in eighth-grade mathematics. *Applied Measurement in Education, 18*(2), 129–161.

Elliott, S. N. (2006, March). *Selecting accommodations wisely: facilitating test access and enhancing implementation integrity.* Presentation at the Accommodating Students with Disabilities on State Assessments: What Works? Conference, Savannah, GA.

Emick, J. & Kopriva, R. J. (2007, April). *The validity of large-scale assessment scores for ELLs under optimal testing conditions: does validity vary by language proficiency?* Presentation at the American Education Research Association Annual Meeting, Chicago, Il.

Emick, J., Kopriva, R. J., Monroe, R., & Malagon-Sprehn, M. (2006). Culture, education, and testing in the United States: A novel response. *Educational Measurement: Issues and Practices*. Manuscript submitted for publication.

Fuchs, L. S., & Fuchs, D. (1999) Fair and unfair testing accommodations. *School Administrator, 56*(10) 24–29.

Fuchs, L., Fuchs, D., Eaton, S. B., & Hamlett, C. B. (2005). *Dynamic assessment of test accommodations*. San Antonio, TX: Psych Corporation.

Fuchs, L. S., Fuchs, D., Eaton, S. B., Hamlett, C. B., Binkley, E., & Crouch, R. (2000). Using objective data sources to enhance teacher judgments about test accommodations. *Exceptional Children, 67*, 67–81.

Fuchs, L., Fuchs, D., Eaton, S. B., Hamlett, C. B., & Karns, K. M. (2000). Supplementing teacher judgments of mathematics test accommodations with objective data sources. *School Psychology Review, 29*(1), 65–85.

Helwig, R., & Tindal, G. (2003). An experimental analysis of accommodation decisions on large-scale mathematics tests. *Exceptional Children, 69*, 211–225.

Hipolito-Delgado, C., & Kopriva, R. J. (2006, April). *Assessing the Selection Taxonomy for English Language Learner Accommodation (STELLA)*. Paper presented at the annual meeting of the American Educational Research Association, San Francisco, CA.

Hollenbeck, K., Rozek-Tedesco, M. A., Tindal, G., & Glasgow, A. (2000). An exploratory study of student-paced versus teacher-paced accommodations for large-scale math tests. *Journal of Special Education Technology, 15*(2), 27–36.

Hollenbeck, K., Tindal, G., & Almond P. (1998). Teachers' knowledge of accommodations as a validity issue in high-stakes testing. *Journal of Special Education, 32*(3), 175–183.

Individuals With Disabilities Education Act of 2004, Public Law print of P.L.108-446, reauthorization. Retrieved June 21, 2006, from http://frwebgate.access.gpo.gov/cgi-bin/getdoc.cgi?dbname=108_cong_public_laws&docid=f:publ446.108

Jayanthi, M., Epstein, M. H., Polloway, E. A., & Bursuck, W. D. (1996). A national survey of general education teachers' perceptions of testing adaptations. *Journal of Special Education, 30*(1), 99–115.

Ketterlin-Geller, L. R., 2003. *Establishing a validity argument for using universally designed assessments*. Unpublished doctoral dissertation, University of Oregon, Eugene.

Kopriva, R. J. (2000). *Ensuring accuracy in testing for English language learners*. Washington, DC: Council of Chief State School Officers.

Kopriva, R. J. (2002). *Application for Taxonomy for Testing English Language Learners (TTELL)*. Title IV, Subpart 1, Section 6112: Enhanced Assessment Instruments. Washington, DC: U.S. Department of Education.

Kopriva, R. J. (2005a, June). *Language, literacy, and psychosocial factors: Preliminary findings of the interaction related to the interaction of ability, student variables and large-scale testing characteristics*. Presentation at the National Conference on Large-Scale Assessment, San Antonio, TX.

Kopriva, R. J. (2005b). *Final performance report for the Taxonomy for Testing English Language Learners Project*. Washington, DC: U.S. Department of Education.

Kopriva, R. J. (in press). *Improving testing for English language learners: A comprehensive approach to designing, building, implementing, and interpreting better academic assessments*. Mahwah, NJ: Lawrence Erlbaum.

Kopriva, R. J., & Carr, T. (2005, June). *Introducing STELLA*. Presentation at the National Conference on Large-Scale Assessment, San Antonio, TX.

Kopriva, R. J., Carr, T., & Cho, M. Y. (2006, June). *Application of STELLA system and relevant findings*. Presentation at the National Conference on Large-Scale Assessment, San Francisco, CA.

Kopriva, R. J., Carr, T., & Koran, J. (2006, April). *STELLA: A computerized system for test accommodations to English language learners*. Presentation at the annual meeting of the

American Educational Research Association, San Francisco, CA.

Kopriva, R .J., Emick, J. E., & Hipolito-Delgado, C. P. (2006). *Do proper accommodation assignments make a difference? Examining the impact of improved decision-making on scores for ELLs.* Manuscript submitted for publication.

Kopriva, R. J., Emick, J. E., Winter, P., & Chen, C. S. (2006). *Examining the item level interaction of ability, student variables and language characteristics for English language learners and others.* Manuscript submitted for publication.

Kopriva, R.J., & Hedgspeth, C. (2005). *Technical manual, Selection Taxonomy for English Language Learner Accommodation (STELLA) Decision-Making Systems.* College Park, MD: University of Wisconsin, Center for the Study of Assessment Validity and Evaluation.

Kopriva, R. J., Hedgspeth, C., Koran, J., & Carr, T. (2007). *Using the Selection Taxonomy for English Language Learner Accommodations (STELLA) to make defendable large-scale assessment accommodations decisions.* Manuscript in preparation.

Kopriva, R. J., & Mislevy, R. (2001). *Application for Valid Assessment of English Language Learners* (PR No. R305T010846). Washington, DC: U.S. Department of Education.

Kopriva, R. J., & Mislevy, R. (2005). *Narrative final performance report Valid Assessment of English Language Learners* (PR No. R305T010846). Washington, DC: U.S. Department of Education.

Koran, J., & Kopriva, R. J., (2006). *Teacher assignment of test accommodations for English language learners.* Article submitted for publication.

Koran J., Kopriva, R. J., Emick, J., Monroe, J. R., & Garavaglia, D. (2006, April). *Teacher assignment and a multi-source computerized approach for making individualized test accommodation decisions for English language learners.* Presentation at the meeting of the American Educational Research Association, San Francisco, CA.

Mislevy, R. J. (1994). Evidence and inference in educational assessment. *Psychometrika, 59,* 439–483.

National Center for Education Statistics. (2005). National Assessment of Educational Progress. Washington, DC: U.S. Department of Education, Institute of Education Sciences. Reading, mathematics, and science assessments retrieved September 29, 2006, from http://nces.ed.gov/nationsreportcard/about/inclusion.asp

No Child Left Behind. (2001). Public Law print of PL 107-110, reauthorization of the Elementary and Secondary Education Act, Retrieved March 10, 2006 from http://www.ed.gov/policy/elsec/leg/esea02/107-110.pdf

Plake, B. S., & Impara, J. C. (2006) Report, Accommodation Station Expert Panel Meeting #2, Unpublished. U.S. Department of Education, Title IV, Subpart 1, Section 6112: Enhanced Assessment Instruments. Washington, DC.

Rivera, C., & Collum, E. (Eds.). (2006). *A national review of state assessment policy and practice for English language learners.* Mahwah, NJ: Lawrence Erlbaum.

Sharrocks-Taylor, D., & Hargreaves, M. (1999). Making it clear: A review of language issues in testing with special reference to the National Curriculum Mathematics Tests at Key Stage 2. *Educational Research, 41*(2), 123–136.

Shriner, J. G., & DeStefano, L. (2003). Participation and accommodation in state assessment: The role of individualized education programs. *Exceptional Children, 69,* 147–161.

Sireci, S. G., Li, S., & Scarpati, S. (2003). *The effects of test accommodation on test performance: A review of the literature.* (Center for Educational Assessment Research Report. No. 485). Amherst, MA: University of Massachusetts School of Education.

Siskind, T. (2004). *Application for Achieving Accurate Results for Diverse Learners: Accommodations and access enhanced item formats for English language learners and students with disabilities (AARDL).* Title IV, Subpart 1, Section 6112: Enhanced Assessment Instruments. Washington, DC: U.S. Department of Education.

Solano-Flores, G., & Nelson-Barber, S. (2001). On the cultural validity of science assessments. *Journal of Research in Science Teaching, 38*(5), 553–573.

Solano-Flores, G., Trumbull, E., & Nelson-Barber, S. (2002). Concurrent Development of dual language assessments: An alternative to translating tests for linguistic minorities. *International Journal of Testing 2*(2), 107–129.

Solomon, C., Jerry, L., & Lutkus, A. (2001, August). *The nation's report card: State mathematics 2000* (NCES 2001-519). Washington, DC: National Center for Education Statistics).

Swierzbin, B., Anderson, M. E., Spicuzza, R., Walz, L., & Thurlow, M. L. (1999). *Feasibility and practicality of a decision-making tool for standards testing of students with disabilities* (Minnesota Report No. 21). Minneapolis, MN: University of Minnesota, National Center on Educational Outcomes. Retrieved May 2, 2005, from http://education.umn.edu/NCEO/OnlinePubs/MnReport21.html

Thurlow M. L., Moen, R. E., and Wiley, H. E. (2004). *Biennial performance reports: 2002–2003 state assessment data.* Minneapolis: University of Minnesota, National Center on Educational Outcomes.

Thurlow M. L., Wiley, H. I., & Bielinski, J. (2002). *Biennial performance reports: 2000–2001 state assessment data.* Minneapolis: University of Minnesota, National Center on Educational Outcomes.

Tindal, G. (2006, April). *A journey through the reliability of a decision-making model for testing students with disabilities.* Presentation at the annual meeting of the American Educational Research Association, San Francisco, CA.

Tindal, G., & Ketterlin-Geller, L. R. (2004). *Test accommodations: Research, focus, and validation.* Manuscript in preparation.

Weston, T. J. (2003). *NAEP validity studies: The validity of oral accommodations in testing* (NCES 2003–06). Washington, DC: National Center for Education Statistics.

Wright, G., & Bolger, F. (1992). *Expertise and decision support.* New York: Plenum Press.

Ysseldyke, J., Thurlow, M., McGrew, K. S., & Shriner, J. (1994). *Recommendations for making decisions about the participation of students with disabilities in statewide assessment programs* (Synthesis Report No. 15). Minneapolis: University of Minnesota, National Center on Educational Outcomes. (ERIC Document Reproduction Service No. ED 375588)

Author Note: Portions of this chapter have been adapted from *Improving Testing for English Language Learners: A Comprehensive Approach to Designing, Building, Implementing, and Interpreting Better Academic Assessments.* Book in press, Mahwah, NJ: Lawrence Erlbaum.

Assessment Accommodation Considerations for Middle School Students With Disabilities

JAMES SHRINER

LIZANNE DESTEFANO

University of Illinois at Urbana-Champaign

At the time IDEA '97 was enacted, most students with disabilities were not meaningfully included as participants in large-scale assessment programs. The original assessment provisions, initiated research and training efforts to promote useful processes to include students in district and state assessments testing programs (e.g., DeStefano & Shriner, 1998; Elliott, Kratochwill, & McKevitt, 2001; Hollenbeck, Tindal, & Almond, 1998). Based on the law and regulations, Rouse, Shriner, and Danielson (2000) presented six combinations for student participation/accommodation ranging from full participation in general assessments without accommodations to participation in an alternate assessment. *Accommodations* for students were viewed primarily as alterations that allowed students with disabilities to participate. At that time, *alternate assessments* generally were intended for students for whom the general education curriculum was thought to be inadequate in addressing their specific needs.

Since the original law's passage, much work has been done, especially with respect to accommodations use and effect on scores (e.g. Sireci, Scarpati, & Li, 2005; Tindal, 2006) and alternate assessment (e.g., Browder et al., 2004; Kleinert & Kearns, 2004; U.S. Department of Education, 2005). Another aspect of participation and accommodation research has been on individualized education program (IEP) team decision making for inclusion of students with disabilities in testing programs. IEP teams, then and now, bear the responsibility for all decisions about the participation of an individual student with a disability in district and state assessments (Yell, Katsiyannis, & Shriner, 2006). Much progress has been made and an increasing research and literature base are helping. However, IEP teams still tend to hold low expectations for students with disabilities and to lack knowledge about both assessments, in general, and implications of accommodation decisions, specifically.

ACCOMMODATIONS: DEFINITIONS AND BACKGROUND

Accommodations for testing are quite numerous and varied. Technological advances continue to expand the types of accommodations that might be considered. Generally, however, most accommodations in use fall into four broad categories: setting, timing/scheduling, presentation, and response. These accommodation types are described earlier in this book (see Chapter 1 by Thurlow) and in earlier writings by Thurlow, Elliott, and Ysseldyke (2003).

Recently, Clapper, Morse, Thurlow, and Thompson (2006) have used the term *access assistance* to describe test accommodations that are implemented using an additional person (e.g., read aloud, dictated response, and sign language interpretation). Other authors (e.g., Elliott, Braden, & White, 2001) use accommodation classification strategies that build upon those listed above, and describe types of accommodations or assistance in temporal terms. The Assessment Accommodation Checklist (Elliott, Kratochwill, & Schulte, 1998) includes (a) assistance prior to testing (practice items), (b) motivational accommodations (encouragement), (c) assistance during testing (pointing to items), and (d) equipment/technology (amplification devices). Regardless of the classification option used, it is important that the IEP team discuss and document changes to assessments that will be used by students with disabilities.

The authors have been participants in the research and development efforts related to accommodation decision making through two Office of Special Education Programs (OSEP)-sponsored grants. The first effort, Project PAR (No. H324D980070; DeStefano & Shriner, 1998) included several investigations concerning the participation, accommodation, and reporting of assessment decisions immediately following IDEA '97. Project PAR included an intervention research component in which we trained personnel from several school districts on the existing regulations and guidelines, as well as the then current best practices for both participation and accommodation choices. The follow-up effort is a Personnel Preparation and Technical Assistance grant, Project IEP-D (No. H325N020081; Shriner & DeStefano, 2002). For this project we have worked with local level decision makers on how district personnel and school building personnel could use information from testing to improve the programmatic decisions for all students, including the students with disabilities served in those programs.

Project PAR findings and implications illustrated the relative newness of the full participation of students with disabilities in large-scale assessment. Posttraining decisions were found to be better documented on students' IEPs and team members reported being more confident in their understanding and application of assessment and accommodation principles (DeStefano, Shriner, & Lloyd, 2001). The participation of students with disabilities and assignment and use of accommodations was found to be highly variable. Though IEP planning processes were improved, a general disconnect between the intended and actual participation and accommodation patterns was evident. Often, the departures from planned actions were attributable to a lack of capacity to handle the logistics involved in actual accommodation delivery or to the emergence of unplanned student accommodation need on the day of testing (Shriner & DeStefano, 2003). In some cases, test administrators resorted to group-based solutions to accommodation delivery. (e.g., all special education students reported to the resource room for testing) in lieu of the individual considerations that had been planned. On the day of testing, students with disabilities often received more accommodations than had been documented on their IEPs. Sometimes these were more of the motivational or access accommodation type (c.f., Clapper, et al., 2006; Elliott, Braden et al., 2001) that reflected the instructional styles of the teachers who were administering the assessments. In other cases, the additional accommodations were assigned because students' skills and characteristics had changed substantially in the interim period of the IEP that was developed the spring of the *previous year* for the current year's test. Participation and accommodation choices documented on the IEP were sometimes considered irrelevant given the student's present circumstances (Shriner & DeStefano, 2003).

With the initial work to guide us, we began Project IEP-D to work on issues at a local level with a focus on the use of participation and accommodation data produced by the inclusion of students with disabilities in district and state assessment programs. One main purpose of our work is to help school decision makers and IEP teams place in proper perspective the program and policy decisions that emphasize group actions with the determination and assignment of accommodations for individual students. By working at the district level, we address the policy-level requirements for states to determine appropriate accommodation guidelines. At the same time, we can assist at the practice level, at which IEP teams must be fully informed of policy and use reasoned judgment to determine accommodation use on a case-by-case basis.

In this chapter, we report on our technical assistance efforts with one middle school to improve the inclusion of students with disabilities in both district and state assessments. A focus on appropriate accommodations for both instruction and testing was used to frame other important programmatic decision making based on assessment results. Our work at the middle school level is important given both No Child Left Behind (NCLB) and Individuals with Disabilities Education Improvement Act of 2004 (IDEA, 2004) requirements that students with disabilities be part of the accountability measures (i.e., Adequate Yearly Progress, AYP) of schools, districts, and states. Because AYP is tied to reading and mathematics performance many middle schools are "singled out" for not reaching AYP goals, often because the elementary schools from which they receive students have insufficient numbers of students in the IEP subgroup to trigger reporting requirements (Yell et al., 2006). The willingness of the middle school to participate in our project was fortunate, because relatively little IEP and assessment/accommodation effort has focused on the experiences and academic performance of students at the middle school level (Espin, Deno, & Albayrak-Kaymak, 1998; Sopko, 2003).

This project was a technical assistance/professional development effort and not a research effort in its focus. Throughout the process, no attempt was made to establish control or comparison conditions for any questions we addressed. We began our work with a focus group and needs assessment in order to establish the school's most important concerns for data summary, data analysis, and possible changes in programmatic actions. Our initial advice to all persons involved rested upon the premise that the data we collected and/or examined for the school should help identify "actionable" points of intervention. Although we recognized that possible alternate explanations for why the data might appear as they did that could suggest the "problem" rested outside the middle school's control, our efforts were to be concentrated on variables that the middle school could alter in their current form. We wanted to focus the school's attention on aspects other than a student's status as a special education student.

The focus group and needs assessment yielded three main questions that would frame our technical assistance with the school:

- How are middle school students performing on tests of reading and mathematics?

- What are the participation and accommodation use patterns for students with disabilities?

- What is the instructional and testing accommodation status for students with disabilities in both general education and special education environments?

Because the middle school receives students from different elementary schools and backgrounds, the initial desire of nearly all persons was to have a complete, yet easily understandable, analysis of performances profiles of the students who entered the middle school. Thus, they placed a high priority on gaining some background information on how students performed on the district chosen standardized test, the Iowa Tests of Basic Skills (ITBS, Hieronymus, Hoover, & Lindquist, 1986; 1992), prior to addressing current participation and accommodation patterns and policies.

DESCRIPTION OF THE COMMUNITY AND SCHOOL

The Midwest School District is situated in East-Central Illinois, and serves a community of approximately 40,000 people. It includes six elementary schools, one middle school, and one high school. The district employs over 300 teachers, the majority of whom are White (89.8%) and female (78.5%). Midwest Middle School (MMS), which is the focus of this chapter, serves a racially mixed population with a total enrollment of 1,033 students based on Illinois School Report Card (Illinois State Board of Education, ISBE, 2005a). The racial composition of MMS is comparable with the composition of the Midwest School District (50.1% White, 33.4% African American, and 16.5% Bi/multi racial or other). More

than half of students attending MMS come from low-income families.

MMS serves students in sixth, seventh, and eighth grade. For this work, we followed seventh- and eighth-grade students with disabilities for the ITBS (administered in November) and Illinois Standards Achievement Test (ISAT) respectively. Typically, the ISAT is given in early to mid-March, with make-up periods extending through the end of the month. In general, these students reflect the diversity of the larger community. Demographic information for these students is shown in Table 11-1. The number of cases for which information was missing or not listed for fall ITBS testing reflects a combination of two factors—an oversight of identifying those students served in alternative placements, and missing fields on the electronic IEPs. This extent of missing information was a high priority for correction before spring ISAT testing.

A total of 58 general education teachers and 14 special education teachers served in the school in the 2004 to 2005 school year (ISBE, 2005a). Midwest Middle uses a team approach to service delivery in which students and teachers are assigned to different instruction teams to create a small learning community where students can receive attention and support from their team teachers.

PRIMARY DECISION-MAKING GROUP

The principal and assistant principal of MMS, lead general and special education teachers from each grade's team, and both the director and assistant director of special education for the district were our primary contacts for this work. In all, 10 people were part of the primary decision-making group. The assistant principal for MMS previously had served as an assistant director of special education for a nearby district. Throughout the year, biweekly meetings were held with this group; if a member from each "subgroup" was not available (e.g., administrators,

TABLE 11-1

Student Demographic Information

| | ITBS Fall 7th Grade | ISAT Spring 7th & 8th Grade | |
| | | Reading and Math N = 64 | Science N = 69 |
	Frequency (%)	Frequency (%)	Frequency (%)
Gender			
Male	41 (54.7)	41 (64.1)	45 (65.2)
Female	21 (28.0)	23 (35.9)	24 (34.8)
Not listed	13 (17.3)		
Total	75 (100.0)		
Ethnicity			
American Indian or Alaskan Native	0	0	0
African American	29 (38.7)	29 (45.3)	32 (46.4)
Asian or Pacific Islander	0	0	0
Hispanic, regardless of race	3 (4.0)	2 (3.1)	3 (4.3)
White (not of Hispanic origin)	26 (34.7)	26 (40.6)	28 (40.6)
Multiracial	4 (5.3)	6 (9.4)	6 (8.7)
Not listed	13 (17.3)	1 (1.6)	0
Total	75 (100.0)		
Age			
12	36 (48.0)	0	39 (56.5)
13	24 (32.0)	16 (25.0)	30 (43.5)
14	1 (1.3)	44 (68.8)	0
15		4 (6.3)	0
Not listed	14 (18.7)		
Total	75 (100.0)		
Grade/Level			
7	75 (100.0)	0	69 (100.0)
8		64 (100.0)	0
Not listed	0		
Total	75 (100.0)		
Primary Disability			
Learning Disabilities	39 (52.0)	30 (46.9)	33 (47.8)
Behavioral Disorders	6 (8.0)	7 (10.9)	6 (8.6)
Mental Retardation	3 (4.0)	2 (3.1)	3 (4.3)
Speech / Language	5 (6.7)	1 (1.6)	2 (2.9)
Multiple Disabilities	0	0	0
Orthopedic Impairments	0	2 (3.1)	0
Other Health Impairments	4 (5.3)	7 (10.9)	5 (7.2)
Visual Impairments	0	0	0

continues

TABLE 11-1 *(Continued)*

| | ITBS Fall 7th Grade | | ISAT Spring 7th & 8th Grade | | | |
| | | | Reading and Math N = 64 | | Science N = 69 | |
	Frequency (%)		Frequency (%)		Frequency (%)	
Primary Disability cont.						
Hearing Impairments	1	(1.3)	0		1	(1.4)
Autism	4	(5.3)	1	(1.6)	2	(2.9)
Traumatic Brain Injury	1	(1.3)	0		1	(1.4)
Deaf-Blindness	0		0		0	
504 only	2	(2.8)				
Not listed	10	(13.3)	3	(4.7)	1	(1.4)
Total	75	(100.0)				
Related Services						
Speech/Language	7	(9.4)	14	(21.9)	6	(8.7)
Physical Therapy	0		2	(3.2)	0	
Audiological Services	1	(1.3)	0		1	(1.4)
Transportation	1	(1.3)	8	(12.6)	4	(5.8)
Assistive Technology	0		0		0	
Counseling	0		0		1	(1.4)
Occupational Therapy	1	(1.3)	3	(4.8)	0	
Orientation/Mobility	0		0		0	
Social Work	12	(16.0)	20	(31.3)	15	(21.7)
Other	3	(4.0)	12	(18.8)	1	(1.4)
Not listed	50	(66.7)				
Total	75	(100.0)				

teachers) then the planned meeting was rescheduled if possible.

PERFORMANCE DATA FOR CURRENT MIDDLE SCHOOL STUDENTS

Across the district, students with disabilities in fifth grade who were tested on the ITBS obtained scores in both reading and mathematics that were roughly the same as those obtained by students without disabilities in third grade. Beginning MMS students with disabilities are about 2 years behind their peers without disabilities in both content areas. As requested, we provided analyses to show the ITBS performance of students with disabilities from all feeder schools who enter the middle school at two points in time: (a) as fifth graders, 1 year prior to attending MMS, and (b) as seventh graders, after 1 year at MMS. Figure 11-1 (reading) and Figure 11-2 (mathematics) show the scores for the 2004 cohort of MMS students as a combined group and as smaller subgroups as fifth graders. The different numbers of students reported for MMS reflects the fact that of the current group of seventh graders ($n = 63$, reading; $n = 64$, math), same student scores (as fifth graders) were retrievable for lesser numbers of students ($n = 46$; $n = 48$, respectively). Separating the scores of the additional students did not significantly change the mean reported in either content area.

Scores for reading and math of the students from the feeder schools are quite variable, with Schools B, C, and D having higher mean scores than Schools A, E, and F in both areas. In reading, students with disabilities as a group score below the ITBS Developmental Mean in both fifth and seventh grades, and although a 16 point (191–207) increase in the scores across 2 years of instruction is shown, the group mean for students with disabilities at seventh grade is well below the district and national mean scores.

There appears to be a stronger effect of MMS instruction for mathematics than for reading. A 30-point increase (191–221) over the same time period is noted, and the developmental mean for seventh-grade students with disabilities is close to the district and national means. Further evidence of the effect of instruction can be seen in the scores for students coming from the lower-scoring feeder schools. Students from Schools A and E have scores (M = 213, M = 217) that are close to the overall mean score for seventh graders (M = 221).

The Midwest Middle School staff, although disappointed, had a possible explanation for the data we shared with them. A decision to drop targeted instruction in reading and initiate a content area literacy approach coincided with the entrance of this student cohort. Beyond a return to separate reading instruction, the information had implications for accommodation provisions during instructional and testing activities. It is to these issues that we focused our subsequent attention.

ACCOMMODATIONS FOR DISTRICT ASSESSMENT (ITBS)

In the focus group sessions, most team members felt the decisions about accommodations were managed adequately by the special edu-

cation staff. Although the district did use an online IEP generation template, special education teachers thought they were, perhaps, overly reliant on the template forms for accommodation options. In addition, staff was interested in technical assistance/support to examine accommodation use on the district assessment (ITBS), which all persons agreed was a lower-stakes test than the ISAT. Doing so, they thought, would allow for an examination of the accommodations used in testing situations across both general and special education settings, and would inform the teams of effective and ineffective accommodation strategies prior to the higher stakes spring testing.

DATA COLLECTION: FALL ITBS

The ITBS is given only to students in seventh grade at MMS; reading, mathematics, science, and social studies are tested. We collected participation and accommodation information in two ways: teacher-completed inventory (2 forms) and direct observation on the day of testing. The teacher-completed inventories were adapted from one used for prior research as part of Project PAR (DeStefano et al., 2001). The checklist-style form was organized in sections that corresponded to the major accommodation categories: *scheduling/timing, setting, presentation,* and *response.* A separate area in which teachers could write accommodations that were not on the form or could write notes/questions for our consideration was included. Teachers (or other test administrators) were to mark the accommodations (if any) received by a student for all content area tests in which he/she participated. One form per student (covering all testing sessions) was used. This form was most often completed by the special education teacher on whose caseload the student appeared

A second version of the teacher-completed inventory was developed for use by the general education teacher who

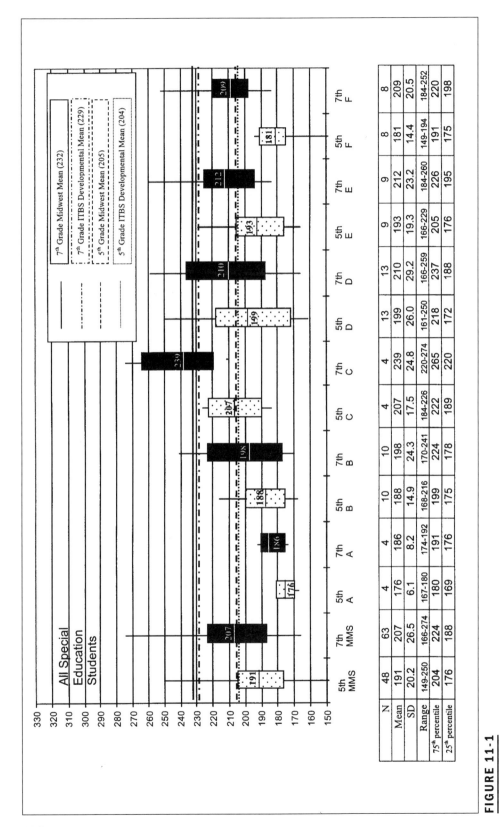

FIGURE 11-1

ITBS Mean Reading Total Scores for Special Education Students for Middle School (MID) by Feeder School (A-F) Administered 5th: Fall 2002, 7th: 2004

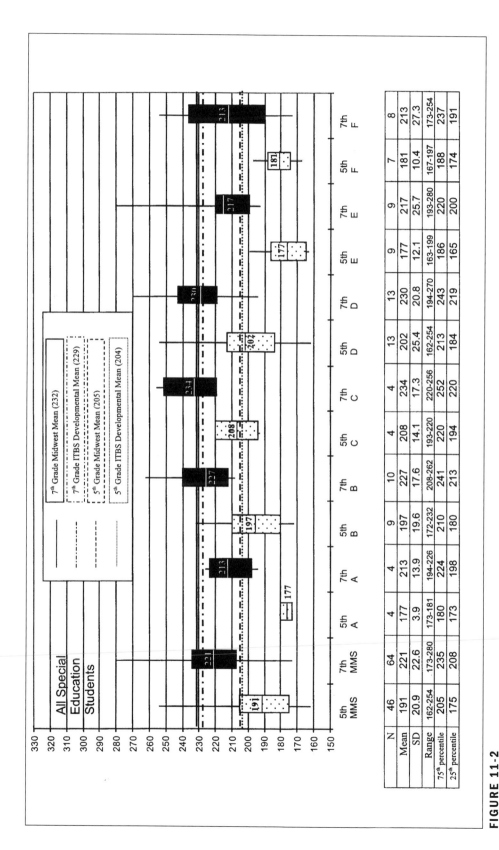

	5th MMS	7th MMS	5th A	7th A	5th B	7th B	5th C	7th C	5th D	7th D	5th E	7th E	5th F	7th F
N	46	64	4	4	9	10	4	4	13	13	9	9	7	8
Mean	191	221	177	213	197	227	208	234	202	230	177	217	181	213
SD	20.9	22.6	3.9	13.9	19.6	17.6	14.1	17.3	25.4	20.8	12.1	25.7	10.4	27.3
Range	162-254	173-280	173-181	194-226	172-232	208-262	193-220	220-256	162-254	194-270	163-199	193-280	167-197	173-254
75th percentile	205	235	180	224	210	241	220	252	213	243	186	220	188	237
25th percentile	175	208	173	198	180	213	194	220	184	219	165	200	174	191

FIGURE 11-2

ITBS Mean Math Total (With Computation) Scores for Special Education Students for Middle School (MID) by Feeder School (A-F) Administered 5th: Fall 2002, 7th: 2004 administered ITBS subtest(s) in general education settings. These forms were similar to the primary form, but included a section for documenting *whole-classroom* changes/adaptations/accommodations that they made (e.g., scheduling changes due to late-arriving students, providing an extra practice item to the whole group). Collection of these data was something we had not done in our original research. Because the team approach was an important consideration to this technical assistance, the opportunity to gather general and special education setting data was thought to be especially important. General education teachers completed one form per testing session. All teachers were asked to complete the forms after the testing sessions ended to reflect the actual accommodation provided.

Inventory/checklist use was explained by the first author to all teachers at a general faculty meeting in late October. Questions that were raised were answered and followed up with an explanatory message delivered to the teachers' school mailboxes prior to testing.

The first author and a doctoral student working on the project conducted direct observations on testing days. Prior to each observation, the teacher was asked for permission to conduct the observation. At no time did either observer interact with the teacher or student(s). After each session, the teacher was asked if they wished to comment about the testing that had occurred and to point out any event that he/she thought deserved particular attention. Because this project was not a research effort, we did not seek permission to interview students. Comments and questions they directed to their teachers, however, were noted. At times, these student comments were the basis for follow-up questions asked of the teachers or administrators. Across the 4 days of testing, we observed 40 test sessions (25 special education, 15 general education). Field notes for all sessions were compiled into a casebook format.

FALL ITBS PARTICIPATION AND ACCOMMODATIONS

After testing was completed, we compared our teacher inventories with the roster of students with disabilities provided by MMS and the enrollment data provided to the state of Illinois by the district. It became clear that the rosters of names and the forms we collected did not match. Both the MMS and state rosters included 10 students who were not on the absentee lists for the days within the testing period. These 10 students were being served in out-of-building placements. (e.g., residential day treatment or full-time residential placements) at the time of testing. Midwest Middle School personnel confirmed that they had not planned for their participation in districtwide assessment, although they knew these students eventually would be counted as MMS students for state testing and AYP participation purposes. Therefore, these students' exposure to the general education curriculum and use of accommodations were unknown factors at this time. For the time being, then we were limited to analyzing the data for those students with disabilities ($N = 63$) who were within the building and who took ITBS subtest(s). Participation was over 90% for all subtests.

Teacher Inventories

With respect to accommodation use reported by teachers, all 13 general education teachers administered ITBS subtest(s) and returned their teacher inventories of general classroom changes made during testing that might also serve as accommodations for special education students. Seven teachers indicated making specific changes (accommodations) to the classroom setting, beyond the written administration instructions. Six of the seven reported a single setting accommodation of "seating alteration/proximity to test administrator." Of all other accommodations on the teacher inventory, only "reread directions/items" and "praise/encouragement to keep working" were reported ($n = 2$; $n = 1$, respectively).

Table 11-2 is a list of accommodations used by students with disabilities that is organized by the major groupings described earlier (*scheduling, setting, presentation, response*) and reported via the teacher inventory for all content area tests. A strong majority (60%–98%) of students received *scheduling* accommodations (e.g., "extended time," "extra testing sessions"). Most of these students also received *setting* accommodations and were either in "small groups" or with the "special education teacher in a separate room" (> 50%). *Presentation* accommodations for all areas tended to cluster around those requiring the teacher and/or test administrator to "read or simplify the directions and items." About 30% of the students were also recipients of "praise and encouragement statements" to keep them engaged in the testing situation at hand. For the reading and math subtests, about one third of students were provided a "reminder of a test-taking skill" during testing. Finally, although calculators were provided for nearly 90% of test takers, a fewer number of *response* accommodations and assistance for completing test items were recorded. "Praise and encouragement" to complete test responses were noted for about 20% of students.

Direct Observations

Field notes from the direct observations of ITBS sessions supplemented the teacher inventories. The day of testing observations helped us to provide the middle school personnel with a very complete accounting of the testing and accommodation scenarios encountered by the students. We found that this step, though labor intensive, was important to do so that meaningful, technical assistance and feedback could be provided.

Our observations of the general education environment suggested that there was an overall supportiveness for students (including those with disabilities), that was not reflected on the data forms that were completed by the general education teachers. This supportiveness was illustrated by several teachers' statements that referred to the "team nature" of the testing. For example, prior to beginning a test session in mathematics, one teacher spent a few minutes reminding the students of what she referred to as "the big ideas" of area and volume that they had covered earlier. She asked a student with a learning disability (LD) to share the one or two main ideas about these principles that she "thought her team members should remember" once testing began. The student responded quite competently, and was praised for her statements by the teacher and several of her peers. Similarly, another teacher gave a team-focused "pep talk" to the students who were awaiting a science subtest. In this instance, he reminded all students of a test-taking strategy he had taught previously, and asked a follow-up clarification question of a student with LD. We noticed, also, that when students were moved to be in closer proximity to the test administrator, these changes were presented in a very matter of fact, natural manner.

Across all testing days, observations of special education teachers documented a dedicated staff doing its best to provide testing environments in which the student could demonstrate what they had learned. In MMS, a very strong connection between students with disabilities and their teachers is noticeable. Because so many students with disabilities (> 90%) were tested with some degree of accommodation provided by the special educator (e.g., small group in special education room), we found that most teachers were required to be "multitasking" during the testing sessions. It was a common event to see a teacher answering specific questions from individual students (Is this the question I'm supposed to be on?) and trying to administer directions to a group at the same

TABLE 11-2

ITBS Participation/Accommodation of Specific Students With Disabilities by Subtest, November 2004 Testing Accommodations Used

	(%) Reading (N = 56)	(%) Math (N = 57)	(%) Science (N = 55)	(%) Social Studies (N = 55)
Scheduling				
Extended time	55 (98.2)	55 (96.5)	54 (98.2)	54 (98.2)
Additional breaks	35 (62.5)	35 (61.4)	34 (61.8)	34 (61.8)
Multiple test sessions	48 (85.7)	50 (87.7)	42 (76.4)	41 (74.6)
Setting				
Individual testing	0	2 (3.5)	1 (1.8)	1 (1.8)
Small group testing	54 (96.4)	53 (93.0)	52 (94.6)	52 (94.6)
Use of carrels	0	2 (3.5)	0	0
Special seating/proximity to monitor	0	1 (1.8)	0	0
Adaptive furniture	0	0	0	0
Tests in separate room	24 (42.9)	21 (36.8)	24 (43.6)	24 (43.6)
Test in special education room	32 (57.1)	34 (59.7)	31 (56.4)	31 (56.4)
Presentation				
Braille	0	0	0	0
Large print	0	0	0	0
Modified spacing between lines	0	0	0	0
Templates	0	0	0	0
Fewer items/lines per page	1 (1.8)	1 (1.8)	1 (1.8)	1 (1.8)
Highlighted important words/directions	0	0	0	0
Read aloud directions and/or items	39 (69.6)	40 (70.2)	39 (70.9)	38 (69.1)
Simplified directions	22 (39.3)	22 (38.6)	21 (38.2)	21 (38.2)
Paraphrasing directions/items	28 (50.0)	28 (49.1)	28 (50.9)	28 (50.9)
Sign language	1 (1.8)	1 (1.8)	1 (1.8)	1 (1.8)
Lighting/acoustics	1 (1.8)	1 (1.8)	0	0
Magnification equipment	0	0	0	0
Provide practice item	1 (1.8)	1 (1.8)	0	0
Praise/encouragement	17 (30.4)	17 (29.8)	16 (29.1)	16 (29.1)
Reminder of test-taking skill	19 (33.9)	20 (35.1)	5 (9.1)	5 (9.1)
Redirection to the correct item	4 (7.1)	4 (7.0)	2 (3.6)	2 (3.6)
Student use of self-management	1 (1.8)	1 (1.8)	1 (1.8)	1 (1.8)
Response				
Scribe to record answers	2 (3.6)	2 (3.5)	2 (3.6)	2 (3.6)
Tape recorder	2 (3.6)	0	0	0

continues

TABLE 11-2 *(Continued)*

	(%) Reading (N = 56)		(%) Math (N = 57)		(%) Science (N = 55)		(%) Social Studies (N = 55	
Response cont.								
Communication device	1	(1.8)	1	(1.8)	1	(1.8)	1	(1.8)
Computer/word processor	0		0		0		0	
Write on materials/test booklet	2	(3.6)	2	(3.5)	2	(3.6)	2	(3.6)
Calculators	8	(14.3)	51	(89.5)	7	(12.7)	7	(12.7)
Number tables	0		0		0		0	
Braille	0		0		0		0	
Templates	0		0		0		0	
Altered test materials format	0		0		0		0	
Provide practice item	1	(1.8)	1	(1.8)	0		0	
Praise/encouragement	11	(19.6)	11	(19.3)	10	(18.2)	10	(18.2)
Reminder of test taking skill	9	(16.1)	10	(17.5)	0		0	
Redirection to the correct item	2	(3.6)	3	(5.3)	2	(3.6)	1	(1.8)
Student use of self-management	1	(1.8)	1	(1.8)	1	(1.8)	1	(1.8)

time. As the week of testing progressed, students' test completion rates became more varied. At later stages, teachers may have had several students taking portions of two or three content area subtests. Still, the teachers strived to remain positive and took opportunities to provide praise/encouragement statements to support not only students' cognitive/academic needs, but also their social/behavioral needs as well (see Table 11-2, Presentation).

Student comments of note during the test week included several about how the test made them feel inadequate and was frustrating. We heard several pleas for "help" with items during many test sessions. Notably, several students being tested in special education settings asked if they could use supports "like those we get in class," and if their general (math or science) teacher could assist them. We asked both teachers and administrators to elaborate on these statements, and learned that the degree of consistency of supports provided varied by both individual teachers and by "team."

The extent to which the sometimes "chaotic" nature of the special education setting during testing exerted a negative effect upon the student performance is unknown, but it was clear that the special education teachers were experiencing a degree of stress, some of which was being passed onto the students. Finally, though the special education staff as a whole extended themselves during ITBS testing, individual special education teachers' behavior in terms of providing individual or small group supports varied significantly.

Feedback and Technical Assistance

We provided in-person feedback and technical assistance to administrators and all team members for Grades 6, 7, and 8. We shared the data and observational summaries with the primary decision-making group first (December) in order to plan the technical assistance they wanted. Although the primary group generally was pleased to have the fall accommodation and participation information, there was a sense that testing scenarios did not provide an overt consideration of the instructional and assessment supports available to students. In addition, coordination of accommodations across teachers and teams seemed to be an important need for the technical assistance that was to follow. This project occurred prior to enactment of the NCLB requirement for the reading and mathematics assessment of students in each of the grades third through eighth. Therefore, although seventh-grade students would be tested in science on the state assessment, the primary group requested that attention focus on the decisions to be made for the eighth-grade assessments of reading and mathematics.

The first author met in person with all teams (first as a group, followed by team specific meetings) after the winter break. At the initial meeting, data and observations from the fall testing were shared and discussed. This meeting allowed teams to review what was planned for group use (general accommodations/supports) as well as for individual student's needed accommodations. The connection between what was planned and what was actually provided during instruction and assessment became a very important issue after the fall test data was presented.

Content of the technical assistance presentations and discussions was organized around PAR training materials, and focused on the key principles for accommodation assignment (Shriner & DeStefano, 2001; Yell, Shriner, & Katsiyannis, in press). All discussions occurred in the context of MMS and those students with disabilities to be tested in the spring. First, accommodations that are recommended should relate to the student's particular educational need, not the type of disability for which he/she is receiving special education services. Student characteristics that warrant an accommodation should be documented in educational terms and not categorical labels. Second, accommodations for testing generally should

be those that have been used for instructional purposes. One consideration that teams should include in assigning assessment accommodations is experience with an accommodation for a student with disabilities during his or her instruction. This particular principle was afforded extra attention given our observation that the general education teachers and environments were, perhaps, supporting student performance in ways not recognized by all team members.

We provided all teams with an Accommodation Monitoring Form (Ganguly & Shriner, 2004) to help promote discussion among team members regarding the provision of accommodations (see Figure 11-3). Because accommodations are often planned during an IEP meeting and revisited only at the time of the next one (Shriner & DeStefano, 2003), the form was developed as a tool for teachers to use to document the extent to which students were using supports that were provided to all students in a class (routine classroom practices) as well as those listed specifically in the student's IEP. Although this form does yield accommodation use data, it does not, in any way, provide for an evaluation of the score impact effect of any accommodation. Teams were allowed to discuss accommodation strategies and individual student cases. Use of the Accommodation Monitoring Form was voluntary as this was not a research intervention and only a limited time period remained in the effective instructional year.

Third, a discussion on the importance of matching student-specific characteristics with accommodation choices was presented. As the research on accommodation use has evolved, researchers have recommended with increasing frequency that accommodation decisions be made at the most precise level possible. Authors of other chapters in this book (e.g., Sireci et al., 2005; Tindal, 2006) have documented that the combination of student characteristics with the task demands of individual test items is the optimal level

Name: _____ **Grade:** _____ **Teacher:** _____

Content Area(s): _____

ACCOMMODATION(S)	How Often Used?			How Helpful?		
	Routine Classroom Practice for **All Students**	All the Time	Occasionally	Never	Very Helpful	Somewhat Helpful	Not Helpful
Presentation							
Response							
Scheduling/Timing							

Notes about accommodations: _____

_____

_____

FIGURE 11-3

Accommodation Monitoring Form

From "Academic and Social-Behavioral Accommodations for Students With Emotional-Behavior Disorders" by R. Ganguly & J. G. Shriner, February, 2004. Paper presented at the annual meeting of the Midwest Symposium for Leadership in Behavior Disorders, Kansas City, MO.

for decision making about the effect of an accommodation on student performance and the resulting inferences that can be made. Although this level of detailed accommodation assignment was not presented as a viable option in this context, consideration of the key principle resonated with the MMS administrators and teachers. This issue is especially important in relation to the overall testing program in Illinois. For students in Grades 3 through 8, the IEP team's recommendations for accommodations are examined by district administrators in almost all cases. At the high school level, however, IEP teams must submit their accommodation recommendations to the State Board, which, in turn sends them to the testing contractor for verification. Central to the approval process, is the need for a clear demonstration of the connection between student characteristics and the requested accommodation. Technical assistance ended with a thorough examination of the *ISAT Test Administrators' Manual* (ISBE, 2005b). The standard procedures for all subtests were reviewed. General education teachers' roles and responsibilities in providing test supports for all students were highlighted.

DATA COLLECTION: SPRING ISAT

Procedures and tools similar to those used for the fall testing were also used for this round of data collection. Both versions of the teacher-completed inventories (general education, special education) were modified to highlight test procedures/supports that appeared in the *ISAT Test Administrators' Manual* (ISBE, 2005b). Routine practices that occurred in the general education setting were gathered for all test sessions. The ISAT was administered over a period of 4 days with 80 total testing sessions. Fifteen general education test administrators each completed six teacher inventories. We also gathered teacher inventories from the special education teachers who tested students with

disabilities. One form per student was used for each subtest area. Direct observations were done on a more limited basis because of the high stakes nature of the ISAT. Each of the 15 general education test administrators' rooms was observed only once, and each special educator's room on no more than two occasions. In all we conducted 36 total observations. As in the fall, we asked for permission to conduct the observations, and remained in the room until the teacher announced a break in the session.

After discussing the issue of IEP team documentation of accommodations, we examined the IEPs of the seventh- and eighth-grade students to compare the accommodations listed on their IEPs for instruction and state assessment with those reported as actually used on the ISAT assessment.

SPRING ISAT PARTICIPATION AND ACCOMMODATIONS

We documented the participation and accommodation of all students with disabilities on the roster of MMS at the time of ISAT testing. The placements and status of all seventh and eighth graders on the roster were identified. We gathered data for students who were in the middle school and who were in alternative settings at the time of testing. Accommodation data were not gathered for students in the Illinois Alternate Assessment or who were listed as "non-participants" because of hospitalization or incarceration. A total of 69 seventh-grade students took the science assessment. Of these students, 13 took the assessment *without planned* accommodations in a general education room, and 56 took the assessment *with* accommodations and with the involvement of a special education teacher. In eighth grade, 64 took the reading and mathematics tests. For reading, 12 students took the assessment *without planned* accommodations in a general education room, and 52 took the assessment *with* accommodations and with the involvement of a special education teacher. For mathematics, 13 students took the assessment *without planned* accommodations in a general education room, and 51 took the assessment *with* accommodations and with the involvement of a special education teacher.

Teacher Inventories

The general education classroom accommodations for all sessions in each subtest area (32 reading; 24 math; 24 science) are reported in Table 11-3. Because the ISAT manual includes specific guidelines for the time period of test sessions, changes in *scheduling* of the test are not listed. Accommodations that are highlighted appear in the ISAT manual, and when considered within the context of all accommodations listed, give an indication of the extent to which the environment was a supportive one for student testing.

Noticeable within Table 11-3 is that the test administrators did a thorough job of following directions and offering supports listed in the ISAT manual. This is especially the case for the reading and math assessments. In addition, it appears the general education environment included more supports for testing than were listed in the ISAT manual. For example, test administrators for all 24 (100%) testing sessions in mathematics included an "extra practice item(s) prior to the beginning of the testing session." In both reading and mathematics, approximately 80% of the test administrators reported "paraphrasing or using simplified language" in administering directions to the test, thus providing further clarification of what was expected of the students. From a social/behavioral perspective, "praise, encouragement and motivational statements" in both the *presentation* and *response* categories are reported for a minimum of 47% of the testing sessions. These types of social/behavioral supports to keep students on task seemed particularly important within the mathematics and science sessions.

Accommodations provided to students with disabilities are reported in Table 11-4, including *scheduling* accommodations. Again, specific supports from the ISAT manual are highlighted. As is often reported for *scheduling* accommodations, the provision of extra time on the assessments was used by the vast majority of students. The reported use of the individual accommodations within the *setting* and *presentation* groups must be interpreted with caution because of the last minute rules change by the State Board of Education. Just prior to testing, the state board issued a memorandum to all schools indicating that the "read-aloud" accommodation could be done in small group test administration settings, rather than restricting its use to "individual testing," as before. The reported 24% of students who received the read-aloud accommodation in mathematics is probably an underestimation of actual use. We believe that the read-aloud accommodation was offered to several of the students with disabilities who were part of small group administrations not reported on the general education form of the inventory form. In addition, during mathematics tests within the special education setting, our observations recorded multiple situations in which the teacher was administering tests to small groups of students and reading aloud (pronouncing) individual words from the materials, if not complete items.

Over 75% of students received social/behavioral supports in reading and mathematics, including "praise and encouragement" throughout the testing sessions. This percentage was slightly higher than reported in science (approximately. 50%). Special education teachers also issued "reminders of test-taking skills" to the majority of students in all areas.

On the ISAT accommodation forms, two questionable numbers appear. We are

TABLE 11-3

General Classroom Accommodations for 2005 ISAT Testing Provided to ALL STUDENTS
Test Administrators and Sessions: 15 Administrators (total testing sessions N = 80)

Area	Frequency (%)
Reading	32 (40)
Math	24 (30)
Science	24 (30)
Total	80 (100)

Frequency and Percentage of Sessions in Which Accommodations Were Used

	Reading (%)	Math (%)	Science (%)
Setting			
Make sure room was well lit, ventilated, free of distractions	32 (100.0)	24 (100.0)	24 (100)
Displayed materials in room to help on test	6 (18.8)	23 (95.8)	0
Use of carrels or dividers	0	0	0
Provided special seating/proximity to monitor	16 (50.0)	12 (50.0)	9 (37.5)
Presentation			
Pointed out important aspects of test booklet	21 (65.6)	20 (83.3)	0
Repeated or reread directions	19 (59.4)	19 (79.2)	8 (33.3)
Paraphrasing directions/used simplified language	25 (78.1)	20 (83.3)	8 (33.3)
Clarified direction/explained task(s)	22 (68.8)	23 (95.8)	7 (29.2)
Read aloud item or section dividers	5 (15.6)	5 (20.8)	0
Read aloud individual items or prompts	4 (12.5)	5 (20.8)	0
Highlighted/circled important words in directions	6 (18.8)	12 (50.0)	0
Highlighted/circled important words in test items	2 (6.3)	11 (45.8)	0
Provided additional sample item(s) as a prompt during testing	0	11 (45.8)	0
Provided practice items leading up to (before) testing	11 (34.4)	24 (100.0)	8 (33.3)
Praised/encouraged students to begin item	15 (46.9)	15 (62.5)	16 (66.7)
Redirected students to the correct test item	2 (6.3)	11 (45.8)	0
Made sure students had hand-held calculator	0	24 (100.0)	0
Reminded students of test-taking skills (e.g., look for key word)	20 (62.5)	16 (66.7)	8 (33.3)
Encourage students done early to check work	27 (84.4)	24 (100.0)	8 (33.3)

continues

TABLE 11-3 *(Continued)*

	Reading (%)		Math (%)		Science (%)	
Response						
Read aloud possible answers	1	(3.1)	1	(4.2)	0	
Helped marks response(s) on answer sheet	0		4	(16.7)	0	
Allowed students to write on materials/test booklet	26	(81.3)	24	(100.0)	9	(37.5)
Highlighted/circled important words in response options	2	(6.3)	14	(58.3)	0	
Encouraged use of calculators	0		22	(91.7)	0	
Provided sample response as prompt	3	(9.4)	13	(54.2)	0	
Praise/encouraged students to continue working on test	18	(56.3)	16	(66.7)	16	(66.7)
Reminded students of test-taking skills (e.g., look for key word)	16	(50.0)	16	(66.7)	8	(33.3)
Redirected to the correct test item	2	(6.3)	8	(33.3)	1	(4.2)
Redirected students to the correct place on answer sheet	9	(28.1)	11	(45.8)	0	

Note. Shaded items are from the ISAT administration manual.

unsure why "read aloud" and "calculator" appear as accommodations for a handful of students (< 4) in the reading test. We observed no teacher reading any portion of the reading subtest, and did not see a calculator on the desk of any student in the reading sessions we observed.

Direct Observations

General educators and special educators alike were very busy during the test sessions we observed. Procedures in ISAT manuals were followed precisely, and we observed significant active monitoring in most sessions. As general education teachers scanned the room, they did not hesitate to move toward a student they thought was struggling. We observed numerous instances of verbal and nonverbal support and prompting. Thus, the high percentages of "praise" and "redirection" statements on the inventories are not surprising.

Our field notes contained very few instances of multiple assessments being given simultaneously in special education settings. Although it did occur, teachers' "multitasking" observed during ISAT was typically limited to addressing students' needs or questions related to the particular test item they were attempting. Thus, as was the case in fall testing, we again heard multiple help requests from students in the special education settings we observed. During math testing, both observers heard student comments to the effect that they "could not think about math in the [testing] room and would rather go there [general education classroom]." After the sessions, both teachers were asked why they thought the student had made the comment. They thought the students might have been missing the normal cues about their math work that were available in the general education math rooms. (e.g., posters, displays). Their frame of reference for math work, in essence, was not available in the special education or alternate room.

In discussing the assessment with the primary decision-making team, we found the

TABLE 11-4

ISAT Accommodation of Students With Disabilities—Spring 2005 Grades 7 and 8: Reading, Math, and Science Frequency and Percentage of Accommodations for Students for Whom Accommodations Were Recorded

	Reading N = 52 (%)		Math N = 51 (%)		Science N = 56 (%)	
Scheduling						
Provided extended time	44	(84.6)	49	(96.1)	56	(100)
Provided additional breaks	16	(30.8)	16	(31.4)	13	(23.2)
Provided multiple test sessions	17	(32.7)	26	(51.0)	13	(23.2)
Setting						
Made sure room was well lit, ventilated, and free of distractions	50	(96.2)	49	(96.1)	36	(64.3)
Displayed materials in room to help on test	5	(9.6)	14	(27.5)	15	(26.8)
Used of carrels or dividers	8	(15.4)	8	(15.7)	2	(3.6)
Provided special seating/proximity to monitor	13	(25.0)	20	(39.2)	22	(39.3)
Provided small group testing (not with special educator)	1	(1.9)	1	(2.0)	0	
Provided individual testing (not with special educator)	0		0		0	
Administered test in special education room	18	(34.6)	43	(84.3)	45	(80.4)
Provided individual test with special educator	11	(21.2)	9	(17.7)	7	(12.5)
Presentation						
Pointed out important aspects of the test booklet	34	(65.4)	37	(72.9)	25	(44.6)
Repeated or reread directions	45	(86.6)	41	(80.4)	26	(46.4)
Paraphrased directions/used simplified language	42	(80.8)	42	(82.4)	43	(76.8)
Clarified direction/explained task(s)	42	(80.8)	41	(80.4)	28	(50.0)
Read aloud item or section dividers	4	(7.7)	12	(23.5)	36	(64.3)
Read aloud individual items or prompts	15	(28.9)	38	(74.5)	29	(51.8)
Highlighted/circled important words in directions	1	(1.9)	1	(2.0)	2	(3.6)
Highlighted/circled important words in test items	1	(1.9)	1	(2.0)	1	(1.8)
Provided additional sample item(s) as a prompt during testing	0		0		9	(16.1)
Provided practice items leading up to (before) testing	17	(32.7)	29	(56.9)	15	(26.8)
Praised/encouraged student to begin items	41	(78.9)	40	(78.4)	27	(48.2)
Redirected student to the correct test item	2	(3.9)	5	(9.8)	3	(5.4)
Used sign language	0		0		0	
Used adaptive lighting/acoustics to present test	0		0		20	(35.7)
Reminded student of test-taking skill (e.g., look for key word)	42	(80.8)	33	(64.7)	28	(50.0)

continues

TABLE 11-4 *(Continued)*

	Reading N = 52 (%)		Math N = 51 (%)		Science N = 56 (%)	
Presentation cont.						
Encouraged student done early to check work	35	(67.3)	39	(76.5)	17	(30.4)
Encouraged student use of self-management	16	(30.8)	10	(19.6)	16	(28.6)
Response						
Read aloud possible answers	3	(5.8)	33	(64.7)	25	(44.6)
Helped mark response(s) on answer sheet	2	(3.9)	2	(3.9)	2	(3.6)
Recorded students responses verbatim (scribe)	5	(9.6)	4	(7.8)	3	(5.4)
Allowed students to write on materials/test booklet	49	(94.2)	49	(96.1)	15	(26.8)
Highlighted/circled important words in response options	0		0		0	
Used communication device	0		0		1	(1.8)
Allowed student to use a calculator	4	(7.7)	50	(98.0)	3	(5.4)
Provided sample response as prompt	0		0		11	(19.6)
Praised/encouraged student to continue working on test	42	(80.8)	39	(76.5)	29	(51.8)
Reminded student of test taking skills (e.g., look for key word)	36	(69.2)	30	(58.8)	25	(44.6)
Redirected student to the correct test item	2	(3.9)	3	(5.9)	9	(16.1)
Redirected student to the correct place on answer sheet	2	(3.9)	2	(3.9)	10	(17.9)
Encouraged student use of self-management	16	(30.8)	11	(21.6)	18	(32.1)

Note. Shaded items are from the ISAT administration manual.

staff felt that the spring testing process for ISAT was better run than the fall testing sessions for ITBS. However, similar to what they experienced earlier, on the day of testing many teachers reported they felt they were in the position where they needed to make decisions without being fully sure of exact accommodation delivery or if they were assigning more accommodations than were planned for individual students.

IEP-ISAT Accommodation Agreements

As mentioned earlier, the Midwest District special education teachers were able to use an online IEP generation template for all grades. The form includes all IDEA-required information and statements related to students' needs for accommodations and modifications and for participation in district and state assessment. In our preliminary examination of the IEPs for seventh- and eighth-grade students with disabilities, we noticed that planned accommodations for reading and mathematics instruction and assessment were more fully documented than for other content areas. This difference in available information is most likely an artifact of the IEP form itself (which does not list content areas) and the current level of attention given to these areas by NCLB. Therefore, we prioritized, the eighth-grade students' IEP–ISAT accommodation agreement.

Table 11-5 contains both the simple agreement and Kappa values that result when the planned accommodations listed on eighth grade students' IEPs are compared to those reported across testing sessions. Specifically we examined the individual accommodations in each of the main categories of *scheduling, setting, presentation,* and *response.* For this table, the IEP is the anchor point of all comparisons. Thus, if an IEP had an accommodation listed and the student in fact received that accommodation then an exact match existed. If the IEP listed an accommodation that was not provided during testing, then the IEP would *overrepresent* the accommodation use by that student. Alternately, if the IEP did not have an accommodation listed that was used during testing, then the IEP would *underrepresent* the accommodation. This IEP–ISAT accommodation relationship is shown in the right-hand column of Table 11-5.

The reported values in the table must be interpreted with some qualifying cautions. Some accommodations listed reflect those listed in the *ISAT Test Administration Manual* (e.g., "well-lit, distraction-free room," "checking work if done early"). Thus, although these data inform us of the conditions of testing actually experienced, some accommodations would not be expected to be found on IEPs. In addition, recall the State's last-minute rules change allowing "read-aloud" within group arrangements. Finally, in the *setting* accommodation group, the "test in special education room" shows that of the 52 students with disabilities for whom this was planned, only 18 received this accommodation. In actuality, 52 students did take the assessment *with* accommodations and with the involvement of a special education teacher (see Table 11-5); however, they may have taken the test in an alternate room and not their teacher's assigned room.

Across all accommodation categories, the IEPs of eighth-grade students tend to *underrepresent* accommodations actually used

by a nearly 3:1 ratio, inclusive of the ISAT manual items. Within, *scheduling* accommodations, it appears that although more students took ISAT reading in "multiple sessions" than had planned to do so, the accommodation of "extended time" was reportedly used by fewer students than expected. In the *setting* group, it appears more test administrators' attention was provided than had been planned. "Proximity to the monitor" occurred often in general education settings, and "individual testing" although not appearing on IEPs, was provided for 11 students.

The *presentation* and *response* accommodation categories reflect the provision of many test-taking supports and social/behavioral accommodations that were not listed on students' IEPs. "Praise and encouragement" and "reminders of test-taking and self-management skills" are among those provided often. We should point out that our observations documented that students in the individual and small-group testing sessions often got similar packages of accommodations as has been reported in earlier studies (e.g., Elliott, Kratochwill, et al., 2001; Shriner & DeStefano, 2003.) Although the IEP process serves as the focal point for accommodation planning decisions, day-of-testing logistics and changes in students' accommodation needs during the year are important factors in accommodation decisions that are made during the testing program implementation.

LESSONS LEARNED AND DISCUSSION

The technical assistance and professional development activities in which we engaged, though not controlled interventions, were guided by research-to-practice principles as applied within the operational environment of MMS. From the work throughout the entire school year with MMS and district special education staff, we cannot report results or effect sizes, but can make several interre-

TABLE 11-5

Agreement (Kappa) Between Planned IEP Accommodations for State and Districtwide Assessments and Accommodations Provided During 2005 ISAT Testing for Specific Students With Disabilities: Grade 8

IEP Accommodations for State and District Assessments for all SWD (N = 74)		
	Accommodations for Testing in IEP (%)	No Testing Accommodations in IEP (%)
Participated in ISAT	60 (81.1)	4 (5.4)
Did not participate in ISAT	7 (9.5)	3 (4.0)[a]

Agreement of Planned and Provided IEP Accommodations (N = 64)					
	Planned (%)	Actual (%)	Agreement	Kappa	Direct
Scheduling					
Provided extended time	57 (89.1)	44 (68.6)	.67	.07	over
Provided additional breaks	10 (15.6)	16 (25.0)	.72	.14	under
Provided multiple test sessions	2 (3.1)	17 (26.6)	.70	−.06	under
Setting					
Made sure room was well lit, ventilated, and free of distractions	2 (3.1)	50 (78.1)	.25	.02	under
Displayed materials in room to help on test	0	5 (7.8)	.92	b	under
Use of carrels or dividers	0	8 (12.5)	.88	b	under
Provided special seating/proximity to monitor	0	13 (20.3)	.80	b	under
Administered test in Special Education Room	52 (81.3)	18 (28.1)	.41	.07	over
Provided individual test with Special Educator	0	11 (17.2)	.83	b	under
Presentation					
Pointed out important aspects of the test booklet	0	34 (53.1)	.47	b	under
Repeated or reread directions	0	45 (70.3)	.30	b	under
Paraphrased directions/used simplified language	4 (6.3)	42 (65.6)	.38	.02	under
Clarified direction/explained task(s)	11 (17.2)	42 (65.6)	.45	.09	under
Read aloud item or section dividers	40 (62.5)	4 (6.3)	.44	.08	over
Read aloud individual items or prompts	36 (56.3)	15 (23.4)	.64	.33	over
Highlighted/circled important words in directions	0	1 (1.6)	.98	b	under
Highlighted/circled important words in test items	0	1 (1.6)	.98	b	under

continues

TABLE 11-5 *(Continued)*

	Planned (%)	Actual (%)	Agreement	Kappa	Direct
Presentation cont.					
Provided additional sample item(s) as a prompt during testing	0	0	1.0	[b]	same
Provided practice items leading up to (before) testing	0	17 (26.6)	.73	[b]	under
Praised/encouraged student to begin items	0	41 (64.1)	.36	[b]	under
Redirected student to the correct test item	0	2 (3.1)	.97	[b]	under
Used sign language	0	0	1.0	[b]	same
Used adaptive lighting/acoustics to present test	0	0	1.0	[b]	same
Reminded student of test taking skill (e.g., look for key word)	0	42 (65.6)	.34	[b]	under
Encouraged student done early to check work	0	35 (54.7)	.45	[b]	under
Encouraged student use of self-management	0	16 (25.0)	.75	[b]	under
Response					
Read aloud possible answers	36 (56.3)	3 (4.7)	.48	.07	over
Helped mark response(s) on answer sheet	2 (3.1)	2 (3.1)	.97	.48	same
Recorded students responses verbatim (scribe)	5 (7.8)	5 (7.8)	.94	.57	same
Allowed students to write on materials/ test booklet	0	49 (76.6)	.23	[b]	under
Highlighted/circled important words in response options	0	0	1.0	[b]	same
Used communication device	1 (1.6)	0	.98	[b]	over
Allowed student to use a calculator	40 (62.5)	4 (6.3)	.34	–.08	over
Provided sample response as prompt	0	0	1.0	[b]	same
Praised/encouraged student to continue working on test	0	42 (65.6)	.34	[b]	under
Reminded student of test taking skills (e.g., look for key word)	10 (15.6)	36 (56.3)	.36	–.04	under
Redirected student to the correct test item	0	2 (3.1)	.97	[b]	under
Redirected student to the correct place on answer sheet	2 (3.1)	2 (3.1)	.94	–.03	same
Encouraged student use of self-management	0	16 (25.0)	.75	[b]	under

[a]Two of the three students with no testing accommodations were identified as taking an alternate assessment. [b]Kappa is not computed because one variable is a constant (zero).

lated summary statements of lessons learned about the use of accommodations by students with disabilities in the middle school.

First, within the building, disparate ideas and levels of engagement regarding accommodations are potentially problematic and should be addressed. At the outset of the year, there was very limited tracking of the accommodations that were planned and their subsequent use in either instruction or assessment. General educators, in particular, gave the impression of low levels of interest and awareness of planning and delivering accommodations for individual students with disabilities. Perhaps, not surprisingly, the special education teachers (as leaders of most IEP teams) were assigning accommodations with implicit approval of other school-related team members. (We did not address parent involvement in this work.) Moreover, although the middle school operated on team-based principles, accommodation in district and state assessment were rarely discussed in team meetings. During the fall discussions, special education teachers more than others felt they were in a type of "catch-up" mode. Accommodation use and strategy decisions had been given to them, and some felt that the existing demands were already significant.

Second, data-based discussions of accommodations will reveal the positives and negatives of the supports students receive. School personnel reported that the data from fall ITBS testing provided a combined pleasant surprise and rather unexpected challenge. General educators were doing an overall good job with respect to accommodations support for students. Data gathered through fall observations revealed involvement of general educators that reflected the team orientation of MMS and that were appropriately inclusive of students with disabilities. In addition, was a surprise to most staff that student comments expressed a preference for the general education room because it had a positive influence on their attitude and thinking that was not available in the special

education room. This issue was a focal point for technical assistance discussions regarding spring ISAT testing. The *ISAT Administration Test Manual* allowed wall posters and other displays of general information about a subject that were part of the original décor to remain posted during ISAT tests, although "posting or [displaying new items] immediately prior to or during testing" (ISBE, 2005b, p. 7) was prohibited. Items that did not provide direct support for answering test questions were acceptable. Thus, for *all* students, the typicality of the atmosphere of the math or science testing rooms may serve to support thinking about a content area and reduce test-related anxiety to some degree.

Another aspect of this lesson is that the IEP, as a source of accommodation information, often must be supplemented in order to provide a complete description of a student's status. Although most IEPs had planned accommodations marked, rarely were they clearly specified by *content area*. Accommodation delivery was often inconsistent and their actual need and effect was rarely evaluated. At the middle school, in particular, promoting accommodation issues as a topic of team meetings could be of benefit for both instructional and assessment considerations.

Bringing this information to their attention caused school personnel to better understand and incorporate the input and contributions of general educators and, when coupled with the comparatively high-demand environments experienced in special education settings, to question the real benefit of the special education pullout accommodations over the general education testing situation for some students.

Third, the social/behavioral and affective supports that students experience in testing environments are important considerations and require effective communication between general education and special education staff. Praise statements, prompting and redirecting, and reminders of test-taking skills may not be viewed by all personal as accommodations for assessment; some might consider them routine teacher practice. The "social event(s) within tests" (Tindal, 2006), however, are components of most assessments, whether or not they are formally labeled accommodated tests. We observed (and teachers reported) many instances of teachers interacting with students in an attempt to keep students on task, bolster their motivation, and support effective test-taking behaviors. Though we neither counted the exact frequencies and types of these statements, nor attempted to ascertain their actual behavioral function, teachers clearly thought their behaviors were helpful to the students. For students of middle school age, in general, and for certain students with disabilities, in particular, teacher attention and interaction could, perhaps, be perceived as not supportive in all cases. Information about the extent to which these types of support exist in the regular instructional environment and their typical effect on student behavior, are important data to share.

JOINT RECOMMENDATIONS AND DISTRICT PLANS

We engaged in this technical assistance for MMS with the express purpose of addressing their self-identified high priority programmatic issues using data-supported decision processes. As technical assistance providers, our one expressed requirement was that both general education and special education decision makers be involved. This work occurred in the year prior to the NCLB requirement for yearly testing of students, a factor that when coupled with the increasingly stringent AYP criteria, weigh heavily in their choices of action plans. Following, we share the four recommended plans that Midwest will follow in order to improve the quality of assessment and accommodation strategies afforded students with disabilities in both general education and special education environments.

Recommended Plan #1: Explore/Enhance the General Education Accommodation Environment

The first plan MMS staff created addresses not only accommodations as they are typically considered, but also the routine instructional supports and teacher behaviors that students experience in the general education setting. The degree to which the instructional and assessment tasks reflect principles of universal design (Dolan & Hall, 2006) is something that the staff wishes to know. To design learning environments so that the learning is accessible to a wide range of students without the need for adaptation and that also maintains the learning goals may help students better remember what they were taught and to think better during the test (Thompson, Johnstone, Anderson, & Miller, 2005). In addition, the extent of social/behavioral support availability (e.g., opportunity for responding and reinforcement) within general education, and the sustainability of those supports are important considerations.

All teams at MMS are participating in meetings to share their information about regular classroom practices with considerations of those students with disabilities served by the team members. They are hopeful that the observed supportiveness of the general education environment exists over the long term, and that the often troublesome logistics of testing students with the involvement of special educators will be minimized. General education setting "retention" for a larger percentage of students may reduce the need for separate testing and "access assistance" (Clapper et al., 2006) that require another person to be involved. The need for and use of accommodation strategies, a reality addressed by the second recommended plan, will not be eliminated,

Recommended Plan #2: Periodically Monitor Accommodation Use and Effect

The Accommodation Monitoring Form (Figure 11-3), which was distributed to all teams after fall testing, will be used to summarize accommodation and support availability, to promote discussions at team meetings, and to reference as IEPs for the next year are developed. The use of such a form allows a teacher-friendly assessment of the types and frequency received in both general education and special education settings. It can supplement the judgment of teachers and is an important addition for the students' IEP and other records. In Illinois, the student's history of use of accommodations is required information in accommodation decisions for the high school level test, the Prairie State Achievement Examination (PSAE). The Accommodation Monitoring Form might be useful in these decisions. In addition, provisions for minor changes to the IEP as provided in proposed section 300.324 of IDEA 2004 may not require reconvening and IEP team meetings. At this time, it is not known if an accommodation decision will be considered a minor change. Still, policy researchers and technical assistance providers (e.g., Thurlow, 2006; Yell, et al., in press) recommend that IEP teams should continue to exercise their best, reasoned judgment when determining accommodation plans and use. The documentation of teachers' ongoing decisions seems a prudent strategy that could support such a minor adjustment to the IEP.

Recommended Plan #3: Evaluate the Role of Social/Behavioral Accommodations and Supports

The MMS staff and the special education administrators were keenly interested in a closer examination of the testing experiences of students at the middle school and at the alternative education sites that served their students. The stressors that most students experience during end-of-year tests are sometimes more of a concern for students with disabilities, although specific accommodations of this type are less often documented on IEPs than are changes to test format and response options (Shriner & Wehby, 2004) Staff members expected increased anxiety as a result of the NCLB requirements for yearly testing. Special educators, with the support of staff members at one of the alternative placements, planned to systematically evaluate the frequency and effect of social/behavioral supports on the ITBS test performance of several students for whom appropriate behavior during assessments was a high priority concern. This ambitious plan seemed important to members of the primary decision-making group given the relatively high number of students for whom these accommodations and supports were provided in both fall ITBS and spring ISAT testing.

Recommended Plan #4: Empower IEP Teams With Knowledge Regarding "Valid" Accommodations

A final, forward-looking plan for action revolves around the ongoing professional development needs of the Midwest School District. The administrators, in particular, want to be ahead of the curve with respect to NCLB and IDEA 2004 requirements for states in assuring that accommodation use does not compromise the validity of assessment inferences. Some of their motivation for planning periodic staff updates on accommodations is the result of the "read-aloud" accommodation changes discussed earlier. In the past, differing opinions about the provision of this accommodation were based on differing views about the construct(s) being measured by items on the reading test and the purpose of the test. Adding to their concern is the fact that, for Grades 3 through 8, Illinois currently allows nothing to be read aloud, however, at the high school level, reading aloud is permitted on the PSAE, provided that the student's characteristics warrant the accommodation. This disconnect of rules, they thought, placed the students moving from middle school to high school at a disadvantage. (Recall that documentation of a history of accommodation use is one factor considered in the assigning of accommodations for the PSAE.)

Further, some teachers requested a definitive list of accommodations that were allowed for each ISAT subtest, and they had a particular concern for reading. Under IDEA 2004, it is the states' responsibility to determine what types of accommodations may be used on a particular test, while ensuring that students with disabilities receive appropriate accommodations (70 FR 74632), yet there exist no publicly reported data to define which part(s), if any, of the ISAT reading test (passage, question stem, possible answers) can be read aloud without invalidating the assessment of intended constructs. Special educators were experiencing first hand the challenge of balancing the requirements for states' delineations of valid accommodations and their appropriateness with the IEP teams' authority to determine and assign accommodations for individual students. By implementing this action plan, the Midwest Middle School's special education leadership is trying to help them achieve this balance, however fragile it may be.

REFERENCES

Browder, D., Flowers, C., Ahlgrim-Delzell, L., Karvonen, M., Spooner, F., & Algozzine, R. (2004). The alignment of alternate assessment content with academic and functional curricula. *The Journal of Special Education*, 37(4), 211–223.

Clapper, A. T., Morse, A. B., Thurlow, M. L., & Thompson, S. J. (2006). *How to develop state guidelines for access assistants: Scribes, readers, and sign language interpreters.* Minneapolis, MN: University of Minnesota, National Center on Educational Outcomes.

DeStefano, L., & Shriner, J. G. (1998). *Project PAR: Investigating participation, accommodation, and reporting practices with the Illinois Standards Achievement Test.* Unpublished manuscript, University of Illinois at Urbana Champaign.

DeStefano, L., Shriner, J. G., & Lloyd, C. (2001). Teacher decision making in participation of students with disabilities in large-scale assessment. *Exceptional Children*, 68, 7–22.

Dolan, R., & Hall, T. (2006, March). *Developing accessible tests with universal design and digital technologies.* Presentation at the Educational Testing Service Conference on Accommodation of Students with Disabilities on State Assessments. Savannah, GA.

Elliott, S., Braden, J, & White, J. (2001). *Assessing one and all: Educational accountability for students with disabilities.* Reston, VA: Council for Exceptional Children.

Elliott, S., Kratochwill, T., & McKevitt, B. (2001). Experimental analysis of the effects of testing accommodations on the scores of students with and without disabilities. *Journal of School Psychology*, 39, 3–24.

Elliott, S., Kratochwill, T., & Schulte, A. (1998). The assessment accommodation checklist: Who, what, where, when, why, and how? *TEACHING Exceptional Children*, 31(2), 10–14.

Espin, C. A., Deno, S. L., & Albayrak-Kaymak, D. (1998). Individualized education programs in resource and inclusive settings: How "individualized" are they? *Journal of Special Education*, 32(3), 164–74.

Ganguly, R., & Shriner, J. G. (2004, February). *Academic and social-behavioral accommodations for students with emotional-behavior disorders.* Paper presented at the annual meeting of the Midwest Symposium for Leadership in Behavior Disorders, Kansas City, MO.

Hieronymus, A. N., Hoover, H. D., & Lindquist, E. F. (1986). *Iowa Tests of Basic Skills.* Chicago: Riverside. (Form K, 1992 norms).

Hollenbeck, K., Tindal, G., & Almond, P. (1998). Teachers' knowledge of accommodations as a validity issue in high-stakes testing.

The Journal of Special Education, 32(3), 175–183.

Illinois State Board of Education. (2005a). *Teacher Service Record*. Retrieved December 9, 2005, from http://www.isbe.state.il.us/pubs/tsr_data/default.htm

Illinois State Board of Education. (2005b). *ISAT Test Administration Manual: Grades 3–8*. Springfield, IL: Author.

Kleinert, H., & Kearns, J. (2004). Alternate assessments. In F. Orelove, D. Sobsey, & R. Silberman (Eds.), *Educating children with multiple disabilities: A collaborative approach* (4th ed., pp. 115–149). Baltimore: Paul Brookes.

Rouse, M., Shriner, J., & Danielson, L. (2000). National assessment and special education in the United States and England and Wales. In M. McLaughlin & M. Rouse, (Eds.), *Special education and school reform in the United States and Britain* (pp. 66–97). London: Routledge.

Shriner, J. G. (2001, April). *Effective IEPs: Decisions for standards and assessment*. Paper presented at the annual meeting of the Council for Exceptional Children, Kansas City, MO.

Shriner, J. G., & DeStefano, L. (2001). Participation in statewide assessments: Views of district-level personnel. *Assessment for Effective Intervention, 26*, 9–16.

Shriner, J. G., & DeStefano, L. (2002). *Project IEP-D: Improving Education Professionals' Decision Making*. Unpublished manuscript, University of Illinois at Urbana Champaign.

Shriner, J. G., & DeStefano, L. (2003). Participation and accommodation in state assessment: The role of Individualized Education Programs. *Exceptional Children, 69*, 147–161.

Shriner, J. G., & Wehby, J. H. (2004). Accountability and assessment for students with emotional and behavioral disorders. In R. Rutherford, M. Quinn, & S. Mathur (Eds.), *Handbook of research in behavioral disorders* (pp. 216–231). New York: Guilford.

Sireci, S. G., Scarpati, S., E., & Li, S. (2005). Test accommodations for students with disabilities: An analysis of the interaction hypothe-

sis. *Review of Educational Research, 75*, 457–490.

Sopko, K. M. (2003). *The IEP: A synthesis of current literature since 1997* (Report for Project FORUM). Alexandria, VA: Project FORUM at National Association of State Directors of Special Education (ERIC Document Reproduction Service No. ED 476 559)

Thompson, S. J., Johnstone, C. J., Anderson, M. E., & Miller, N. A. (2005). *Considerations for the development and review of universally designed assessments* (Tech. Rep. No. 42). Minneapolis, MN: University of Minnesota, National Center on Educational Outcomes. Retrieved March 20, 2006, from http://education.umn.edu/NCEO/OnlinePubs/Technical42.htm

Thurlow, M. L. (2006, March). *Accommodations in state policies: What a wonderful world of diversity*. Presentation at the Educational Testing Service Conference on Accommodation of Students with Disabilities on State Assessments, Savannah, GA.

Thurlow, M. L., Elliott, J. L., & Ysseldyke, J. E. (2003) *Testing students with disabilities* (2nd ed.). Thousand Oaks, CA: Corwin Press.

Tindal, G. (2006, March). *Accommodations research: Reconsidering the test accommodation validation process*. Presentation at the Educational Testing Service Conference on Accommodation of Students with Disabilities on State Assessments. Savannah, GA.

Title I—Improving the Academic Achievement of the Disadvantaged; Individuals with Disabilities Education Act (IDEA)— Assistance to States for the Education of Children with Disabilities; Proposed Rule, 70 Fed Reg. 74624 (2005) (34 C.F.R. § 200 and 300)

U.S. Department of Education. (2005, August 9). *Alternate achievement standards for students with the most significant cognitive disabilities: Non-regulatory guidance*. Retrieved July 11, 2006, from http://www.ed.gov/admins/lead/account/saa.html#guidance

Yell, M. L., Katsiyannis, A., & Shriner, J. G., (2006). No Child Left Behind Act, Adequate Yearly Progress, and students with disabilities. *TEACHING Exceptional Children, 38*(4), 32–39.

Yell, M. L., Shriner, J., G., & Katsiyannis, A. (in press). Individuals with Disabilities Education Improvement Act of 2004: Implications for special and general educators, administrators, and teacher trainers. *Focus on Exceptional Children*.

Author Note: Preparation of this chapter was supported, in part, by a grant (H325N020081) from the U.S. Department of Education, Office of Special Education and Rehabilitative Services, Office of Special Education Programs awarded to the authors. Opinions expressed herein do not necessarily reflect those of the U.S. Department of Education or Offices within it.

12

How States Use Assessment Results to Improve Learning for Students With Disabilities

DANIEL J. WIENER

Massachusetts Department of Education

INTRODUCTION AND OVERVIEW

This chapter explores the effects that the enactment of federal education reform laws beginning in the 1990s (IDEA, NCLB) and state education reform initiatives (particularly Massachusetts Education Reform Act of 1993) have had on students with disabilities. The new policies have had a major impact on the internal reorganization within state departments of education, which have led to restructuring and reordering the priorities in the schools and districts under their supervision.

The new and far-reaching requirements of these laws have led state departments to expand their traditional responsibilities and capacities in order to develop new, comprehensive statewide academic assessments; collect and report vast quantities of data on assessment results for every child; and determine and report on the academic progress of each school and district. These new mandates and policy directions have caused state departments to rethink their approaches to instruction, assessment, and accountability in

order to include and account for all students, including students with disabilities, and to justify these new policies to the public.

However, before states can presume to use results from new, fully inclusive assessments to improve learning and inform state policies, they must be certain the assessment system itself is validly measuring students' academic knowledge and not other factors, such as:

- The degree to which instruction was or was not provided to all students. (For example, is it clear to special educators what is meant by "access to the general education curriculum," and what is expected to be taught to students with disabilities?)

- The appropriateness of test accommodations and assessment formats used to measure the student's level of achievement. (For example, does the lack of availability of accommodations prevent the student from demonstrating his or her knowledge and skills?)

- The effects of a student's disability, which can interfere with measurement of knowledge and skills. (For example, would the student be more appropriately assessed using an alternate assessment?)

States are still struggling to get maximum benefits from their assessment systems. They refine and make improvements to appropriately assess all students and they continually learn how to use the data these assessment systems collect. This chapter describes what Massachusetts has learned as it analyzes data from its statewide assessment (the Massachusetts Comprehensive Assessment System, MCAS, and the alternate assessment, MCAS-Alt) and its technical and policy advisory committees.

The application of a uniform graduation requirement is also discussed, because of its impact on teaching, learning, assessment, and accountability for students with disabilities in Massachusetts since first implemented for the class of 2003. Data will be presented to demonstrate that students with disabilities "close the gap" with their nondisabled peers beyond Grade 10 in terms of meeting the state's graduation requirement.

STATE ROLES ARE CHANGING

State departments of education collect an extensive array of student demographic information, assessment results, and school performance data with increasing precision and sophistication. To improve instruction and student achievement, they have set up elaborate systems to report test results and help schools target limited resources. State education departments are evolving into warehouses for data collection, laboratories for data analysis, and comprehensive information systems. They rely not only on test results and locally reported student identification data, but also on scientific research, public opinion, feedback from practitioners, and education law to make informed deci-

sions that continuously drive change and improvement. States are uniquely and ideally situated to obtain immediate feedback on the impact their policy decisions have on schools and districts. They can review the effects of these policies quickly by analyzing test data and reviewing concerns from practitioners. Often this requires that they modify their assessment system accordingly.

States receive a continual stream of information from schools and parents in the form of inquiries, requests for technical assistance, and anecdotal reports from the field as well as the input of numerous stakeholder advisory groups, all of which serve to inform development of new methods and policies for school improvement and student assessment. This revolution in information management and in the mandate for schools to account for and improve the achievement of *all* students has had its most dramatic effects on those student subgroups that have historically lagged behind the mainstream in academic performance and opportunities to participate in all the learning activities of schools. The educational experiences of students with disabilities, in particular, have undergone radical changes as a result of these academic reforms with almost 80% of the subgroup meeting graduation requirements, and those with the most significant disabilities being provided expanded academic opportunities. (Massachusetts Department of Education, 2005b and c).

REORGANIZATION OF STATE DEPARTMENTS OF EDUCATION

In the aftermath of state and federal standards-based reform laws enacted in the 1990s, the internal structures of state departments of education began to change dramatically to respond to the new mandates for improving student achievement. In Massachusetts, the Education Reform Law of 1993 addressed the apparent educational disparities between students in poor and in affluent communities and mandated a new funding formula to provide schools with the equitable means to accomplish the provisions of the law. The Education Reform Law specified, among other things, that the state identify academic standards for all students, and that a minimum academic performance on statewide MCAS tests be defined in order to meet requirements to graduate from high school. The Individuals With Disabilities Education Act Amendments of 1997 (IDEA '97), in turn, required the full participation of students with disabilities in statewide academic achievement assessments that measure their performance on the same learning standards as other students, rather than on the functional skills that had been the traditional mainstay of most programs for these students (Browder et al., 2005). IDEA '97 also stipulated the use of accommodations and alternate assessments, as needed, for students with disabilities so they could participate fairly and meaningfully in state and district assessments.

These laws had the effect of galvanizing the leadership within the Massachusetts Department of Education to explore ways to collaborate internally in order to promote academic improvements and fully inclusive assessments. In order to include students with disabilities in its state assessments, the offices of special education, curriculum and instruction, and assessment and accountability found it necessary to collaborate to a greater extent, and to adapt to their new roles by developing new approaches to deal with constituents, the public, and each other. (See Figure 12-1 which illustrates how each Department office adapted to these new requirements.)

Office of Student Assessment

The student assessment office found it necessary to make testing policies more flexible by expanding and promoting the use of an expanded array of new test accommodations

for students with disabilities who had previously been excused from testing when appropriate accommodations were not available (Browder et al., 2005). Massachusetts incorporated many of these accommodations (e.g., untimed testing) into its new assessment system (MCAS) for all students. New test policies acknowledged the need for other accommodations as well (e.g., flexible testing schedules, scribes, development of test adaptations for Braille, electronic text readers). The use of calculators and math formula sheets were added to a growing list of "commonly used" accommodations, which in turn created a need to train local educators how to determine test accommodations and designate students for alternate assessments. After a 2-year development and field testing process, a statewide alternate assessment (MCAS-Alt) was launched based on evidence compiled in a portfolio throughout the school year. New participation guidelines and publications with extensive training specifically for educators working with students with disabilities were developed (Massachusetts Department of Education, 1999) to help individualized education program (IEP) and 504 teams decide which students should take alternate assessments.

Office of Special Education

As the student assessment office became more flexible in allowing multiple approaches and testing formats for students with disabilities, the state special education office needed to acknowledge in its literature and training that all students with disabilities would now participate in these assessments. These assessments would be based on student performance of state academic standards, rather than on social, behavioral, and daily living skills. Special educators would require extensive retraining and resources in order to provide academic instruction to all students, even those with significant cognitive disabilities. Almost 10 years after the passage of

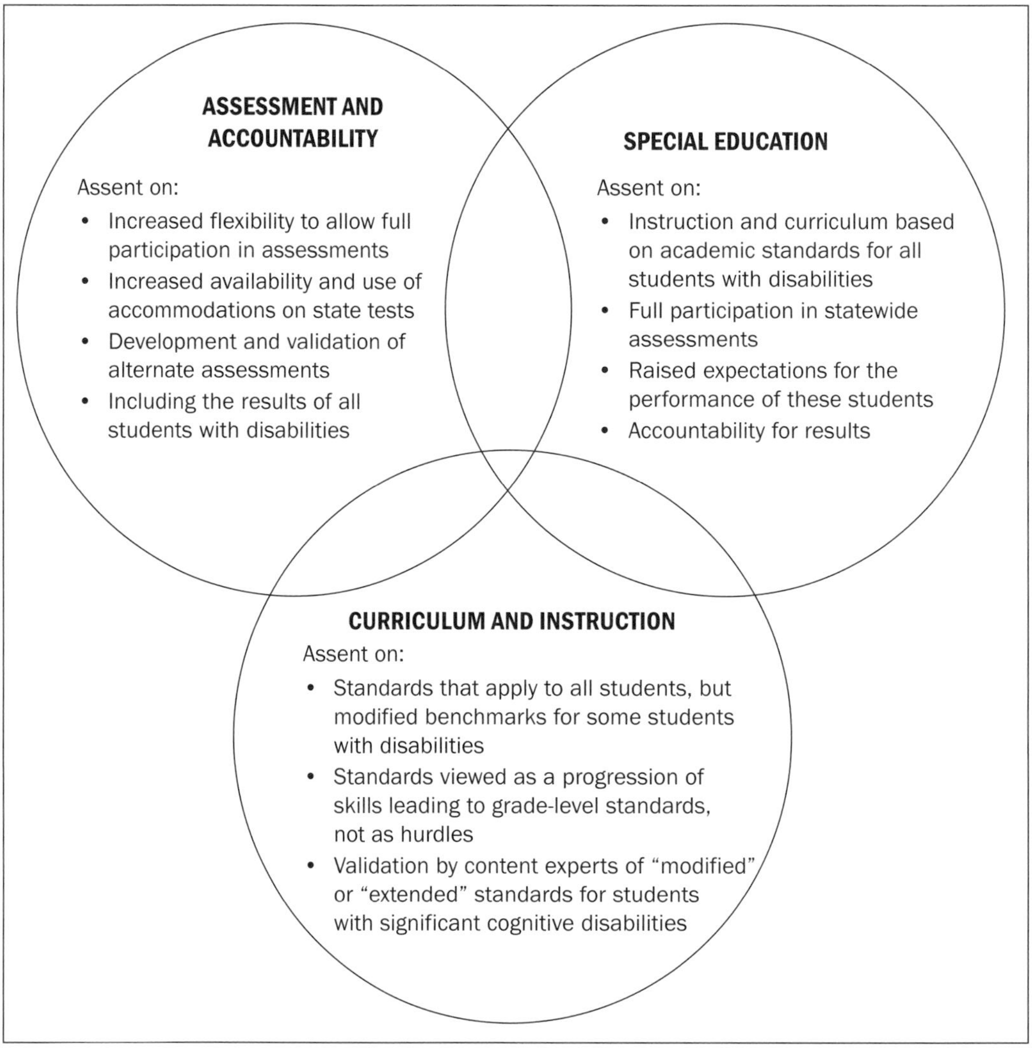

**ASSESSMENT AND
ACCOUNTABILITY**

Assent on:

- Increased flexibility to allow full
  participation in assessments
- Increased availability and use of
  accommodations on state tests
- Development and validation of
  alternate assessments
- Including the results of all
  students with disabilities

SPECIAL EDUCATION

Assent on:

- Instruction and curriculum based
  on academic standards for all
  students with disabilities
- Full participation in statewide
  assessments
- Raised expectations for the
  performance of these students
- Accountability for results

CURRICULUM AND INSTRUCTION

Assent on:

- Standards that apply to all students, but
  modified benchmarks for some students
  with disabilities
- Standards viewed as a progression of
  skills leading to grade-level standards,
  not as hurdles
- Validation by content experts of "modified"
  or "extended" standards for students
  with significant cognitive disabilities

FIGURE 12-1

Adaptation and Collaboration Within State Departments of Education in Order to Promote Fully
Inclusive Standards, Assessments, and Accountability

IDEA '97, extensive reorganization within
the field of special education and in preser-
vice training programs for prospective teachers continues today in response to:

- The mandated participation of students
  with disabilities in state academic testing.

- The process for decision making on use
  of test accommodations and alternate
  assessments.

- A graduation requirement for all students in many states, including Massachusetts.

Perhaps more significantly, traditional
assumptions began to change, though slowly
at first, as to what students with disabilities
could (and should) learn.

Office of Curriculum and Instruction

The office of curriculum and instruction is
responsible for developing state curriculum

frameworks, content standards, and performance benchmarks. Staff was required to lend their expertise to the task of adapting state standards and grade-level benchmarks for a broader range of students, many of whom were working well below grade-level expectations and for whom it was not readily apparent how performance expectations would apply (Kleinert and Kearns, 2001). With collaboration and assistance from content experts, special educators, and others, the Massachusetts Department of Education completed a comprehensive guide in 2001, the *Resource Guide to the Massachusetts Curriculum Frameworks for Students With Significant Disabilities*, and expanded this guide in 2006. The curriculum guide conceptualized academic instruction for students with the most significant cognitive disabilities along a progression of skills that allowed them to access key ideas, skills, and content by addressing the standards at modified "levels of complexity." Students would address specific outcomes by mastering a progression of skills moving toward and based on, the grade-level standards taught to nondisabled students. This process of expanding the learning standards along a continuum entailed support not only from education leadership, but the cooperation of the offices of special education, curriculum and instruction, and student assessment, because each would rely on the other for essential information to complete the task. Although the process of modifying standards and benchmarks to address the needs of all students took several years, the instructional approach described in the *Resource Guide* was subsequently embraced by Massachusetts special educators. This approach has helped state and federal education officials redefine the term "access to the general education curriculum" for all students (Massachusetts Department of Education, 2001; U.S. Department of Education, 2003).

How do states know whether test results for students with disabilities are reliable and if the inferences made from these results are valid? Before states can effectively and reliably use the assessment results of students with disabilities, they first must ascertain the following:

- Whether the student had access to the learning opportunities, resources, and materials needed to learn the knowledge and skills being assessed (e.g., textbooks, maps, manipulatives, computers, etc.).

- Whether appropriate test accommodations and assessment formats were used to measure the knowledge and skills.

- Whether lack of familiarity with subject matter by educators prevented effective teaching.

- Whether a student with a disability was unfamiliar with test-taking strategies, or was physically and emotionally unprepared for the test-taking experience.

As a result, it has taken longer than many had anticipated to ascertain that learning has improved for students with disabilities as a result of standards-based instruction and participation in assessments and accountability. However, as issues of capacity, resources, training, and assessment formats are addressed and fine-tuned by state and local educators, it is apparent, at least from the assessment data gathered in Massachusetts, that the performance of students with disabilities on state assessments (including alternate assessments) has improved noticeably. In addition, IEP teams have adjusted to their expanded role in determining standards-based goals and assessment participation formats for students with disabilities. (Massachusetts Department of Education, 2005c).

SUPPORT FOR STATES

States have had to rely on help from both within and outside the state to develop new instruments and policies for measuring student performance and to devise new strategies for training educators and communicating with the public. The challenge of developing an effective alternate assessment system, in particular, continues to perplex many states years after these systems were first mandated (Thompson & Thurlow, 2000; Thompson, Thurlow, Johnstone, & Altman, 2005). States in the vanguard of developing alternate assessments, notably Kentucky, West Virginia, Maryland, and others, lent their support and expertise to other states struggling to meet these requirements. Educators from Kentucky, the first state to require the use of alternate assessments in 1992 (Browder et al., 2005; Kleinert & Kearns, 2001), supported states like Massachusetts in developing their state models. In addition, they prepared state department staff for the magnitude of the task they faced and the likely reactions from the public. Now that NCLB and IDEA 2004 have reinforced the requirement for technically valid alternate assessments, states like Massachusetts continue to provide consultation and assistance to other states in meeting this challenge.

Contractors have also assisted states in developing their alternate assessments. The test industry has geared up to provide this service as evidenced by the increased number of firms providing capacity in this area (anecdotal to author, 2006). Contractors with clients in multiple states are able to share effective practices and have assisted states to document the technical adequacy of their assessment systems (Massachusetts Department of Education, 2006b). Meanwhile, the research and publications of institutes and universities, (such as the National Center on Educational Outcomes, which publishes annual state survey data) allows states to benefit from the wisdom and accomplishments of researchers and other states. Perhaps most important, stakeholder advisory councils have allowed states to strengthen their emergent assessment systems by asking relevant questions and posing challenges, and by assisting in the development of participation guidelines, communications strategies, and new instructional approaches. Each of these contributors plays an important role in shaping the assessment environment for students with disabilities and ensuring that results are as meaningful and available as possible.

EXPLAINING IT TO THE PUBLIC

Although most states continue to involve a cross-section of stakeholders to advise them on state education policies, there is an additional obligation to explain these policies and initiatives in detail to the public. For example, states have had to develop cogent arguments for the likely benefits to students with disabilities of including them in academic instruction and assessments, particularly those with the most significant disabilities. It is not readily apparent to parents, for example, how this might be accomplished, given the severity of the disabilities of many of their sons and daughters, and also why academic skills ought to be considered important in the lives of those students. The prevailing perception of this student population is that they lack the capacity to learn abstract concepts, complex subject matter, and higher-order reasoning. As a consequence, a climate has prevailed in much of special education in which self-esteem is preserved, but low expectations maintained for the achievements of these students (McGrew & Evans, 2003). Instruction for students with significant disabilities has preeminently been in the areas of social, behavioral, and other "life skills" (Browder et al, 2005), because it was presumed that these students should learn only how to address skills of daily care and recreation, rather than the stimulating and enriching academic activities provided to their nondisabled peers. The change in focus toward fulfillment of the academic goals of these students has taken parents largely by surprise, who see this new emphasis as an additional arena in which their children most certainly will fail. Evidence is emerging to the contrary, however, and teachers report that most of their students eagerly participate in demanding learning activities, faring surprisingly well (Massachusetts Department of Education, 2005c and d; Wiener, 2006).

Added to parents' list of concerns is the fear of new graduation requirements in some states, including Massachusetts, that affect whether or not a student with a disability will receive a diploma. Many states with graduation requirements, though not all, hold students with disabilities to the same graduation requirements as general education students (Johnson & Thurlow, 2003). Because a student with a disability will never meet the state's graduation requirement, the reasoning goes, why should he or she be taught the same academic skills as other students or be assessed on his or her progress? The graduation requirement has given rise to predictable reactions from parents, such as the following comments, paraphrased only slightly (Wiener, 2002):

• "He can't learn math! How will he feel if he fails?"

• "She doesn't need academics; she needs life skills!"

• "She'll never meet the graduation requirement, so why bother assessing her?"

• "The state is setting up my child to fail. Why punish him?"

• "He could never pass that test"

Comments such as these reflect parents' natural protective impulse, and no amount of reassurance by local or state officials is likely to provide a satisfactory response. These questions reinforce the highly emotional nature of inclusive state assessments and should serve to remind educators of the very human aspects of this work. It has been a challenge to alter the educational climate for students with disabilities, but at its core, it has raised the inevitable and fundamental question: *What is the purpose of special education?* Is it solely to prepare students to live independently upon leaving public instruction? Or, should special education focus on teaching and learning the knowledge, concepts, and skills that are deemed important for all students?

HOW ASSESSMENT RESULTS CAN HELP STATES

Once state assessment policies and systems stabilize and schools and IEP teams adjust to new expectations and procedures for the instruction, learning, and assessment of all students, the data from those systems can then become useful in determining information and making decisions about the education of students with disabilities. The data can provide answers to important questions, such as the following:

1. Are students participating in assessments fairly and appropriately?

   • Are students receiving all necessary accommodations?

   • Are students being appropriately assigned to alternate assessments?

2. Are *all* students receiving instruction in state standards?

   • Do students receive instruction in *all* content areas?

   • Are they taught grade-appropriate knowledge and skills?

3. Are there areas in need of clarification, support, review, or monitoring for *individual* students?

   • Do most or all students do poorly in certain academic areas?

   • Do individual students need support in specific areas of the curriculum?

Scores alone don't tell schools enough, and by themselves are unlikely to yield improvements in teaching and learning. Systematic analysis throughout the year, however, may lead to improvements. Assistance from detailed test analyses provided by the state that show how students in each school answered test questions, how many students (and in which classrooms) answered each question correctly, and the content standard on which each question is based can assist educators to determine whether test responses reflect *individual* knowledge and skills or a *systemic* lack of instruction in that area. Some states, among them Massachusetts, provide software to schools for downloading and sorting test results. From the state's perspective, the assessment serves as a "searchlight" that exposes areas of strength and challenge and a "mirror" that reflects all aspects of academic teaching and learning in a school, including those areas in need of improvement. Because the results of all students, including students with disabilities, count in the Adequate Yearly Progress rating of each school, there has been a more equitable distribution of resources within schools and greater attention to the needs of all students.

ASSESSMENT RESULTS AND TEST ACCOMMODATIONS

Assessment results plus observation of students during testing can assist IEP teams to identify academic goals and test accommodations needed by the student for the coming year. Decisions made early in a student's education may need to be adjusted to reflect accumulated experience using accommodations on previous assessments (Cortiella, 2005). Accommodations, if used correctly, allow students with disabilities to access and participate in the assessment fairly, and also correct for other factors unique to the testing process and environment (e.g., stress and anxiety, ability to recall facts under pressure,

ability to stay on task, inexperience taking tests of the duration and intensity of most statewide tests). Feedback from IEP teams also informs the state whether or not it should consider the development of, or encourage the use of, additional accommodations resulting from the suggestions of educators and parents, such as:

- Use of new electronic test versions (e.g., on a CD) compatible with specific electronic text-reader software.

- Use of video cameras to record a deaf student's signed responses and then, based on the video playback, have the student transcribe his or her responses in English text.

- Use of preapproved math formula sheets and individualized graphic organizers.

- Use of projection systems to enlarge text beyond standard large print size.

Feedback from test administrators and assessment results can improve the state's perception and understanding of how accommodations are used for routine instruction. This can enable the state to improve its guidance to IEP teams in making appropriate decisions regarding the use of necessary accommodations on state tests.

RESULTS OF ALTERNATE ASSESSMENTS

Alternate assessments, like their standardized counterparts, measure what skills, concepts, and information in the state standards students with significant disabilities have learned. (Browder et al, 2005). Additionally, the purpose of alternate assessments is to provide assessment data on the performance of the students who take them to schools and the public, so schools can be held accountable for what students are learning (Quenemoen, Rigney, & Thurlow, 2002). Only since 1997 have alternate assessment systems been required for each state, and states have taken a variety of approaches to meet this requirement for the widely divergent student population who takes them. Use of data from these assessments, therefore, is still in the relatively early stages. However, the requirement for states to develop and use alternate assessments, and for schools to be accountable for the students with disabilities who take them, has significantly changed the education landscape. It now guarantees that these students won't be forgotten when determinations are made about which students in the school will receive instruction and other resources. It is important to increase awareness of what these students are learning and hold schools accountable for *all* students.

There are important local applications for alternate assessments as well, such as setting instructional goals, sharing this information with parents and IEP team members, and writing periodic progress reports (Browder et al, 2005). Alternate assessments also provide a framework for collecting data on student performance centrally, and then assessing how well and how much each student has learned before deciding what to teach next. The process of alternate assessment in Massachusetts is intended to guide teachers to improve student achievement by requiring that they first set a precise and measurable instructional goal for each student, and then design tasks that measure performance on that goal by recording the student's responses in terms of the accuracy and the independence demonstrated in each response. Once the student attains a sufficiently high degree of accuracy and independence and meets the predetermined performance goal, the teacher is directed to increase the level of complexity of the tasks and begin the process once again. The assessment products (called *evidence*) and the instructional data collected for the student's portfolio result from actual instruction in the classroom and are intimately tied to what is being taught to the student (Massachusetts Department of Education, 2001.)

According to a biannual state survey of Massachusetts teachers who conducted alternate assessments during the previous year, special educators have improved in their capacity to teach academic subject matter, and report that they now feel more included in the life of the school and connected to other faculty. Most special educators in Massachusetts have become thoroughly familiar with the learning standards as a result of regular use of the *Resource Guide to the Massachusetts Curriculum Frameworks for Students with Significant Disabilities* (Massachusetts Department of Education, 2001), and have been included with greater frequency and regularity in meetings to discuss issues of curriculum and instruction. Special educators have increased the frequency with which they consult with general educators on curriculum issues, because they must be aware of what other students are learning in order to adapt it for their own students (Massachusetts Department of Education, 2005c).

STATE GRADUATION REQUIREMENTS

In 2003, 27 states had graduation exit exams that students were required to pass before earning a diploma. Policies vary on whether students with disabilities are held to the same graduation standard as other students, and whether alternative diploma options exist (Johnson & Thurlow, 2003). Although opinions may differ on the effectiveness of such an "exit-exam" policy, experience in Massachusetts has shown that standards, and the expectations for reaching them, have been raised as a result of the graduation exit examination. When schools are held accountable for the achievement of all students, including students with disabilities, and the graduation rates of each high school are publicly reported, as required by NCLB, a state graduation requirement can serve as a stimulus for schools to continue to provide intensive instruction throughout high school

Class of:	On Grade 10 Test	After Retest 1	After Retest 2	After Retest 3	After Retest 4
2003	30	45	55	69	80
2004	32	58	67	75	84
2005	46	57	66	70	77
2006	50	62	70	74	79

FIGURE 12-2

Students With Disabilities: Percentage Meeting the Massachusetts Graduation Requirement By Earning a "Competency Determination"

to students who have not yet passed the required high school assessments. However, states must work to minimize the potential negative consequences, such as increased pressure on schools and students and the narrowing of the curriculum. In addition, schools need to provide opportunities for the small number of students who don't earn diplomas.

The assessment results of students with disabilities in Massachusetts in Grade 10 and beyond are particularly instructive, and two important conclusions can be drawn from the data collected since the graduation requirement was first applied to the class of 2003. First, there has been a notable increase each year in the percentage of students with disabilities who pass the Grade 10 tests in English language arts and mathematics *on their first try,* as shown in Figure 12-2. In spring 2006, 55 percent of students in the class of 2008 passed both Grade 10 tests on their first attempt, compared with just 30 percent in the class of 2003. In addition, the gap in passing rates between students with disabilities and their non-disabled peers has closed significantly after successive administrations of the MCAS retest in Grades 11 and 12, as shown in Figure 12-3 (Massachusetts Department of Education, 2005b).

We acknowledge the controversial nature of assessments that hold all students

to the same standards of performance, and particularly in using test results to determine who will graduate. However, we have seen in Massachusetts schools—and heard firsthand from teachers and parents—that the graduation requirement has fundamentally changed the nature of instruction, especially in high schools for students with disabilities. Schools have intensified instructional support to students in Grades 11 and 12 who have not yet passed the tests in required subjects. Students with disabilities and English language learners are represented disproportionately in the group receiving this support (Massachusetts Department of Education, 2005b; Wiener, 2004).

As a consequence of intensified instruction and support in Grades 11 and 12, students with disabilities are passing subsequent MCAS retests and meeting the state's graduation requirement at a rate approximating 80% of students in that subgroup. Many parents who had questioned whether their children were being set up for failure now openly acknowledge their surprise and delight that their children ultimately did graduate thanks to the diligence of the school and the perseverance of their child. Educators and parents are questioning their earlier assumptions about what these students were capable of learning and have expanded the range of opportunities for these students to participate

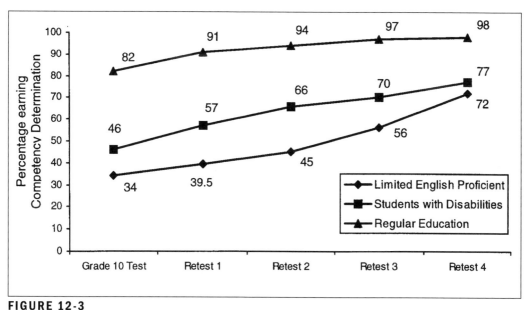

FIGURE 12-3

Class of 2005: Percentage Meeting the Graduation Requirement

in academic activities in their schools. Raised expectations for students with disabilities have fueled another debate, however, as to how to retool the entire special education profession to provide high-level academic instruction to all students.

Still, as the director of a nationally known and respected parent information and advocacy center observed: "Despite early misgivings, the MCAS and the graduation requirement have been some of the most beneficial changes ever for special education students in Massachusetts" (Wiener, 2004).

Despite these encouraging statistics, however, it is evident that a small percentage of students with disabilities may not receive a diploma when they exit public school. A case can be made, though, that even those who do not earn a diploma will have received a more rigorous education and a more varied academic experience than would have been possible prior to education reform. Data also indicates that students with significant cognitive disabilities are learning to read, to perform varied mathematical operations, and to address science

content because of the state's alternate assessment requirement. This requirement not only holds schools accountable for teaching this material, but also guides teachers through the process of aligning their instruction with grade-level standards (Massachusetts Department of Education, 2001; Massachusetts Department of Education, 2006c; Wiener, 2006).

IMPLICATIONS FOR SCHOOL-BASED DECISION MAKING

IEP teams were given new responsibilities under IDEA and NCLB to determine how, rather than *whether*, students with disabilities will participate in statewide assessments. Therefore, in order to make these important decisions, states must be certain IEP and 504 Teams are familiar with at least the following:

- Participation requirements and accommodations policies.

- The state's guidelines for participation in alternate assessments so teams can recognize students for whom it is appropriate to administer alternate assessments.

- Instructional accommodations already in place for the student so their appropriateness can be examined for use on assessments scheduled in the coming year.

- Accommodations used previously by the student on the test and whether these have had the desired effects.

- Accommodations that correct for the unique effects of certain disabilities that interfere with effective demonstration of knowledge and skills during statewide assessments.

Informed participation decisions must be made by teams to ensure that assessments truly and validly represent the student's demonstration of knowledge and skills before results are used to make long-range educational decisions.

Principals, too, must be aware of state-assessment policies and must make sure that all students, including students with the most significant disabilities, receive programs of instruction based on the full breadth and depth of the state's learning standards for students in that grade. As the range and use of accommodations increases, they must be careful to coordinate staff and the resources of the school to ensure that all accommodations listed in students' IEPs are provided during testing. Principals must be aware of test results for students in the school and be skilled at using the tools and materials available for analyzing those results to improve instruction.

IMPLICATIONS FOR POLICY MAKERS

States must be certain their assessments reflect the standards they are intended to measure and that are taught in schools. States must be careful to train school personnel in the selection and use of appropriate accommodations for students with disabilities and on the careful analysis of test results, so they can be certain the assessments reflect the knowledge and skills of each student.

Using a variety of media and methods, states must communicate regularly with the public on the rationale and requirements of the assessment system. States should also be able to respond to feedback from the field to make continuous refinements and improvements to the assessment system.

States should be careful to articulate which accommodations are acceptable and the consequences, if any, of using certain accommodations, such as those that might lead to invalidation of the score. States are increasingly asked by schools and parents to consider the use of novel test accommodations which should lead states to increase the range of accommodations that are acceptable. However, the lack of explicit and clear guidelines on their use may result in misinterpretation of the state's policy (Massachusetts Department of Education, 2006a).

States should be certain the assessment system "works" for students with disabilities and that the assessments measure what students are being taught, rather than magnifying the effects of the student's disability due to an inappropriate accommodation or assessment format. Open lines of communication with stakeholders will reveal important information about the nature of the system and how it can be improved. Assessment results will be useful for improving instruction only when policy makers are certain of what those results represent. At the very least, assessment results should provide important information to assist states to improve the assessment system itself. At best, states should be able to report clear and timely assessment data to schools on the performance of all their students as well as provide educators with the necessary tools to analyze and interpret those results to improve instruction and curriculum alignment. Over time, as educators enhance their familiarity with learning standards, they can be increasingly confident that assessment results truly indicate what every student has learned because they have provided appropriate instruction in the content area being assessed.

IMPLICATIONS FOR RESEARCH

We have much to understand about how students' disabilities interact with their ability to show what they know on statewide tests and if accommodations and alternate assessments are accomplishing their primary purposes. Following, several areas are described in which previous research appears inconclusive or contradictory, and for which additional studies may be beneficial.

Research should be continued on students with significant disabilities and their capacity to learn complex subject matter when skillful teaching methods are applied. Early indications show that these students learn more efficiently than anyone had anticipated, but more information is needed.

Additional research is also needed on the validity and effectiveness of certain test accommodations, particularly those that appear to change a portion of the construct being measured by the test. For students with severe learning disabilities, these might include providing the read-aloud accommodation for the English Language Arts test, or using a calculator for non-calculator sessions of the math test. Policy direction is needed on how to handle such students, because many appear to be "caught between assessments"—prevented from using the accommodation they need, but that would invalidate their score, yet inappropriate for alternate assessments.

Research on how schools use (or do not use) statewide assessment results may also enhance development of more efficient state reporting systems that improve the timing, specificity, and general usefulness of those results. Additional research and data is needed on how states have (or have not)

closed the achievement gap between students in general and special education that also considers the different learning profiles of each group, the need for differentiation and additional time to learn the same concepts, and whether schools are using effective teaching methods with this population. The reader is directed to the Section II of this book for further discussion of some recent research studies and their implications for policy and practice.

REFERENCES

Browder, D., Algrim-Dalzell, L., Flowers, C., Karvonen, M., Spooner, F., & Algozzine, R. (2005). How states implement alternate assessments for students with disabilities. *Journal of Disability Policy Studies*, 15(4), 209, 215, 218.

Cortiella, C. (2005). *No Child Left Behind: Determining appropriate assessment accommodations for students with disabilities*. New York: National Center for Learning Disabilities. Retrieved May 12, 2006, from http://education.umn.edu/NCEO/Online Pubs/NCLD/Accommodations.pdf

Individuals With Disabilities Education Act of 1997, 120 U.S.C. (1997).

Johnson, D. R., & Thurlow, M. L. (2003). *A national study on graduation requirements and diploma options for youth with disabilities* (Tech. Rep. No. 36). Minneapolis, MN: University of Minnesota, National Center on Educational Outcomes. Retrieved July 11, 2006, from http://education.umn.edu/NCEO/OnlinePubs/Technical36.htm

Kleinert, H. L., & Kearns, J. F. (2001). *Alternate assessment: measuring outcomes and supports for students with disabilities*. Baltimore: Brookes.

Massachusetts Department of Education. (1999). *Participation guidelines for IEP/504 team decision making*. Malden, MA: Author.

Massachusetts Department of Education. (2001; revised 2006c). *Resource guide to the Massachusetts Curriculum Frameworks for students with significant disabilities*. Malden, MA: Author.

Massachusetts Department of Education. (2004). *MCAS Alternate Assessment (MCAS-Alt): Spring 2003 state summary of participation and performance.* Malden, MA: Author.

Massachusetts Department of Education. (2005a). *2006 Educator's Manual for MCAS-Alt.* Malden, MA: Author.

Massachusetts Department of Education. (2005b). *Progress report on students attaining the competency determination statewide and by school and district: Classes of 2005 and 2006.* Malden, MA: Author.

Massachusetts Department of Education. (2005c). *Statewide survey of teachers who conducted MCAS Alternate Assessments.* Malden, MA: Author.

Massachusetts Department of Education. (2005d). *MCAS Alternate Assessment (MCAS-Alt): Spring 2004 and spring 2005 state summary of participation and performance.* Malden, MA: Author.

Massachusetts Department of Education. (2006a). *Requirements for the participation of students with disabilities in MCAS: a guide to educators and parents.* Malden, MA: Author.

Massachusetts Department of Education. (2006b). *MCAS technical report.* Malden, MA: Author.

Massachusetts Education Reform Act of 1993, Chapter 71 of the Acts of 1993: An Act Establishing the Massachusetts Education Reform Act: Boston 1993. M.G.L. c: 69, §1E (1996); c. 69, §§ 1B (2006) and 1D (1996); c. 70, § 2 (2006).

McGrew, K. S., & Evans, J. (2003). *Expectations for students with cognitive disabilities: Is the cup half empty or half full? Can the cup flow over?* (Synthesis Report 55). Minneapolis, MN: University of Minnesota, National Center on Educational Outcomes. Retrieved June 6, 2006, from http://education.umn.edu/NCEO/OnlinePubs/Synthesis55.html

No Child Left Behind Act of 2001, Pub. L. No. 107-110, 115 Stat. 1425 (2002).

Quenemoen, R., Rigney, S., & Thurlow, M. (2002). *Use of alternate assessment results in reporting and accountability systems: Conditions for use based on research and practice* (Synthesis Report 43). Minneapolis, MN: University of Minnesota, National Center on Educational Outcomes. Retrieved July 10, 2006, from http://education.umn.edu/NCEO/OnlinePubs/Synthesis43.html

Thompson, S. J., & Thurlow, M. L. (2000). *State alternate assessments: Status as IDEA alternate assessment requirements take effect* (Synthesis Report No. 35). Minneapolis, MN: University of Minnesota, National Center on Educational Outcomes. Retrieved May 12, 2006, from http://education.umn.edu/NCEO/OnlinePubs/Synthesis35.html

Thompson, S. J., Thurlow, M. L., Johnstone, C. J., & Altman, J. R. (2005). *2005 State special education outcomes: Steps forward in a decade of change.* Minneapolis, MN: University of Minnesota, National Center on Educational Outcomes. Retrieved May 12, 2006, from http://education.umn.edu/NCEO/OnlinePubs/2005StateReport.htm/

U.S. Department of Education. (2003, December). 34 CFR Part 200. Final regulations: Title I-Improving the Academic Achievement of the Disadvantaged; Final Rule. *Federal Register,* Volume 67, No. 231.

Wiener, D. (2002, June). *Assessment is the answer, but what is the question?* Presentation at Council of Chief State School Officers (CSSO) National Conference on Large-Scale Assessment, Palm Desert, CA.

Wiener, D. (2004, June). *How states use assessment data.* Presentation at Council of Chief State School Officers (CSSO) National Conference on Large-Scale Assessment, Boston, MA.

Wiener, D. (2006, June). *Mining the data: finding out what students with significant disabilities have learned in math?* Presentation at Council of Chief State School Officers (CSSO) National Conference on Large-Scale Assessment, San Antonio, TX.

13

Individualized Education Program Teams and Assessment Accommodation Decisions: Rhode Island's Assessment Accommodation Study, 2002 to 2003

JANE EWING
Rhode Island College

This chapter is based on data from the Rhode Island Assessment Accommodation Study (2003), funded by the National Center of Educational Outcomes (NCEO) and co-developed by the Rhode Island Office of Special Needs, Office of Assessment, and the Paul V. Sherlock Center. The primary goals of this effort were to determine (a) how individualized education program (IEP) teams make assessment accommodation decisions for students, (b) how assessment accommodations compared to instructional accommodations, and (c) how assessment accommodations were implemented during statewide assessments within a small set of participating Rhode Island schools (2002 student sample, $N = 66$; 2003 $N = 39$). As the starting point for the investigation of assessment accommodation practices among Rhode Island special educators, the author wanted to know what relationship, if any, existed between instructional accommodations, recommended assessment accommodations (i.e., accommodations as they appeared on student IEPs), and assessment accommodations provided for students on the day of the assessments. The author looked at 107 student IEPs; observed 66 students in nine schools during class instruction and during state assessments; and interviewed proctors, instructors, and administrators. In addition, 246 educators were surveyed about their accommodation practices. According to the IEPs, practitioners most frequently recommended the same five assessment accommodations: (a) alternate location; (b) oral administration of directions; (c) clarified and repeated directions; (d) extended time; and (e) for elementary students, frequent breaks, regardless of the instructional accommodations. Further, *where* a student tested was a better predictor of what accommodations he or she might receive on the day of testing than the student's IEP. Accommodations were almost always *batched*; that is, students assigned to an alternate setting generally received identical accommodations regardless of their IEPs.

On average, high school students had fewer assessment accommodations than the elementary students, who had the most.

Additionally, instructional accommodations were much more detailed and individualized than assessment accommodations for the student samples.

During assessments, observed proctors seemed hesitant when implementing assessment accommodations that involved some discretionary decision making. This uncertainty, as well as lack of awareness as to how to implement accommodations to match students' needs, seemed to inhibit the strategic use of accommodations available for students with disabilities during testing.

Other recent studies that have examined the accommodations for students with disabilities during large-scale assessments have found similar trends. These trends included giving students the "same set of accommodations . . . regardless of instructional accommodations because it was easiest to test these students together" (DeStefano, Shriner, & Lloyd, 2001, p. 19) and using performance or demographic factors (such as retention data, race, or grade point average) to decide which students should receive assessment accommodations (Fuchs et al., 2000, p. 79).

DeStefano and others have concluded that "testing accommodations should be selected from the domain of instructional accommodations provided during routine instruction and classroom assessments" (DeStefano et al., 2001, p. 19). However, according to our sample of professionals, in practice this was only possible with the most basic accommodations. More individualized accommodations (such as having a reader or scribe) were often difficult for schools to implement.

Our observations and document review also suggested a general lack of awareness among special and general educators as to how they might tailor a set of assessment accommodations that matched an individual student's testing needs. This apparent lack of awareness and/or effort to fit assessment accommodations to individual need was not the result of any single factor. Interviews with

the 2002 and 2003 participants in the Assessment Accommodations Study revealed many reasons why personalized accommodations did not occur with great frequency, at least within the sample of schools that were observed, including lack of proficiency developing assessment accommodations during the development of IEPs and lack of preparation for the assessments.

Implications for school-based professionals include the need for schools to (a) hold sessions with administrative/instructional personnel to develop implementation practices, (b) allocate resources, and (c) develop or revisit IEP test accommodations for students during the same school year as the state assessments. Policy makers must address the need for clear guidelines for individualized support or accommodations that involve discretionary decision making, more resources and support for schools to implement individualized accommodations, and more practice-based trainings or training guidance. Directions for further research might include case studies of states and schools where accommodations can be shown to result in greater student success on standardized assessments.

IMPLICATIONS FOR SCHOOL-BASED DECISION MAKING

Differences Between Instructional and Assessment Accommodations

Assessment accommodations repeatedly did not appropriately parallel instructional accommodations for the students in the sample, even on the IEPs. When compared to a student's very specific instructional accommodations, assessment accommodations seemed rather perfunctory. Feedback from some special educators indicated that the same process of selection was not possible for assessment accommodations, most frequently because of institutional obstacles. A few examples of instructional accommodations are:

- A rubric or some type of form for student to look at during independent work period to keep oriented to the task at hand (elementary student).

- Modified tests and quizzes in mainstreamed setting (word banks, shortened length, multiple choice; middle school student).

- Notes provided for academic classes due to processing limitations and written output (high school student).

Rhode Island teachers reported feeling quite proficient when it came to the development of instructional modifications for students, and this was borne out by the length and specificity of these items. However, they reported less certainty about how to develop similarly useful assessment accommodations. According to the 246 individuals who responded to the 2002 Rhode Island Assessment Accommodation survey, 53% of the sample felt they knew a lot about the variety of possible instructional accommodations, whereas 43% felt they knew a lot about assessment accommodations.

Perhaps more telling was the relatively few resources that special educators used to assist them in developing accommodations for state assessments. Following are some of these resources; note that very few educators cited classroom accommodations as a likely place to begin the development of assessment accommodations:

- Rhode Island State Assessment Guidebook (44% of the sample).

- State Assessment Program Requirements for Student Participation and Assessment Accommodations (40%).

- IEP Guidebook (38%).

- Guidance from special education teachers (11%).

- Discussion with peers (7%).

- Student's IEP (6%).

- Individual need of student (4%).

- Background/training/judgment (3%).

- Supervisor's guidelines (3%).

- Regional/district resources (3%).

- Classroom accommodations (2%).

According to state-developed guidelines, assessment accommodations should "parallel the accommodations used for that student in daily instruction" (*Testing Guidelines for Rhode Island's State Assessment Program*, Sec. III, "Testing of Students with Special Needs," 2003, p. 4). Again, a very small percentage of our 2002 sample of Rhode Island educators identified instructional assessments as important when determining a student's need for assessment accommodations (see Table 13-1).

More recently, interviews with special educators revealed that they often simply chose assessment accommodations from the list available in the drop-down box of their school's IEP development software package.

Despite the lack of resources and preparation during the development of assessment accommodations during team meetings, educators reported that they always based their decisions on the students' individual needs. Because it was repeatedly seen that assessment accommodations were fairly generic, this suggested that educators viewed the testing accommodations differently than instructional accommodations—almost as if the test accommodations had no real utility. Selecting a greater number of test accommodations or exactly matching a set of instructional and assessment supports on an IEP isn't enough. Test accommodations can only be useful for students if they are implemented—and properly.

TABLE 13-1

How Do IEP Teams Determine a Student's Need for Assessment Accommodations? (2002 teacher sample, N = 246)

Response	Percent
Recommendations from IEP team	23
Based on current classroom performance	20
Follows instructional accommodations	18
Based on student need	16
Per IEP	13
Based on recent evaluations	12
Performance on other tests	10
Teacher input	9
Guided by disability needs	8
Use state guidelines/checklist	7
Consultation with parent/student	7

Comparison of Recommended Versus Observed Assessment Accommodations

Overall, the author saw greater agreement between recommended and implemented assessment accommodations for the 2003 sample of students. However, both sets of students (2002 and 2003) had the most generic assessment accommodations including, alternate location, oral administration of directions, clarified and repeated directions, extended time, and for elementary students, frequent breaks.

In general, high school students had fewer assessment supports—both recommended on their IEPs and implemented in practice. These students were recommended for and generally received two accommodations: alternate location and extended time. In addition, high school students were often given oral administration of directions even though this was rarely written into their IEPs. Because most of the high school students observed did not use extra time, in reality these students had two accommoda-

tions during assessments, alternate location and oral administration of directions. They actually received only a small number of assessment accommodations when compared to the six or more instructional accommodations found on their high school IEPs. This indicates that other factors were influencing the selection process. Every elementary student received all five of the commonly recommended accommodations: alternate location, oral administration of directions, clarified and repeated directions, extended time, and frequent breaks, However, middle school students received four accommodations (not frequent breaks), again regardless of their IEP recommendations. (Because of the numerous breaks teachers built in during assessments for elementary students, extended time was actually used, although not by student choice.) Again, there were many more instructional accommodations for elementary and middle school students and these also tended to be very specific and individualized.

As noted earlier, flawed implementation rendered some assessment accommodations practically useless. For example, two students who required "distraction-free" setting recommendations were in small group/alternate settings, but the rooms were too full of other students to be quiet. In another setting, a student who requested additional time had to try to finish her assessment while people knocked repeatedly on the classroom door.

Implementation was also affected when assessment accommodations were not clear. For example, one IEP listed "reader," which may have meant "tests read orally." This accommodation was not listed on the proctor's testing sheet, and thus the student did not have reading assistance. At another location, two students had IEP accommodations for "tests read orally," but an observer noted that no one read to these students at all, not even directions. The author was told of repeated instances where students had reportedly "foregone" their accommodation (i.e., refused them). This included accommodations such as extended time, access to a computer, and scribing assistance. Finally, the author saw instances where proctors did not implement student accommodations because they felt they weren't necessary or they weren't sure what to do. These included flexible scheduling of tests, scribing, and one-to-one student support.

It is not sufficient to focus only on how many assessment accommodations an IEP team puts into a student's IEP. In many of the assessment sessions that were observed, schools simply did not plan enough or allocate enough personnel, space, or time to properly implement assessment accommodations for their students with IEPs. Thus, many of the assessment accommodations that more closely paralleled students' instructional accommodations were not often made available during the state exams.

Lack of Clear Process Within Schools to Create Testing Accommodations

Relatively few individuals that were surveyed or interviewed described any kind of shared process to prepare special education staff and students for the assessments, and certainly nothing as extensive as the process recommended in the Rhode Island testing guidelines (2003, Sec. 6, "Testing Accommodations for all Students," p. 14). Even if a student's IEP recommended a more tailored set of assessment accommodations rather than a selection from the usual five, there was no guarantee that the accommodations would be implemented (e.g., that a reader would be available for the student) or utilized (e.g., employing the flexible schedule of testing accommodation when a student seemed to need it).

Except for their strict adherence to protocols for administrative paperwork and test security, the sample of schools in the study differed noticeably in how they approached structuring test conditions. (An example is the "Dos and Don'ts of Test Security" issued by the Office of Assessment for the state assessments, Spring 2003, App. 3. Despite the high priority of test security, not every teacher/proctor had a copy of this.) For example, there was considerable range in the degree of collaboration between administration and classroom staff in developing assessment accommodations. In one school, individual teachers managed every detail of preparing accommodations for their own group of students (e.g., securing a free room for the alternate location, getting back-up assistance from aides or other teachers, making sure that certain students did not test together, obtaining the *Testing Guidelines* from the Office of Assessment). This meant that teachers did things differently within the same school, particularly in those areas where teacher discretion (e.g., coaching, encouraging a student) was involved. In another school, where the teachers themselves apparently had little to do with developing the testing conditions, they seemed confused and uninformed about procedures.

In one elementary school where a strong and shared process was established, the principal made resources available to the staff as they prepared for the assessments, such as providing substitutes so that teachers could attend the Office of Assessment's statewide training sessions. Additionally, he increased the number of hours that aides worked for the month of testing. Since this school assigned its aides by grade cohort, rather than by classroom or teacher, the aides knew every child in the grade level. This practice had the unintended (but positive) effect of creating a considerably larger pool of competent proctors for the school's assessments. Perhaps not surprisingly, a proctor's lack of knowledge about a student also had a clear effect on how the accommodations and assessment were handled.

IMPLICATIONS FOR STATE POLICY MAKERS

Rhode Island's study participants identified several factors that interfered with providing more suitable assessment accommodations for students with disabilities. As noted, some of these issues could be addressed by providing specific training to the district and/or school personnel who proctor the assessments. This type of training is not currently available, at least not from sources that could best address the many questions that school professionals had. There are yearly training workshops offered by the Rhode Island Office of Assessment. However, most of the attendees were administrators rather than teaching personnel. Because many of the topics covered at these sessions were not related to proctoring practices, the general lack of teachers in attendance did not seem inappropriate. Guidelines from these trainings, such as the 2003 *Testing Guidelines for Rhode Island's State Assessment Program*, sometimes called the "Periwinkle Booklet," and "Dos/Don'ts" lists (Rhode Island Department of Education, 2003), are supposed to be made available to school-level staff. Surprisingly, many staff members at the participant schools did not know about these resources. In addition, the testing booklet did not answer every question proctors had, particularly about coaching students.

The author also received many questions from school professionals that required both policy and practical interpretations. States may need to be more explicit about the use of certain accommodations; or if these guidelines do exist, guarantee a much wider distribution (such as providing one-to-one support, scribing, oral response into recorders, flexible scheduling, visual aids, and use of resources). For example, many professionals in our sample felt that scribing was "difficult" to use, apparently this was a result of the lack of guidelines available to school professionals to make this accommo-

dation useable during instructional time and assessments. Currently, the 2003 *State Testing Guidelines* offer only the following on scribing (Rhode Island Department of Education, 2003):

> When transcription or oral dictation is used, scribes should attend to making a fair representation of the spelling, punctuation, grammar, and pictorial representation skills of the student. When writing skills are being assessed, a stronger criterion of verbatim transcription should be applied. (*Testing Guidelines for Rhode Island's State Assessment Program*, Sec. 6, "Testing Accommodations for All Students," p. 15).

Authorizing and distributing clear and detailed procedures for scribing and other assessment accommodations might well guarantee students greater access. However, states must also consider whether they truly endorse the widespread use of scribing for "any student, if warranted." Other accommodation, such as providing a reader, may give an unfair boost to the relatively few students who are eligible to receive them. Further research as well as policy discussions are clearly required.

Judging from the observational data, students with distractibility or anxiety issues and older students did not necessarily benefit from extended time, which was by far the most common accommodation used during assessments. However, school officials were reluctant to alter the school schedule to make use of accommodations such as flexible scheduling of tests. More individualized time-related accommodations pose a difficult choice (i.e., maintaining a normal environment for the many students in schools who are not testing that year or at that particular time, or creating conditions that may improve the testing performances of a very small percentage of students with particular needs).

Other factors in accommodation selection were related to fixed institutional limitations that could not be remedied at the school level. With a condensed testing schedule for schools in Rhode Island, a growing numbers of students needing accommodations, and an increased number of high-stakes assessments added to the schedule, creating conditions that enhance student performance seemed to require resources beyond what school districts could easily provide. Many school professionals said they could not implement more individualized accommodations because the numbers of students requiring accommodations were too great (scribing and computer assistance) or too small (flexible scheduling) to warrant it. However, if schools received incentives to make a greater effort or met with increased penalties when their special needs populations underachieved, then maximizing student testing performances through more strategic and individualized use of accommodations might be forthcoming.

It was also clear from interactions with the participating schools that Rhode Island professionals were eager for more specific training and guidance in how to make better use of individualized testing accommodations. The following set of practices are offered as a possible starting point. These are based on recommendations from current studies on the development of assessment accommodations for students with disabilities:

- Develop the IEP during the same school year as state testing taking into consideration the curriculum and instructional accommodations currently used. Involve the teacher who will implement the assessment accommodations (Shriner & DeStefano, 2003, p. 160).
- Establish a link between assessments and accommodations used for instructional needs. Document their use and evaluate their effectiveness and impact (DeStefano, 1998).
- Provide IEP teams with a local research and policy base on which to make testing accommodation decisions (Chard, 1999).
- Focus training and professional development resources on teachers who make instructional and assessment accommodations "more often than just at the IEP meeting" (Fuchs et al., 2000, p. 9).

IMPLICATIONS FOR RESEARCH

The author sees three potential areas for researching assessment accommodations for students with disabilities: developing, choosing, and implementing accommodations.

Researchers will undoubtedly continue to assess whether individual accommodations actually assist students with disabilities during large-scale assessments or during instruction. Because accommodations will affect individual students differently, how can special educators make decisions about which accommodations to use and in what combinations? How might schools develop a means to test whether accommodations work for students?

It may be worthwhile to rethink the process of developing accommodations. Is there another model for choosing accommodations rather than the team process during IEP development? Who else might be involved in the process?

Finally, are there specific schools and school districts that have solved the issues created for students with disabilities taking large-scale assessments, particularly during implementation? What resources made the difference? What resources didn't matter? Can schools create testing conditions flexible enough to adapt to student needs, without invalidating the results of the assessment?

Collected findings indicate that students with disabilities can more effectively participate in large-scale assessments when they have the accommodations that best meet their needs. However, the Rhode Island Assessment Accommodation Study demonstrated that providing these accommodations proved more challenging than expected. Hopefully, information presented here provides some direction to educators for meeting these challenges head-on.

REFERENCES

Chard, D. J. (1999). Case in point: Including students with disabilities in large-scale testing. *Journal of Special Education Leadership, 12*(1), 39–42.

DeStefano, L. (1998, April). *Translating classroom accommodations in large-scale assessments.* Paper presented at the annual meeting of American Educational Research Association, San Diego, CA.

DeStefano, L., Shriner, J. G., & Lloyd, C. A. (2001). Teacher decision making in participation of students with disabilities in large-scale assessments. *Exceptional Children, 68,* 7–22.

Fuchs, L. S., Fuchs, D., Eaton, S. B., Hamlett, C., Binkley, E., & Crouch, R. (2000). Using objective data sources to enhance teacher judgments about test accommodations. *Exceptional Children, 67,* 67–81.

Rhode Island Department of Education. (2003). *Rhode Island assessment accommodation study: Research summary.* Minneapolis, MN: University of Minnesota, National Center on Education Outcomes. Retrieved October 2003, from http://education.umn.edu/NCEO/TopicAreas/Accommodations/RhodeIsland.htm

Rhode Island Department of Education. (2003). *Testing Guidelines for Rhode Island's State Assessment Program.* Providence, RI.

Shriner, J .G., & DeStefano, L. (2003). Participation and accommodation in state assessment: The role of individualized education programs. *Exceptional Children, 69,* 147–161.

CHAPTER 14

Navigating the Test Accommodation Process for Students With Learning Disabilities: Accommodations on College Board Tests and Accommodations in Postsecondary Settings

DEBORAH LAZARUS
The College Board
NICOLE S. OFIESH
California State University, East Bay

Students with learning disabilities (LD) are the fastest growing group of individuals with disabilities in postsecondary settings (Henderson, 2001). For many of these students, test accommodations are an important aspect of their access to higher education (Kurth & Mellard, 2006; Nelson-Lignugaris-Kraft, 1989) and this often begins with college admissions exams (e.g., SAT). Later in an individual's academic career, this might include postgraduate or professional licensing exams such as the Graduate Record Exam (GRE) or the United States Medical Licensing Exam (USMLE). The right to test accommodations for persons with disabilities stems from regulations accompanying statutory law (e.g., Americans With Disabilities Act, ADA, 1990; Section 504 of the Rehabilitation Act, Individuals with Disabilities Education Act, IDEA), which require institutions to provide access to education both in terms of physical structure and information, to a degree similar to that of their non-disabled peers. Test accommodations are one part of this access.

Of the various ways to accommodate students with LD on standardized exams, extended time is the most frequently requested and provided test accommodation (Cahalan, Mandinach, & Camara, 2002; Ofiesh & McAfee, 2000). The appropriation of this accommodation is built on a growing body of literature that supports the contention that some individuals with LD characteristically take longer to complete timed tasks (Bell & Perfetti, 1994; Hayes, Hynd, & Wisenbaker, 1986; Ofiesh, Mather, & Russell, 2005; Wolff, Michel, Ovrut, & Drake, 1990). Although extended test time is the most commonly provided accommodation, many other kinds of test accommodations are requested and provided on standardized exams. It is also important to note that not all students who request test accommodations receive them. In practice, the process of deciding who receives a test accommodation, as well as what kind of test accommodation is multifaceted. The ADA, Section 504, and IDEA have profoundly influenced the policies and practices surrounding accommodation decisions. With respect to these laws, consultants for testing agencies dealing with admissions tests and postsecondary disability service providers rely on the information provided by students with disabilities to determine the appropriateness of a request. The decision to provide an accommodation is important because the purpose of a test accommodation is to provide students with disabilities the opportunity to demonstrate their true ability as measured by the assessment. In order to promote fair test administrations, a test accommodation should not accommodate nondisability related factors that can impact test taking for all students (e.g., test jitters, motivation, test-taking skills). However, for those students with LD who are genuinely entitled to test accommodations, many are able to perform similarly to their nondisabled peers and thus attain greater scores than they would have without the accommodation (Alster, 1997; Camara, Copeland, & Rothschild, 1998; Camara & Schneider, 2000; Cahalan et al., 2002; Jarvis, 1996; Mandinach, Bridgeman, Cahalan-Laitusis, & Trapani, 2005; Ofiesh, 2000; Runyan, 1991). This chapter provides an overview of current trends and procedures that influence the acquisition of test accommodations for students with learning disabilities particularly as they apply to College Board Tests.

COLLEGE BOARD TEST ACCOMMODATION PROCESS

Similarities and Differences Between K to 12 and Postsecondary Settings

Applying for testing accommodations either at the K to 12 level or at the postsecondary level can be a complicated process for students. Although there are some similarities between the two situations, there are also significant differences which often create difficult adjustments for students and their families. At both junctures, accommodations are granted if it is determined that they are nec-

essary and appropriate because of a diagnosed disability. In other words, a relative cognitive or academic weakness will not support the need for testing accommodations. In addition, a student can still be eligible for accommodations under Section 504 or ADA regulations at the K to 12 level if it is found that the disability is not sufficiently substantial and that the academic implications are not severe enough to support classification with an educational disability under IDEA guidelines. At the college or postcollege level, the student could still qualify for accommodations under Section 504 or ADA if he had not met the more stringent criteria for classification according to IDEA guidelines when he was younger.

There are several major differences between school-age and postsecondary environments. First, delivery of services, including testing accommodations is guided at the school-age level both by IDEA and 504 regulations. Until recently, before the reauthorization of IDEA, eligibility for a learning disability determination was almost always governed by a discrepancy model which schools and school districts across the country have interpreted differently. The implications of the revisions to IDEA and the Response to Intervention (RTI) model will be discussed in detail later in this chapter. Decisions at the postsecondary level are made utilizing 504 or ADA regulations because IDEA regulations only refer to the K to 12 population. Second, the focus for school-age children is prescriptive and emphasizes remediation and helping them to perform optimally in school. Postsecondary institutions, however, are not focusing on remediation. Students have been accepted into the institution and are presumed capable of completing the work with extra help (including testing accommodations), so remediation of skills is not the focus. Third, decisions made by individualized education program (IEP) and child study teams rely on curriculum-based or performance-based tests as well as psychoeducational evaluations. Until now, decisions at the postsecondary level have been based primarily on the nature of the disability and diagnostic evaluations. Some of this may also be changing as we see how the Summary of Performance model plays out. Finally, a very important difference in the school-age and postsecondary arenas is that with the school-age group parents are the students' advocates, and at the postsecondary level students must learn to self-advocate.

Testing Accommodations on College Board Tests

Students with disabilities who require test accommodations on the Preliminary SAT (PSAT), SAT, or Advanced Placement (AP) examinations must apply to the College Board to obtain the appropriate accommodations. The College Board began implementing the current eligibility process and the guidelines for documentation in the mid-1990s.

There are two ways to qualify for accommodations on College Board tests. The way that most students in the country qualify is through the school verification process. To be eligible through this process, the student must:

- Have a disability that necessitates test accommodations.

- Have documentation on file at his school that supports the need for the requested accommodations and meets the Board's Guidelines for Documentation.

- Receive and use the requested accommodations due to the disability, for school-based tests, for at least the last 4 school months.

If the student does not meet the criteria, he may still apply for test accommodations, but he needs to send in all of his documentation for the Board's review. Through the school

verification process, in most instances, the services for students with disabilities coordinator (SSD coordinator) just fills out the eligibility form and indicates that the student has met the Board's eligibility criteria and the guidelines for documentation (The College Board, 1986).

When a student's documentation is reviewed, the College Board utilizes the help of a national panel of experts to advise if the student's documentation meets the Board's guidelines and if the student qualifies for the requested accommodations. The panel members work in higher education institutions as professors, researchers, or directors of disability support services; work as school psychologists at the high school level; or work as psychologists in private practice.

The guidelines for documentation are key to the process of determining eligibility. The student must have a diagnosed disability. Subtle or relative learning weaknesses do not constitute a disability. Students that apply for test accommodations present with a wide range of disabling conditions, including learning, attention, psychiatric, developmental, and physical disabilities. Documentation must be current for all requests: Academic testing must be administered within 5 years. Although cognitive testing from the student's initial diagnosis or classification will be accepted, child study teams must use clinical judgment to determine if an update is indicated. Psychiatric evaluations or updates should be within 1 year of applying for accommodations and medical documentation should be as current as possible. In all situations, relevant educational, developmental, and medical documentation should be provided. The early history is extremely important, particularly for students with attention issues or developmental delays, as many of the observable symptoms and behaviors begin in early childhood.

In most cases, comprehensive psychoeducational testing is required to provide documentation of the diagnosed disability as well as the presence of significant functional limitations in learning. Parents and educators often question the need for this testing if the student does not have a learning disability. But, even if the disability is a psychiatric or an attentional one, the psychological testing is required to demonstrate academic impact. The mere presence of a disability does not qualify a student for testing accommodations. There needs to be functional limitations in learning because of the disability, and at the present time, the College Board determines this in part, by using a discrepancy model. Cognitive ability tests often given include the Wechsler scales (WISC-IV (Wechsler, 2003) or WAIS-III (Wechsler, 1997)) the Woodcock-Johnson Cognitive Ability Scales (WJ-III; Woodcock, McGrew, Mather, 2001b), the Stanford-Binet, 5th Edition (SB5; Roid, 2003), the Differential Ability Scales (Elliott, 1990), and the Kaufman Assessment Battery for Children, Second Edition (KABC-II; Kaufman, 2004a), although this is by no means an exhaustive list. Achievement tests typically given include the Wechsler Individual Achievement Test (WIAT; Wechsler, 2002), the Woodcock-Johnson Achievement Tests, Third Edition (WJ-III; Woodcock, McGrew, & Mather, 2001a), and Kaufman Tests of Educational Achievement, Second Edition (KTEA II; Kaufman, 2004b). Again, this is not an exhaustive list. Although school districts across the country vary in the discrepancy required to classify a student with a learning disability (Reschly, 2005), and although each request for accommodations is reviewed individually, in general, College Board guidelines look at a one and one half standard deviation discrepancy to indicate the student has a substantial functional impairment. If students are requesting extended time, evaluators are advised to administer timed academic measures such as fluency testing, reading rate, and timed reading comprehension. If a student has been diagnosed with an attention or psychiatric

disability, rating scales or questionnaires are often useful in documenting the disability. Input from teachers documenting the student's learning style and use of testing accommodations can also help to support the need for specific accommodations.

Once it is ascertained that a student presents with a disability, the evaluator and child study team need to demonstrate that this student experiences a substantial functional limitation in learning as a result of his or her disability. Usually, this is indicated by the presence of significant discrepancy between cognitive potential and academic achievement. The discrepancy needs to be substantial, and the presence of one or two discrepant scores does not necessarily support the need for testing accommodations. The student's entire picture should be examined, including his history, learning style, school performance, and so forth.

When evaluating the need for accommodations, school staff and evaluators need to consider how a student's disability impacts him and think carefully about what accommodations make sense. The first author knows from her experience as a school psychologist that often child study teams automatically conclude that a student who has been diagnosed or classified with a disability needs extended time, the most commonly requested accommodation. In many instances, however, and often for students with attention problems, the appropriate accommodations are small group setting and extra breaks between test sections. On the current SAT, students with extended time are not permitted to self-pace and must remain on each section for the allotted time. In other words, if a section is 30 minutes with standard time and 45 minutes with 50% extended time, the student is not permitted to go on to the next section until the entire 45 minutes are up. This situation can be very difficult for a student with attention deficit disorder. Similarly, in the case of a highly anxious student, the extra time may only result in the student second guessing himself and changing his already correct responses. School districts should carefully review the student's use of the accommodations on school-based tests when making the decision to recommend test accommodations. Again, from the first author's personal experience, she remembers instances on state tests where the students who had extended time finished the examination even before the standard test takers. Students can request either 50% extended time (time and one half) or 100% extended time (double time). Students receiving 100% extended time take the SAT I over a 2-day period. SAT II Subject tests and most AP tests are generally taken within 1 day. Examples of other accommodations available include:

- A reader or a cassette for students who are unable to read on their own.
- Enlarged print.
- Large block answer sheet.
- Permission to record answers in the test booklet.
- Braille editions.
- American Sign Language (ASL) presentations.
- A scribe or a computer.

Many students request the computer accommodation for essay sections, and in all instances, requests for a computer must be accompanied by supporting documentation. Students cannot receive this accommodation through the school verification process. There are three ways to qualify for a computer:

1. If a student has a physical disability such as cerebral palsy which necessitates a computer or a scribe, he needs to submit the appropriate medical documentation.
2. If a student has dysgraphia, he can qualify for a computer. In this case, the documentation needs to establish that there are fine motor delays and because of this,

the student's written expression skills are substantially impaired.

3. If the student has a language-based learning disability and, because of this disability, is unable to organize his thoughts effectively and elaborate on concepts using a paper and pencil.

Some of the common tests that are acceptable by the professional community to document fine motor skills are the Coding subtest of the Wechsler Cognitive Test or the Beery Buktenica Developmental Test of Visual Motor Integration (VMI) or Rey Complex Figure Test. As for the writing area, tests such as written expression subtest of the WIAT II, Broad Writing cluster of WJ-III (Woodcock, 2001a), TOWL III or OWLS can document the functional impact. It is always helpful to include a timed measure such as WJ-III writing fluency especially if timed testing is an issue.

Changes to IDEA, RTI, and the Implications for College Board's Policies

A key element in the recent revisions to the IDEA is RTI (*Federal Register*, 34 CFR Part 300.307-300.311), and depending on how it is implemented, the future of the discrepancy model employed by the College Board may be affected in a significant way. The revisions indicate the following points:

- States may prohibit the use of a severe discrepancy between achievement and intellectual ability criterion to determine whether a child has a specific learning disability.
- States may not require local education agencies (LEAs) to use a discrepancy model to determine a learning disability.
- States would be permitted to allow a process that examines whether the child responds to scientific, research-based

intervention as part of the evaluation procedures.

The current IDEA regulations permit classification of a student with a specific learning disability (SLD) if a child is not achieving commensurate with his or her age and ability levels, and if the LEA finds that the child exhibits a severe discrepancy between intellectual ability and academic achievement. Under the proposed regulations, two elements would be required to determine the existence of an SLD. The first element is a finding that the child does not achieve commensurate with his age in one or more of eight specified areas when provided with learning experiences appropriate to his age. The second element is a finding that the child failed to make sufficient progress in meeting state-approved results after experiencing a scientific, research-based intervention process, or the child exhibits a pattern of strengths and weaknesses that the team determines is relevant to the identification of an SLD.

In other words, under the revised guidelines, a student could be classified if he is not achieving age-level expectations and if he fails to respond to a scientific, research-based intervention process. It is not clear how students would be evaluated in relation to their peers. Three- and four-tiered intervention approaches have been suggested (Reschly, 2005). It seems that if one follows these guidelines, there may no longer be a need for psychoeducational testing, as the discrepancy model may be a moot point.

The RTI model has generated a fair amount of controversy. Supporters of RTI claim that the discrepancy model is a "wait-to-fail model." RTI has been presented as a system to screen all students by mid-kindergarten, at least three times, and routinely afterward in order to identify learning disabilities (Reschly, 2003; Chamberlin, 2005). Supporters also stipulate that many students have been placed in special education

because of an SLD and, in part because of achievement/ability discrepancies, show minimal gains in achievement with few actually ever leaving special education. The problem with the current LD definition (using a discrepancy model) is that students are often inappropriately classified. The old IDEA regulations state that to classify a student with an SLD, a severe discrepancy between intellectual ability and academic achievement needs to be present. However, schools, school districts, and states interpret the definition of *severe or significant* differently which results in variability from state to state in the percentages of students who have been classified LD (Reschly, Hosp, & Schmeid, 2003). Further, supporters claim that scientifically based RTI programs can pick up problems at any age, intervene right away, figure out who needs additional help, and provide several levels of intervention before referral to special education (Reschly, 2005; Chamberlin, 2005). RTI proponents say it is much more focused on outcomes and that IQ testing does not provide sufficient links to intervention. RTI offers a bridge between general education and special education, as the initial intervention is for the entire class. Then, following the various tiers, certain children, based on their responses, will receive addition help or intervention. The RTI model proposes to reduce the number of unnecessary assessments. RTI proposes to identify more females, the assumption being that girls have as many difficulties as boys, but boys' overt behaviors are more likely to attract attention and consequently result in more referrals and identification with SLDs.

The concerns with the RTI model are numerous. Some feel that RTI is not a process for evaluating the psychological processes found in the definition of learning disabled. Without cognitive testing, one will not be able to evaluate patterns of strengths and weaknesses. Further, the RTI model does not evaluate possible additional problems underlying the learning disorders (i.e.; attention deficit disorder, emotional issues) because it is solely based on academic achievement. How will one measure whether or not a child is achieving commensurate with his or her age if there is no reference to the ability to achieve? And, how will we "scientifically" analyze the results without standard scores? Because successful RTI has not been well defined, competency levels can be set low, and that level will differ among schools, school districts, and states (Mastropieri & Scruggs, 2005; Chamberlin, 2005). To date, "scientifically based" has not been defined, and because RTI has not been consistently applied, its premise lacks research to know if it is effective. The roles of teachers and diagnosticians and how these roles may change have not been addressed or considered.

IDEA revisions were approved by Congress in the summer of 2004. Some districts across the country, primarily in elementary schools, have begun implementing aspects of RTI, and some states are piloting RTI projects. It is too early to know if districts will actually be classifying students with SLDs without the use of psychoeducational testing. However, if IDEA no longer requires a discrepancy formula to classify students and allows districts or local educational authorities to include a process in their evaluation procedures that examines a child's RTI, what in fact, are the implications for IQ testing? The College Board Services for Students with Disabilities has utilized the discrepancy model to help determine if a student demonstrates functional limitations in learning due to a disability and whether because of this is entitled to testing accommodations on College Board tests. How will we determine academic impact without the use of psychoeducational assessment? Many people seem to be advocating a combined approach for classification and diagnosis: an RTI process, as well as psychoeducational testing (Ofiesh, 2006). These are questions

that will have to be answered as the regulations are clarified, and as schools and school districts find their way with the new requirements. At the present time, information on a student's RTIs is additional qualitative information that the College Board will consider as part of the student's entire documentation packet and in conjunction with his psychoeducational testing. The reader is referred to Chapter 15 in this book for an extended discussion of the RTI model and its implications for the classification of students with learning disabilities.

ACCESSING ACCOMMODATIONS AT THE POSTSECONDARY LEVEL AND TRENDS IN DOCUMENTATION

If a student with LD has been admitted to a college or university, and has taken an entrance exam with test accommodations, it is likely he will be eligible for accommodations in college as well. The same laws that influence the accommodation process on college entrance exams pertain to students in the postsecondary setting. Therefore, the process used to determine whether or not a student receives test accommodations is similar to the process used to grant accommodations on standardized college entrance exams. The primary similarity is that decisions often center on the presence and severity of the disability as substantiated by the student's psychoeducational diagnostic evaluation.

It is usually the role of the disability service provider (DSP) or ADA coordinator to determine the reasonableness of a student's request for an accommodation based on a disability in relation to legal precepts from the ADA and Section 504. These precepts are (a) the current impact of the disability on a major life activity, and (b) the functional limitations of the disability. Survey research indicates that most DSPs use a student's diagnostic report to help make decisions about service delivery, including accommodations (Ofiesh & McAfee, 2000). Thus, it is common for DSPs to make their own inferences about functional limitations as they relate to specific course tests.

When relating a disability to specific course tests, two important considerations that DSPs consider are (a) the type of test (e.g., essay, multiple choice) and (b) the informational content on which the student is being tested (e.g., reading comprehension, calculus). If time is not an essential component of the test (e.g., a test of factual knowledge), and a student's disability significantly impacts his ability to demonstrate what is known under timed circumstances, that student may qualify for extended test time. This is the most typical scenario in postsecondary settings. Once extended test time is determined to be appropriate for an individual, DSPs are left with the determination of how much extra time is appropriate.

The same process is followed for all types of accommodations. The DSP needs to make the determination regarding whether or not the accommodation will conflict with the construct being measured. For example, a student may be able to use a calculator for some math tests as an accommodation, but not on math tests which factor in calculations as part of the grade unless approved by the instructor. Or a student with dysgraphia, a disorder impacting written language, may be able to have a scribe as an accommodation for essay exams, but not for a multiple choice exam because filling in bubbles on a scantron sheet is not considered an activity that is related to the nature of the student's disability in writing. Essentially decisions are made independently and often the goals and objectives of the program of study need to be considered.

Two major differences highlight the college process, however. The first is that unlike the process used by major testing agencies, students can represent themselves in a face-to-face interview with the person who will make a decision about their eligibility for accommodations. This difference is important as a student's personal self-report can be compelling. The student can have the opportunity to explain academic performance in a way that may not be fully illustrated through a written psychoeducational report or typed self-statement.

The second difference is that the constructs of most course or classroom tests are knowledge based. Anastasi (1988) referred to these types of tests as "power" tests. Standardized exams are almost always various combinations of speed and power. Classroom tests are often developed by faculty who are more interested in how a student will respond to all test items, rather than the speed with which they respond. Very few course or classroom tests are intended to include speed as part of what is being measured, though many course or classroom tests are timed. However, often the timing is based on the length of the class rather than a psychometric calculation associated with the test items. This distinction is an important one to understand, as it often lowers the "stakes" involved in making decisions about accommodations such as extended test time in postsecondary settings. Students may more easily access accommodations when the stakes are lower, but later in their educational career be required to "re-explain" why they need an accommodation on a high-stakes graduate exam.

Current trends in K to 12 education may soon influence how decisions are made at the postsecondary level. As mentioned previously, a recent movement in the identification of children with LD (RTI) has called for new ways to identify and classify students as LD. If identification through RTI becomes a common practice at the K to 12 levels, students who have received special education services but no psychoeducational evaluation, may be required to provide new documentation, at their own expense, to establish existence of a disability when they graduate from secondary school and transition to postsecondary settings (Ofiesh, 2006). The disconnect between the documentation required at the postsecondary level due to the different laws regarding disability has already been the topic of debate for several years. Even before the RTI movement, many students graduated from high school with documentation that did not meet the requirements of most national test agencies or postsecondary institutions. With this most recent development concerning identification of students with LD at the K to 12 levels, several groups have begun to work together to bridge the gap between secondary and postsecondary settings in order to increase rather than hinder access for students with disabilities to postsecondary settings (Gormley, Hughes, Block, & Lendman, 2005). The notion that all children and adults should have an adequate opportunity to learn is perhaps the one belief that brings most educational professionals together (Ofiesh, 2006). Test accommodations and the processes we employ to provide them, are one way to promote this opportunity to learn and to foster fair testing for students with and without disabilities.

REFERENCES

Alster, E. H. (1997). The effects of extended time on the algebra scores of college students with and without learning disabilities. *Journal of Learning Disabilities, 30,* 222–227.

Americans With Disabilities Act of 1990. 22 U.S.C.A. § 12101 *et seq.*

Anastasi, A. (1988). *Psychological testing* (6th ed.). New York: Macmillan.

Bell, L. C., & Perfetti, C. A. (1994). Reading skill: Some adult comparisons. *Journal of Educational Psychology, 86,* 244–255.

Cahalan, C., Mandinach, E. B., & Camara, W. J. (2002). *Predictive validity of SAT I: Reasoning test for test-takers with learning disabilities and extended time accommodations.* (College Board Research Report No. 2002-5). New York: College Entrance Examination Board.

Camara, W. J., Copeland, T. A., & Rothschild, B. (1998). *Effects of extended time on the SAT I: Reasoning test score growth for students with learning disabilities.* (College Board Report No. 98-7). New York: College Entrance Examination Board.

Camara, W. J., & Schneider, D. (2000, January). *Testing with extended time on the SAT I: Effects for students with learning disabilities.* (The College Board Research Notes RN-08.) New York: College Entrance Examination Board.

Chamberlin, Jamie, & Monitor Staff. A learning disability dialogue: Experts debated learning-disability assessment at APA's 12th annual institute for psychology in the schools. *APA Monitor,* Vol. 36, No. 10, November 2005. Washington, DC: American Psychological Association.

The College Board. (1986). Instructions for Completing the 2006–2007 Student Eligibility Form Educational Testing Service. Graduate Record Examination. New York: College Entrance Examination Board.

Elliott, C.D., (1990). Differential Ability Scales (DAS). San Antonio, TX: Psychological Corporation.

Gormley, S., Hughes, C., Block, L., & Lendman, C. (2005). Eligibility assessment requirements at the postsecondary level for students with learning disabilities: A disconnect with secondary schools? *Journal of Postsecondary Education and Disability, 18,* 63–70.

Hayes, F. B., Hynd, G. W., & Wisenbaker, J. (1986). Learning disabled and normal college students' performance on reaction time and speeded classification tasks. *Journal of Educational Psychology, 78,* 39–43.

Henderson, C. (2001). *College freshmen with disabilities: A biennial statistical profile.* Washington, DC: HEATH Resource Center.

Individuals With Disabilities Education Act of 1997, Pub. L. No. 105-117, 20 U. S. C. § 1400 *et seq.*

Jarvis, K. A. (1996). *Leveling the paying field: A comparison of scores of college students with and without learning disabilities on classroom tests.* Unpublished doctoral dissertation. The Florida State University: Dissertation Abstracts International, 57, 111.

Kaufman, A. S &Kaufman, N. L. (2004a). Kaufman Assessment Battery for Children – Second Edition (KABC-II). Circle Pines, MN: American Guidance Service.

Kaufman, A. S. & Kaufman, N. L. (2004b). Kaufman Tests of Educational Achievement – Second Edition (KTEA-II). Circle Pines, MN: American Guidance Service.

Kurth, N., & Mellard, D. (2006). Student perceptions of the accommodation process in postsecondary education. *Journal of Postsecondary Education and Disability, 19,* 71–84.

Mandinach, E., Bridgeman, B., Cahalan-Laitusis, C., & Trapani, C. (2005). *The Impact of Extended Time on SAT Test Performance.* (College Board Research Report No. 2005-8). New York: College Entrance Examination Board.

Mastropieri, M., & Scruggs, T. (2005). Feasibility and consequences of response to intervention: Examination of the issues and scientific evidence as a model for the identification of individuals with learning disabilities. *Journal of Learning Disabilities, 38,* 521–531.

Nelson, R., & Lignugaris-Kraft, B. (1989). Postsecondary education for students with learning disabilities. *Exceptional Children, 56,* 246–265.

Ofiesh, N. (2006). Response to intervention: Why we need comprehensive evaluations as part of the process. *Psychology in the Schools, 43*(8) 883–888.

Ofiesh, N. S. (2000). Using processing speed tests to predict the benefit of extended time for university students with learning disabilities. *Journal of Postsecondary Education and Disability, 14,* 39–56.

Ofiesh, N., Mather, N., & Russell, A. (2005). Using speeded cognitive, reading, and academic measures to determine the need for extended test time among university students with learning disabilities. *Journal of Psychoeducational Assessment, 23,* 35–52.

Ofiesh, N., & McAfee, J. K. (2000). Evaluation practices for college students with learning disabilities. *Journal of Learning Disabilities, 33,* 14–25.

Reschly, D. J. (2003). *What if LD identification changed to reflect research findings?* December, 2003. Kansas City, Missouri: National Research Center on Learning Disabilities.

Reschly, D. J. (2005). Learning disabilities identification: Primary intervention, secondary intervention, and then what? *Journal of Learning Disabilities, 38,* 510–515.

Reschly, D.J., Hosp, J. L., & Schmied, C. M. (2003). *And Miles to Go. . . . State SLD Requirements and Authoritative Recommendations.* (Report supported in whole or in part by the U.S. Department of Education, Office of Special Education Progams). Washington, DC.

Roid, G. H. (2003). Stanford-Binet Intelligence Scales, Fifth Edition. Itasca, IL: Riverside.

Runyan, M. K. (1991). The effect of extra time on reading comprehension scores for university students with and without leaning disabilities. *Journal of Learning Disabilities, 24,* 104–108.

Wechsler, D. (1997). Wechsler Adult Intelligence Scale – Third Edition (WAIS-III). San Antonio, TX: Psychological Corporation.

Wechsler, D. (2002). Wechsler Individual Achievement Test – Second Edition (WIAT-II). San Antonio, TX: The Psychological Corporation.

Wechsler, D., (2003) Wechsler Intelligence Scale for Children – Fourth Edition (WISC-IV). San Antonio, TX: The Psychological Corporation.

Wolff, P. H., Michel, G. F., Ovrut, M., & Drake, C. (1990). Rate and timing precision of motor coordination in developmental dyslexia. *Developmental Psychology, 26,* 349–359.

Woodcock, R. W., McGrew, K. S., & Mather, N. (2001a). Woodcock-Johnson III tests of Achievement. Itasca, IL: Riverside.

Woodcock, R.W., McGrew, K.S., & Mather, N. (2001b). Woodcock-Johnson III Tests of Cognitive Abilities. Itasca, IL: Riverside.

Cultural Responsiveness in Response-to-Intervention Models

JANETTE K. KLINGNER
GUILLERMO SOLANO-FLORES
University of Colorado at Boulder

Response to Intervention (RTI) provides a different way to think about students who struggle in schools, particularly with reading. Although almost all states previously applied an IQ–achievement discrepancy formula to identify which students qualified for special education as having learning disabilities (LD), the newest regulations governing special education stipulate that states cannot require an IQ-achievement discrepancy when determining special education eligibility (Individuals With Disabilities Education Improvement Act of 2004, IDEA; Department of Education, 2006). Instead states must consider the extent to which students respond to evidence-based interventions when making such a decision. In the sense that RTI is a way of determining who should qualify for special education, it is a form of assessment. Thus, it is important to consider what accommodations are needed so that English language learners (ELLs) and other culturally and linguistically diverse students can be assessed accurately.

RTI has another purpose as well. It was conceptualized as a way to monitor students'

progress and provide them with early intervening services within a general education framework when they do not seem to be progressing (IDEA, 2004). RTI promises to facilitate the provision of quality instruction for students *before* they underachieve (Vaughn & Fuchs, 2003).

We still lack consensus on just what form the RTI model should take or the extent to which its primary purpose should be to provide early support to students who show signs of struggling or to offer an alternative special education identification model. Yet the overall RTI framework remains the same. At the first tier all students receive evidenced-based instruction and on-going progress monitoring within their general education classrooms. Within the second tier those students who are not reaching expected benchmarks (i.e., those students who are not making adequate progress) receive intensive intervention support. When students do not respond to interventions at this level, they either qualify for special education or for an evaluation for possible placement in special education (Fuchs, Mock, Morgan, & Young, 2003).

We are encouraged by this shift from IQ-achievement discrepancy formulae to approaches that emphasize early intervention, focus on ensuring appropriate instruction at the "first tier," or classroom level, for all children, and aim at matching instruction to each child's needs based on ongoing classroom assessment (IDEA, 2004). We believe that the use of an RTI approach can contribute to reducing the number of student misclassifications (i.e., false positives or false negatives)—students who are inappropriately referred to and placed in special education programs, but who do not have a true disability, or students who do have a disability but are not referred to and placed in special education (Klingner & Edwards, 2006).

Yet we are also concerned about what appears to be a significant assumption underlying the adoption of RTI models—that a stronger focus on classroom instruction and classroom formative assessment will suffice to properly address the problem of disproportionate representation (mainly overrepresentation) of traditionally underserved groups in the United States. Historically, students from cultural and linguistic minorities have been over-identified as having high-incidence disabilities (Artiles, Trent, & Palmer, 2004; Donovan & Cross, 2002; Heller, Holtzman, & Messick, 1982). (Disproportionate representation is most apparent among African American and American Indian students when aggregated data are the focus, though there are notable instances of overrepresentation among Hispanics and Asian Americans when data are disaggregated and population subgroups are examined. Hispanic students are overrepresented in some school districts and underrepresented in others.) Although this trend may have been due in part to the conceptual foundations of the models used for identifying and classifying students with LD, it also reflects the views and the training (or the

lack thereof) of the individuals involved in making those identification and classification decisions. We believe that, in spite of RTI's potential for promoting more valid educational decisions for culturally and linguistically diverse students, no significant improvement in educational practices will take place unless closer attention is paid to the ways in which researchers and practitioners think about culture and language and about cultural and linguistic minorities. As with previous criteria for eligibility to special education programs, without proper training about culture and cultural and linguistic diversity individuals implementing RTI models may presume, for example, that a child who does not make progress at a certain pace must have an internal deficiency of some kind. Or they may view cultural differences as cultural deficits, which may influence their interpretations of the behaviors of their nonmainstream students.

In this chapter, we examine the challenges posed by RTI models from the perspective of cultural responsiveness. We examine aspects of culture that we believe researchers and practitioners in the field of special education need to address in order to ensure fair and valid practices for cultural and linguistic minority students. Our discussion is organized in two main sections. In the first section, we provide a conceptual framework for reading and a definition of cultural responsiveness. This conceptual framework addresses instruction and assessment in reading. Klingner and Edwards (2006) argue that it is essential to examine not just what works in a global sense, but *what works with whom, by whom, and in what contexts*. Thus, in the next section we examine how the notion of cultural responsiveness is reflected in four areas of RTI model implementation:

1. The defensibility of the methods and procedures selected as "evidence-based."

2. The accuracy and sufficiency of information about students.

3. The skills and knowledge educators need to use in their classrooms when they implement RTI models.

4. The conditions schools need to meet if they are to properly implement those models.

A FRAMEWORK FOR CULTURAL RESPONSIVENESS IN READING AND LITERACY INSTRUCTION

Moje and Hinchman (2004) make the point that "all practice needs to be culturally responsive in order to be best practice" (p. 321). Effective teachers are able to tap into and connect with students' prior knowledge, interests, motivation, and home language (Au, 2000; August & Hakuta, 1997). From a broader, Vygotskian perspective, knowledge construction does not take place in isolation, aside from culture and society (Vygotsky, 1978). Therefore, effective teaching, as an activity that promotes knowledge construction among students, necessarily has to be culturally responsive.

Current thinking in the field of reading instruction recognizes the cultural dimension of literacy. As shown in Table 15-1, different approaches in this field capitalize on or recognize as critical to promoting literacy experiences students have outside the classroom and outside formal instruction. Literacy instruction is seen as consisting of a wide variety of activities ranging from explicit instruction in phonological awareness, the alphabetic code, vocabulary development, fluency, and comprehension strategies (National Reading Panel, 2000; Reyes, 1992; Snow, 2002; Snow, Burns, & Griffin, 1998). Students receive frequent opportunities to practice reading with a variety of rich materials in meaningful contexts linked with the goals and conditions of reading (Pressley, 2002; Roller, 1996). Motivation is an important focus (Kaplan & Maehr, 1999; Willis, 2002).

These modern views of literacy instruction are compatible with the notion of cultural responsiveness, a term that is used to refer to a broad range of conditions or strategies such as the congruence of educational methods with the students' cultural experiences (Aikenhead & Jegede, 1999), the connection between cultural content and academic content (Nelson-Barber & Estrin, 1996), and the extent to which communities are involved in deciding the kinds of knowledge that are relevant for their children to learn (Lipka, 2000). For the purposes of our discussion, we provide a definition of cultural responsiveness in RTI models:

> **_Cultural responsiveness_** is the extent to which research and practice in instruction and assessment take into consideration the cognitive, linguistic, and social assets of an individual (such as epistemologies, world views, and learning, teaching, and communication styles) that are culturally determined and shape the ways in which that individual learns and makes sense of his or her experiences. Cultural responsiveness refers to the fact that, in order to be fair and effective, education should be compatible with those assets and build on them, rather than disparage or ignore them.

Due to the complexities of language and culture, defining or evaluating the cultural responsiveness of programs, instructional materials, or tests in detail can be a formidable task. For example, understanding the epistemology that explains why a student interprets a test item in a way that initially looks wrong may require the use of individual cognitive interviews (Greenfield, 1997; Solano-Flores & Nelson-Barber, 2001), or addressing the language adequacy of test materials may require the use of sophisticated approaches for test development

TABLE 15-1

A Summary of Culturally Responsive Reading Instruction Approaches

Level of Analysis	Approach	Researchers
Individual	Bilingualism is viewed as an asset. The learning of English is promoted as an additive rather than a subtractive process. Individual literacy differences are viewed as strengths, not deficits.	Alvermann (2003) August & Hakuta (1997) Ladson-Billings (1994)
Family	Partnerships with parents and other caregivers are developed with the intent to enhance home literacy experiences. Parents are taught to interact with their children in ways that promote literacy achievement.	Arnold, Lonigan, Whitehurst, & Epstein (1994) Dickinson & Smith (1994) Valdez-Menchaca & Whitehurst (1992) Whitehurst et al., 1994
Community	Programs are developed to tap into community resources that promote children's literacy. Volunteers serve as reading tutors. Parents and other persons in the neighborhood share their expertise or "funds of knowledge."	Aguilera (2003) Baker, Gersten, & Keating (2000) Fitzgerald (2001) Invernizzi, Juel, & Rosemary (1997) Moll & González (1994) Wasik (1998) Wasik & Slavin (1993)
School	School literacy practices are connected to literacy practices from the home. Although different from school practices, students' discourse and behavioral styles are validated.	Heath (1983) Cazden (1988)
Sociocultural contexts	The contexts in which students learn are viewed as critical to effective literacy instruction.	Artiles (2002) Ruiz (1998)

(Solano-Flores, Trumbull, & Nelson-Barber, 2002; Tanzer, 2005). Thus, also for the purposes of this chapter, we discuss cultural responsiveness according to four criteria that are consistent with the definition provided earlier and which allow efficient identification of areas of improvement in RTI models regarding cultural responsiveness. From our perspective, cultural responsiveness can be examined as the extent to which the following four criteria are met:

1. *Process:* The reasonings, decisions, and actions intended to address cultural and linguistic diversity take place timely, at all stages of development and implementation of instructional models and assessments.

2. *Knowledge:* The reasonings, decisions, and actions intended to address cultural and linguistic diversity are supported by current disciplinary knowledge on the fields of language and culture.

3. *Inclusion:* The numbers of individuals from linguistic and cultural minorities who participate in the development, use, and implementation of instructional models and assessments reflect the proportions of those groups in the entire student population.

4. *Resources:* The amount of resources used to address cultural and linguistic diversity in the process of development, use, and implementation of instructional models and assessments are commensurate with the proportion of linguistic and cultural minority students in the entire student population.

These criteria address the need for examination of the conceptual and methodological soundness of instruction and assessment from a multidisciplinary perspective (Lee & Fradd, 1998; Solano-Flores & Nelson-Barber, 2001). An RTI model fails to be culturally responsive if any of these four criteria is not met. According to these criteria, examples of unacceptable practice are:

- *Process criterion:* Making simple adaptations and add-ons for linguistic and minority students after an instructional model has been developed for and tried out with mainstream students.

- *Knowledge criterion:* Mistakenly thinking that English language learners' errors made because they are transferring linguistic rules from their first language to the second language means that they have cognitive deficiencies.

- *Inclusion criterion:* Using insufficient numbers of students from linguistic and cultural minority groups to try out an instructional model.

- Resources criterion: Allocating only a meager part of financial resources to examine issues of culture and language.

WHAT WORKS WITH WHOM, BY WHOM, AND IN WHAT CONTEXTS

Population validity and ecological validity are vital constructs that affect the extent to which the findings from experimental studies can be generalized (Bracht & Glass, 1968). One size does not fit all, but rather there are important differences in students and contexts that should be considered when determining which aspects of the findings from research studies apply (Klingner & Edwards, 2006). In other words, a practice should not be considered "evidence-based" in a general sense, but only when certain fundamental conditions have been met.

What Works: What Counts as Evidence of Effective Practice

In this time of accountability, numerous debates have taken place around the issue of what counts as evidence (see Eisenhart & Towne, 2003; Pressley, 2002). This issue is particularly relevant to this discussion of RTI, because the RTI model is based on the precept that instructional practices or interventions should be based on scientific evidence about "what works." Our concern is that if the criteria for determining "what works" are based on narrow views of science and learning, practitioners may be misled into using practices that are inappropriate for their students or constrained as to the range of methods that can be used in RTI models.

To ensure cultural responsiveness in RTI models, researchers and practitioners need to address the fact that "evidence-based," as used currently in the context of No Child Left Behind legislation and policy, restricts the possibilities of examining and implementing intervention methods that are methodologically sound, yet are proscribed from fundable research because they do not meet certain criteria such as using randomized control trials or experimental designs. Although randomized control trials and experimental designs are part of the wealth of methods and approaches available to scientists, overemphasizing them as the only way of doing science minimizes the role of theory in scientific research.

The impact of these narrow views can have devastating consequences for linguistic and cultural minorities (Johnson, Kirkhart, Madison, Noley, & Solano-Flores, in press). The notion of construct underrepresentation (Messick, 1995) is critical to understand the magnitude of these consequences. As a consequence of construct underrepresentation, cultural constructs can wrongly be operationalized in narrow ways. For example, linguistic proficiency is reduced to two or three categories that may not reflect the complexity of this construct, or culture and race are treated as interchangeable constructs. Although research using these measures or categories can be regarded as "scientifically based" the results it produces may lead to flawed generalizations about linguistic or cultural groups.

Experimental and quasi-experimental research studies can provide valuable information about which practices are most likely to be effective with a majority of students. However, much can also be learned through qualitative (Pugach, 2001) and mixed methods approaches (Chatterji, 2005; Johnson & Onwuegbuzie, 2004) designed to answer questions about complex phenomena. When a qualitative component is added to an experimental study, it can yield important information about contextual variables that might affect the effectiveness of a practice, enhance our awareness of challenges faced by those implementing the practice, or provide information about the circumstances under which, with whom, and by whom a practice is most likely to be successful (Shavelson & Towne, 2002). Schools are complex settings, influenced by a variety of factors. Thus, the research methodologies we use to study them must be able to account for wide variations in culture, socioeconomic status, financial circumstances, social inter-

actions, and institutional support (Gee, 2001).

This is not to say that there is no value in trying to determine which interventions are most likely to be effective with the majority of students. Of course such research is useful. Yet it is important to keep in mind that experimental research can only help us make an informed guess about which approach to try and can neither guarantee positive results nor tell us what will work best with a particular student or group of students (Dillon, O'Brien, & Heilman, 2000). And when a student is not making adequate progress with a given instructional practice, we should consider that the instruction may not be the best match for the student and keep trying to improve instruction to be more appropriate for the student before concluding that the child has LD or assuming we have done all we can to provide an adequate opportunity to learn.

What Works With Whom: Students

To ensure cultural responsiveness in RTI models, researchers and practitioners need to address two facts. First, information about culturally and linguistically diverse students is usually insufficient or inaccurate. Second, culturally and linguistically diverse students are rarely properly sampled or included in the process of development of instructional and assessment methods.

In their description of the RTI model, Vaughn and Fuchs (2003) note, "When children fail to respond to instruction, the assumption is that some inherent deficit, not the instructional program, explains the lack of response and that some special intervention is required" (p. 142). This kind of assumption reflects a major problem in dealing with diversity—assuming that cultural and linguistic minority students can be easily characterized according to a few categorical labels.

The definition of English language learner (ELL) is a case in point. NCLB defines ELLs based on a series of demographic factors and refers to language proficiency in a way that lends itself for multiple interpretations (see Solano-Flores & Trumbull, in press). Moreover, one of the major criticisms of NCLB-mandated tests of English development for ELLs is that these tests are developed from English language arts standards and on criteria of language development observed in monolingual, native English speakers, rather than second-language development standards (Mahoney & MacSwan, 2005). As a consequence, scores on these tests may not provide all the information educators need to have an accurate idea of the linguistic proficiencies of their students.

Populations of ELLs are tremendously heterogeneous. This heterogeneity influences the dependability of test scores even across groups of students within the same broad linguistic group (i.e., native speakers of a given language) but from different local communities (Solano-Flores & Li, 2006). Unfortunately, too often insufficient demographic data are provided about culturally and linguistically diverse students (Artiles, Trent, & Kuan, 1997; Donovan & Cross, 2002; Gersten & Baker, 2000; Simmerman & Swanson, 2001; Troia, 1999). We recommend that at a minimum, researchers should provide information about language proficiency, ethnicity, socioeconomic status, gender, age, years in school, and, if relevant, years in special education (Keogh, Gallimore, & Weisner, 1997). This information is important because when making decisions about whether an assessment or instructional practice might be suitable to use with certain students as part of an RTI model, it should have been validated with students similar to those in question (Pressley, 2003). For instance, sometimes ELLs are purposely left out of research samples because of their limited English proficiency. This is because a

lack of full proficiency can be a confounding factor that might affect research findings (Ortiz, 1997). However, this practice limits the extent to which the results of these studies can be generalized (i.e., the findings can not be applied to ELLs). Unfortunately, this type of overgeneralizing of findings is common. For example, the National Reading Panel (2000) report did not review studies targeting ELLs or "address issues relevant to second language learning" (p. 3). Yet the report's conclusions are cited in support of NCLB as applying to all students.

What Works By Whom: Teachers

To ensure cultural responsiveness in RTI models, two challenges need to be addressed. First, critical to proper RTI model implementation is the availability of professional development programs that promote the appropriate skills needed to address linguistic and cultural diversity in the classroom. Although legislation states that English proficiency and cultural background should not be the basis for determining if an individual has a disability (Department of Education, 2006), it is not clear how this notion can be translated into practice. Teachers who have culturally diverse classrooms require support so that they can confront their own biases, learn about their students' cultures, and understand other, culturally-determined world views (McAllister & Irvine, 2000). Moreover, learning to mediate academic content with the students' linguistic and cultural backgrounds is a gradual and demanding process that requires teacher reflection, formal training, and extensive support (Lee, 2004). Because only a small percentage of teachers receive any formal training in multicultural education (Darling-Hammond & Bransford, 2005), the chances for successfully implementing RTI models in fair ways will be slim unless educators are prepared to capitalize on current knowledge about appropriate interventions for culturally and linguistically diverse students.

The second challenge derives from the fact that the RTI approach relies heavily on information gathered during instruction and through classroom assessment (Fuchs & Fuchs, 2005). Although informal classroom assessment is as old as teaching, important reviews or conceptual advances in the field have taken place relatively recently and do not focus on linguistic or cultural diversity (e.g., Black & William, 1998; Cowie & Bell, 1996; Sadler, 1998). As a consequence, it is difficult to translate the body of knowledge from the field of formative assessment into principled practice for proper RTI model implementation.

Observations in general education classrooms should occur routinely as part of RTI models (Fuchs et al., 2003; Grimes & Kurns, 2003; Vaughn & Fuchs, 2003). Although it may seem to be common sense, previous research suggests that professionals rarely consider the appropriateness of instruction or of the classroom environment when considering why students might be struggling (Harry & Klingner, 2006). By observing classrooms, we are in a position to assess the nature of the relationship between a teacher and her students, the extent to which students are supported, how the teacher promotes interest and motivation, as well as the quality of instruction (Klingner & Edwards, 2006). As we have already noted, it is essential to determine whether or not students are receiving an adequate opportunity to learn.

What Works In What Contexts: Schools

To ensure cultural responsiveness in RTI models, researchers and practitioners need to consider that the development, use, and selection of instructional and assessment methods neglect to account for the context in which instruction takes place. Instructional programs vary considerably in the fidelity with which they are implemented. In addition, their success is shaped by the characteristics of the schools and local communities in which they are used (Cummins, 1999), as well as by larger societal influences (Bronfenbrenner, 1977). Failure to consider context impedes proper evaluation of the effectiveness of instructional programs.

It is common for program implementation and effectiveness to vary across schools and classrooms (Bond & Dykstra, 1967). To some extent this variance can be explained by differences in teachers' implementation. But teacher variation does not account for all discrepancies. The school context is also an important factor. Schools, in turn, are influenced by the systems in which they operate (Klingner et al., 2005). Therefore, it is important to examine multiple layers of the school, community, and society at large when evaluating program implementation (Miramontes, Nadeau, & Commins, 1997; Shanklin et al., 2003). Such examinations should include considerations of social practice, culture, and power across these levels (Gee, 1999).

All of these factors can affect the fidelity with which teachers are able to implement an evidence-based practice. When teachers do not implement a practice with fidelity, a common reaction can be to criticize the teachers for "not doing it right" (Klingner, Cramer, & Harry, 2006, p. 346). Another reaction may be to deplore the gap between research and practice (e.g., (Gersten, Vaughn, Deshler, & Schiller, 1997). Yet, there can be numerous reasons that teachers do not implement a practice with fidelity. Perhaps the practice they are trying was originally validated in contexts quite different than their own, and with dissimilar students. This was the case with teachers' implementation of Success for All in predominately Black urban schools in which virtually all students received free lunch support (Klingner et al., 2006). The teachers faced very real challenges they tried their best to overcome. When teachers struggle to implement a practice as designed, this is a sign we need to look more closely at what is happening and examine the constraints faced by those using the practice (Herman et al., 2000; Kozol, 1991). By not acknowledging these challenges, we run the risk of holding the students themselves at fault, determining that they have learning deficits, and placing them in special education programs at disproportionate rates. Again, our point is that instruction does not take place in a vacuum. Any conclusions about student performance must take into account the consideration that the school environment may not have been conducive to learning.

FINAL COMMENTS

The RTI model has the potential to improve the learning opportunities provided to culturally and linguistically diverse students. We are optimistic that RTI can lead to enhanced educational experiences for cultural and linguistic minority students and reduce their disproportionate representation in special education. Rather than focusing on categorical labels (e.g., a student qualifies for additional support through special education or does not, or has a disability or does not), RTI strives to provide help to those students who need assistance without labeling them, at least at first.

Yet, because RTI is based on a foundation of research-based practices that presumably have been shown to "work," it is important to examine our assumptions about who counts and what matters when generalizing the findings of experimental studies. If we assume that the findings from research conducted in a predominately middle class school with a majority White population should apply to "all" students, we are privileging the White majority students and discounting very real differences in language, culture, and opportunity to learn in diverse schools in high poverty areas. Therefore, in this chapter we proposed that for RTI models to be valid with culturally and linguistically diverse populations, they must be culturally responsive. We examined aspects of culture that researchers and practitioners should address in order to ensure fair and valid practices for cultural and linguistic minority students. We argued that it is essential to examine not just "what works" in a global sense, but to consider what works with whom, by whom, and in what contexts.

REFERENCES

Aguilera, D. E. (2003). *Who defines success: An analysis of competing models of education for American Indian and Alaskan Native students* Unpublished doctoral dissertation, University of Colorado, Boulder, 2003.

Aikenhead, G. S., & Jegede, O. J. (1999). Cross-cultural science education: A cognitive explanation of a cultural phenomenon. *Journal of Research in Science Teaching, 36*(3), 269–287.

Alvermann, D. (2003). Exemplary literacy instruction in grades 7–12: What counts and who's counting? In J. Flood & P. Anders (Eds.), *Literacy development of students in urban schools: Research and policy* (pp. 187–201). Newark, DE: International Reading Association.

Arnold, D. H., Lonigan, C. J., Whitehurst, G. J., & Epstein, J. N. (1994). Accelerating language development through picture book reading: Replication and extension to a videotape training format. *Journal of Educational Psychology, 86*, 235–243.

Artiles, A. J. (2002). Culture in learning: The next frontier in reading difficulties research. In R. Bradley, L. Danielson, & D. P. Hallahan (Eds.), *Identification of learning disabilities: Research to policy* (pp. 693–701). Hillsdale, NJ: Lawrence Erlbaum.

Artiles, A. J., Trent, S. C., & Kuan, L. (1997). Learning disabilities empirical research on ethnic minority students: An analysis of 22 years of studies published in selected refereed journals. *Learning Disabilities Research & Practice, 12*, 82–91.

Artiles, A. J., Trent, S. C., & Palmer, J. (2004). Culturally diverse students in special education: Legacies and prospects. In J. A. Banks & C. M. Banks (Eds.), *Handbook of research on multicultural education* (2nd ed.) (pp. 716–735). San Francisco, CA: Jossey Bass.

Au, K. H. (2000). A multicultural perspective on policies for improving literacy achievement: Equity and excellence. In M. L. Kamil, P. B. Mosenthal, P. D. Pearson, & R. Barr (Eds.), *Handbook of reading research* (Vol. 3, pp. 835–851). Mahwah, NJ: Erlbaum.

August, D., & Hakuta, K. (1997). *Improving schooling for language minority children: A research agenda*. Washington, DC: National Academy Press.

Baker, S., Gersten, R., & Keating, T. (2000). When less may be more: A 2-year longitudinal evaluation of a volunteer tutoring program requiring minimal training. *Reading Research Quarterly, 35,* 494–519.

Black, P., & Wiliam, D. (1998). Assessment and classroom learning. *Assessment in Education, 5*(1), 7–74.

Bond, G. L., & Dykstra, R. (1967). The cooperative research program in first-grade reading instruction. *Reading Research Quarterly, 2,* 10–141.

Bracht, G. H., & Glass, G. V. (1968). The external validity of experiments. *American Educational Research Journal, 5,* 437–474.

Bronfenbrenner, U. (1977, July). Toward an experimental ecology of human development. *American Psychologist,* 513–531.

Cazden, C. B. (1988). *Classroom discourse: The language of teaching and learning*. Portsmouth, NH: Heinemann.

Chatterji, M. (2005). Evidence on "what works": An argument for extended-term mixed-method evaluation designs. *Educational Researcher, 34*(5), 14–24.

Cowie, B., & Bell, B. (1996). A model of formative assessment in science education. *Assessment in Education, 6*(1), 101–116.

Cummins, J. (1999). Alternative paradigms in bilingual education research: Does theory have a place? *Educational Researcher, 28*(7), 26–32, 41.

Darling-Hammond, L., & Bransford, J. (2005). *Preparing teachers for a changing world: What teachers should learn and be able to do*. San Francisco: Jossey-Bass.

Department of Education (2006). The Individuals With Disabilities Education Improvement Act of 2004. *Federal Register, 71*(156), 46540–46845.

Dickinson, D. K., & Smith, M. W. (1994). Long-term effects of preschool teachers' book readings on low-income children's vocabulary and story comprehension. *Reading Research Quarterly, 29,* 104–122.

Dillon, D. R., O'Brien, D. G., & Heilman, E. E. (2000) Literacy research in the next millennium: From paradigms to pragmatism and practicality. *Reading Research Quarterly, 35,* 10–26.

Donovan, S., & Cross, C. (2002). *Minority students in special and gifted education*. Washington, DC: National Academy Press.

Eisenhart, M., & Towne, L. (2003). Contestation and change in national policy on "scientifically based" education research. *Educational Researcher, 32*(7), 31–38.

Fitzgerald, J. (2001). Can minimally trained college student volunteers help young at-risk children to read better? *Reading Research Quarterly, 36,* 28–47.

Fuchs, D., & Fuchs, L. S. (2005). Responsiveness-to-intervention. A blueprint for practitioners, policymakers, and parents. *TEACHING Exceptional Children, 38*(1), 57–61.

Fuchs, D., Mock, D., Morgan, P. L., & Young, C. L. (2003). Responsiveness to-intervention: Definitions, evidence, and implications for the learning disabilities construct. *Learning Disabilities Research & Practice, 18,* 157–171.

Gee, J. P. (1999). Critical issues: Reading and the new literacy studies: Reframing the National Academy of Sciences Report on Reading. *Journal of Literacy Research, 31,* 355–374.

Gee, J. P. (2001). A sociocultural perspective on early literacy development. In S. B. Neuman and D. K. Dickinson (Eds.), *Handbook of early literacy research* (pp. 30–42). New York: Guilford Press.

Gersten, R., & Baker, S. (2000). What we know about effective instructional practices for

English-language learners. *Exceptional Children, 66,* 454–470.

Gersten, R., Vaughn, S., Deshler, D., & Schiller E. (1997). What we know about using research findings: Implications for improving special education practice. *Journal of Learning Disabilities, 30*(5), 466–476.

Greenfield, P. M. (1997). Culture as process: Empirical methods for cultural psychology. In J. W. Berry, Y. H. Poortinga, & J. Pandey (Eds.), *Handbook of cross-cultural psychology, Second Edition. Vol. 1: Theory and method* (pp. 301–346). Needham Heights, Massachusetts: Allyn & Bacon.

Grimes J., & Kurns, S. (2003, December). *An intervention-based system for addressing NCLB and IDEA expectations: A multiple tiered model to ensure every child learns.* Paper presented at the National Research Center on Learning Disabilities Responsiveness-to-Intervention Symposium, Kansas City, MO.

Harry, B., & Klingner, J. K. (2006). *Crossing the border from normalcy to disability: Culturally and linguistically diverse students and the special education placement process.* New York: Teachers College Press.

Heath, S. B. (1983). *Ways with words: Language, life, and work in communities and classrooms.* NY: Cambridge University Press.

Heller, K. A., Holtzman, W. H., & Messick, S. (Eds.). (1982). *Placing children in special education: A strategy for equity.* Washington, DC: National Academy Press.

Herman, R., Carl, B., Lampron, S., Sussman, A., Berger, A., & Innes, F. (2000). *What we know about comprehensive school reform models.* Washington, DC: American Institutes for Research.

Invernizzi, M., Juel, C., & Rosemary, C. A. (1997). A community tutorial that works. *The Reading Teacher, 50,* 304–311.

Johnson, E. C., Kirkhart, K. E., Madison, A. M., Noley, G. B. & Solano-Flores, G. (in press). The impact of narrow views of scientific rigor on evaluation practices for underrepresented groups. In P. R. Brandon & N. L. Smith (Eds.), *Fundamental issues in evaluation.* New York: Guilford.

Johnson, R. B., & Onwuegbuzie, A. J. (2004). Mixed methods research: A research paradigm whose time has come. *Educational Researcher, 33*(7), 14–26.

Kaplan, A., & Maehr, M. L., (1999). Enhancing the motivation of African American students: an achievement goal theory perspective. *Journal of Negro Education, 68*(1), 23–41.

Keogh, B., Gallimore, R., & Weisner, T. (1997). A sociocultural perspective on learning and learning disabilities. *Learning Disabilities Research & Practice, 12,* 107–113.

Klingner, J. K., Artiles, A. J., Kozleski, E., Harry, B., Tate, W., Zion, et al. (2005). Addressing the disproportionate representation of culturally and linguistically diverse students in special education through culturally responsive educational systems. *Educational Analysis and Policy Archives, 13*(38), 1–39.

Klingner, J. K., Cramer, E., & Harry, B. (2006). Challenges in the implementation of Success for All by four urban schools. *Elementary School Journal, 106,* 333–349.

Klingner, J. K., & Edwards, P. (2006). Cultural considerations with response to intervention models. *Reading Research Quarterly, 41,* 108–117.

Kozol, J. (1991). *Savage inequalities: Children in America's schools.* New York: Harper-Perennial.

Ladson-Billings, G. (1994). *The dreamkeepers: Successful teachers of African American children.* San Francisco: Jossey-Bass.

Lee, O. (2004). Teacher change in beliefs and practice in science and literacy instruction with English language learners. *Journal of Research in Science Teaching, 41*(1), 65–93.

Lee, O., & Fradd, S. H. (1998). Science for all, including students from non-English backgrounds. *Educational Researcher, 27,* 12–21.

Lipka, J. (2000). *Adapting Yup'ik elders knowledge: Pre-K to 6th math and instructional materials development.* Fairbanks, AK: University of Alaska, Fairbanks.

Mahoney, K. S., & MacSwan, J. (2005). Reexamining identification and reclassification of English language learners: A critical discussion of select state practices. *Bilingual Research Journal, 29*(1), 31–42.

McAllister, G., & Irvine, J. J. (2000). Cross cultural competency and multicultural teacher education. *Review of Educational Research, 70*(1), 3–24.

Messick, S. (1995). Validity of psychological assessment: Validation of inferences from persons' responses and performances as scientific inquiry into score meaning. *American Psychologist, 50*(9), 741–749.

Miramontes, O., Nadeau, A., & Commins, N. L. (1997). *Restructuring schools for linguistic diversity: Linking decision-making to effective programs.* New York: Teachers College Press.

Moje, E. B., & Hinchman, K. (2004). Culturally responsive practices for youth literacy learning. In T. L. Jetton & J. A. Dole (Eds.), *Adolescent literacy research and practice* (pp. 3211–3350). New York: Guilford Press.

Moll, L. C., & González, N. (1994). Critical issues: Lessons from research with language-minority children. *JRB: A Journal of Literacy, 26,* 439–456.

National Reading Panel. (2000). *Teaching children to read: An evidence-based assessment of the scientific research literature on reading and its implications for reading instruction: Summary Report.* Washington, DC: National Institute of Child Health and Development.

Nelson-Barber, S. & Estrin, E. (1996). *Culturally responsive mathematics and science education for native students.* San Francisco, California: Far West Laboratory for Educational Research and Development.

Ortiz, A. A. (1997). Learning disabilities occurring concomitantly with linguistic differences. *Journal of Learning Disabilities, 30,* 321–332.

Pressley, M. (2002). Effective beginning reading instruction. *Journal of Literacy Research, 34,* 165–188.

Pressley, M. (2003). A few things reading educators should know about instructional experiments. *Reading Teacher, 57*(1), 64–71.

Pugach, M. C. (2001). The stories we choose to tell: Fulfilling the promise of qualitative research for special education. *Exceptional Children, 67,* 439–453.

Reyes, M. de la Luz (1992). Challenging venerable assumptions: Literacy instruction for linguistically diverse students. *Harvard Educational Review, 62,* 427–446.

Roller, C. (1996). *Variability not disability: Struggling readers in a workshop classroom.* Newark, DE: International Reading Association.

Ruiz, N. (1998). Instructional strategies for children with limited-English proficiency. *Journal of Early Education and Family Review, 5,* 21–22.

Sadler, R. D. (1998). Formative assessment: Revisiting the territory. *Assessment in Education, 5*(1), 77–84.

Shanklin, N., Kozleski, E. B., Meagher, C., Sands, D., Joseph, O., & Wyman, W. (2003). Examining renewal in an urban high school through the lens of systemic change. *International Journal of School Leadership and Management, 23,* 357–378.

Shavelson R. J., & Towne, L. (Eds.). (2002). *Scientific research in education.* Washington, DC: National Academies Press.

Simmerman, S., & Swanson, H. L. (2001). Treatment outcomes for students with learning disabilities: How important are internal and external validity. *Journal of Learning Disabilities, 34,* 221–235.

Snow, C. E. (2002). *Reading for understanding: Toward an R&D program in reading comprehension.* Santa Monica, CA: RAND.

Snow, C. E., Burns, M. S., & Griffin, P. (1998). *Preventing reading difficulties in young children.* Washington DC: National Academy Press.

Solano-Flores, G., & Nelson-Barber, S. (2001). On the cultural validity of science assessments. *Journal of Research in Science Teaching, 38*(5), 553–573.

Solano-Flores, G., & Trumbull, E. (in press). In what language should English language learners be tested? In R. Kopriva (Ed.), *Improving large-scale achievement tests for English language learners.* Mahwah, NJ: Lawrence Erlbaum.

Solano-Flores, G., Trumbull, E., & Nelson-Barber, S. (2002). Concurrent development of dual language assessments: An alternative to translating tests for linguistic minorities. *International Journal of Testing, 2*(2), 107–129.

Solano-Flores, G., & Li, M. (2006). The use of generalizability (G) theory in the testing of linguistic minorities. *Educational Measurement: Issues and Practice 25*(1), 13–22.

Tanzer, N. K. (2005). Developing tests for use in multiple languages and cultures: A plea for simultaneous development. In R. Hambleton, P. Merenda, & C. D. Spielberger (Eds.), *Adapting educational and psychological tests for cross-cultural assessment.* Mahwah, NJ: Lawrence Erlbaum.

Troia, G. A. (1999). Phonological awareness intervention research: A critical review of the experimental methodology. *Reading Research Quarterly, 34,* 28–52.

Valdez-Menchaca, M. C., & Whitehurst, G. J. (1992). Accelerating language development through picture book reading: A systematic extension to Mexican day care. *Developmental Psychology, 28,* 1106–1114.

Vaughn, S., & Fuchs, L. (2003). Redefining learning disabilities as inadequate response to instruction: The promise and potential problems. *Learning Disabilities: Research & Practice, 18,* 137–146.

Vygotsky, L. S. (1978). *Mind in society: The development of higher psychological processes.* Cambridge, MA: Harvard University Press.

Wasik, B.A. (1998). Using volunteers as reading tutors: Guidelines for successful practices. *The Reading Teacher, 51*(7), 562–570.

Wasik, B. A., & Slavin, R. E. (1993). Preventing early reading failure with one-to-one tutoring: A review of five programs. *Reading Research Quarterly, 28,* 178–200.

Whitehurst, G. J., Epstein, J. N., Angell, A. L., Payne, A. C., Crone, D. A., & Fischel, J. E. (1994). Outcomes of an emergent literacy intervention in Head Start. *Journal of Educational Psychology, 86,* 542–555.

Willis, A. I. (2002). Dissin' and disremembering: Motivation and culturally and linguistically diverse students' literacy learning. *Reading and Writing Quarterly, 18,* 293–319.